THE W9-CAO-315

BUSINESS

S·t·y·l·e

HANDBOOK

An A-to-Z Guide for Writing on the Job
with Tips from Communications Experts
at the Fortune 500

Helen Cunningham · Brenda Greene

McGraw-Hill

Chicago   New York   San Francisco   Lisbon   London   Madrid   Mexico City
Milan   New Delhi   San Juan   Seoul   Singapore   Sydney   Toronto

11/07   # 47797967

The **McGraw·Hill** Companies

Library of Congress Cataloging-in-Publication Data

Cunningham, Helen.
    The business style handbook : an A-to-Z guide for writing on the job with tips from
communications experts at the Fortune 500 / Helen Cunningham and Brenda Greene.
        p.   cm.
    Includes bibliographical references and index.
    ISBN 0-07-138230-5 (alk. paper)
    1. Business writing.   2. English language—Business English.   3. Business
communication.   I. Greene, Brenda.   II. Title.

HF5718.3 C86   2002
808'.06665—dc21   2001044553

7 8 9 0   LBM/LBM   1 0 9 8 7

ISBN 0-07-138230-5

Cover and interior design by Monica Baziuk

This book is printed on acid-free paper.

•

TO OUR FAMILIES

•

CONTENTS

ACKNOWLEDGMENTS

WE WOULD LIKE TO THANK THE 50 COMMUNICATIONS professionals from the Fortune 500 (1999) for participating in our survey on writing style and standards at America's largest corporations. This book is relevant and more focused as a result of their input.

Since the time we conducted the survey, some of the companies have merged, have been acquired or no longer rank among the Fortune 500. Some individuals, meanwhile, have moved on to other companies or have been promoted. Our list, for the most part, reflects the status of companies and individuals at the time we received responses to the survey.

Again, we extend our appreciation to the following professionals for their time and thoughtful responses: **AFLAC Incorporated,** Glenn Wells, manager, editorial services; **Ameritech Corporation,** Diane L. Calvert, manager, communications quality; **AT&T Corp.,** Jean Hurt, editor; **Bell Atlantic Corporation** (now Verizon), Ken Terrell, executive director, employee communication; **CIGNA Corporation,** Tony Branco, director, corporate media relations; **Circuit City Stores, Inc.,** Ann Collier, vice president, financial and public relations; **Coca-Cola Company,** Robert E. Byrd, senior manager, executive communications; **CompUSA Inc.,** Suzanne Shelton, director, public relations; **Conseco, Inc.,** James Rosensteele, director, communications;

Cooper Industries, Inc., Victoria Guennewig, vice president, public affairs; **Dana Corporation,** Jeff Cole, manager, marketing communications; **Detroit Edison,** Dan Vecchioni, principal communications specialist, employee communications; **Dominion Resources, Inc.**, James Evans, executive writer; **Eli Lilly and Company,** Gail Sax, associate communications consultant; **FedEx Express,** Anne L. Swearingen, senior communication specialist; **Georgia-Pacific Corporation,** Greg Guest, senior manager, corporate communications; **GTE Corporation** (now Verizon), Peter Thonis, senior vice president, external communications; **Home Depot, Inc.**, Beth Aleridge, director, internal communication; **Ingersoll-Rand Company,** Paul Dickard, director, public relations; **Intel Corporation,** Jeanne Forbis, manager, media relations; **International Paper Co.**, Vicki Tyler, manager of publications, corporate communications/publications; **Kmart Corporation,** Mary Lorencz, director, corporate media relations; **Lockheed Martin Corp.**, Raymond V. Bartlett, director, communications; **McKesson HBOC, Inc.**, Clara Degen, manager and editor, employee communications; **The Mead Corporation,** Doug Draper, vice president, corporate communications; **Monsanto Company,** Sue Courtney, manager, strategic communications; **Nabisco, Inc.**, John Barrows, senior manager, marketing communications; **Newell Rubbermaid Inc.**, Dean L. Werner, director, corporate communications; **Nike, Inc.**, Scott Reames, senior communications manager; **Pharmacia & Upjohn Inc.**, Maury Ewalt, director, corporate internal communications; **PPG Industries, Inc.**, John Ruch, manager, corporate public information; **Praxair, Inc.**, Susan Szita-Gore, associate director, communications; **The Prudential Insurance Company of America,** Marie Pavlick, director, communications; **Quantum Corporation,** Kevin Heney, creative director; **R.R. Donnelley & Sons Company,** Vera C. Panchak, director, corporate communication; **Safeway Inc.**, Tom Conway, vice president, communications; **SCI Systems, Inc.**, Alma Kiss, newsletter editor, publications department; **Sempra Energy,** Ed Struble, manager, publications; **Southern Company,** Marc Rice, communication specialist, corporate communication; **Sprint National Consumer Organization,** Russ Robinson, director, global business markets public relations; **The St. Paul Companies, Inc.**, William Tamlyn, manager, communications; **Unicom**

Corp., Mark Mandernach, manager, corporate internal communications; **UnitedHealth Group Corporation**, Barbara J. Gustafson, manager, corporate communications; **United Technologies Corp.**, David Mackey, manager, publications; **USAA**, Thomas D. Honeycutt, specialist, public affairs; **U S West** (now Qwest), Mike Fernandez, vice president; **Viacom Inc.**, William Bartlett, manager, editorial services; **Wal-Mart Stores, Inc.**, Thomas Williams, senior manager, public relations; **WellPoint Health Networks Inc.**, Lisa Mee-Stephenson, senior consultant, corporate communications; **Williams Communications Group**, Lynne S. Butterworth, senior manager, corporate communications.

In addition to our survey participants, others contributed to the book. They are the people who took the time to painstakingly review our manuscript to make sure it was comprehensive, current, relevant, reality-based and accurate. For their time and input, we would like to thank Susan Brandwayn, Anne Cunningham, Eileen Cunningham, Mary Cunningham, Nora Cunningham, Elaine Donato, Anne Dorney, Melissa Gerardi, Charles Greene, Peter Hudelson, Nicholas Lesnikowski, Ida Lowe, Lisa Marsh, Clara Marshall, Virginia Melvin, Rhonda Price, Nancy Rine, Andrea Sholler, Michael Sinsky and Isabel Uibel.

We thank other family members and friends for their support and encouragement: Helenmarie Cunningham, John Cunningham, Myles Greene, Rose Anna Greene, Marie Elena Greene, Terrence Byrne, Mary D'Annibale, Doreen Murray, Patricia Leonard, Alice Good, Rose Greene, Esther Brandwayn, Thord Palmlund, George Uibel and Yuri Fridman.

We also are grateful for the love and encouragement we received from those who aren't here to see this book in print: Myles Byrne, Martha Byrne, Myles Byrne, Jr., Vincent Cunningham and William Greene.

Finally, we thank our agent, Jöelle Delbourgo; our editor, Danielle Egan-Miller; the senior project editor, Heidi Bresnahan; and the copyeditor, Christine Benton.

INTRODUCTION

IN TODAY'S WIRED BUSINESS ENVIRONMENT, everyone writes for a living. Whether you compose letters, proposals, memos, e-mails or reports, you need to write clearly, concisely and quickly. You must gather information, synthesize it and put it into readable form—all before the next deadline rolls around.

And you've got to get it right. In the workplace you can't afford to have a document full of errors and inconsistencies.

Consider this scenario: It's 5 p.m., and you have to finish proofreading a proposal your boss will send to a new client tomorrow. The more you look at it, the more questions you have. Is the symbol for the British pound £ or *GBP?* Does the period go inside or outside the parentheses? Does *highly complex* need a hyphen? Is it the board of directors *meets* Thursday or the board of directors *meet* Thursday? Is *chairman* capitalized? Is it *Website* or *Web site?* Is it *Euro* or *euro?* Your boss wants to see the final version by 6 p.m. (Is it *p.m.* or *PM?)* Where can you find the answers quickly?

Now you can turn to *The Business Style Handbook,* a stylebook tailored to people who write on the job. Professional communicators have at their disposal myriad stylebooks geared to their needs and industries. Most nonprofessional writers, on the other hand, aren't familiar with these resources. This book is geared to the person who writes on the job but doesn't have a background in communications.

The Business Style Handbook answers questions about usage, grammar, spelling and style in an A-to-Z format that is easy to navigate and written in plain English. The entries have a business focus. They are culled from our experience in corporate America as business writers and editors, various trade resources, business publications, the Internet and information from an extensive survey we conducted of professional communicators at the Fortune 500.

While you may be tempted to throw up your hands and say that you are an engineer, not a writer, that kind of thinking will hold you back. Today the ability to communicate effectively gives you a competitive advantage. An in-depth knowledge of your field may get you in the door, but good communication skills will open many more.

USE A ROAD MAP TO GET THERE

Today everyone must compose and deliver at Internet speed, but most employees have nowhere to turn with questions about style and usage, so they just give it their best effort. It's analogous to driving in an unfamiliar city without a road map. You can manage, but it's unnecessary to put yourself in that position. Every professional communicator relies on a stylebook to manage the issues that arise in writing. In an age when computers put writing skills on display as never before, it makes sense to borrow such a valuable tool from the professionals.

Language is complex and at times unruly. To write well in today's business environment, you need to know the basic rules of grammar, punctuation and style—and then some. That is where *The Business Style Handbook* can help. It provides specific guidelines for the issues that crop up in business writing—in a user-friendly format.

Your time is valuable. Getting your ideas across to the reader is your primary focus. But you still want to get it right. The problem is you can't afford to devote much time to finding out whether to write *e.g.* or *i.e.* It helps if you can look up the answer alphabetically, rather than search under *abbreviations* and then search for the *Latin abbreviations* subentry.

We have written *The Business Style Handbook* in language you can understand. It purposefully veers away from terms like *predicate nominative, appositive* and *parallelism.* You need answers. It's more important to know that too many *There is* or *It is* sentences can sound monotonous than it is to know expletive constructions are symptomatic of weak transitions. Highly grammatical language doesn't register with most people, let alone someone who is under pressure to finish a report. You don't need to get bogged down in abstraction when your boss is hovering nearby and asking for the report on mutual funds.

We stick to the essentials. At the risk of being overly focused, we have limited the A-to-Z entries to the words and questions that frequently arise in the workplace as well as the issues that interrupt the flow of writing on the job. For style questions that are open to interpretation—whether *access* is a verb or *Website* is one word—we give you enough information to make an informed decision.

Style is a "mixed bag of absolute rules, general conventions and individual options," according to Thomas S. Kane, author of *The Oxford Essential Guide to Writing.* Even the best writers need to refresh their memories frequently.

INSIGHT FROM THE FORTUNE 500

In deciding how to focus *The Business Style Handbook,* we conducted a survey of corporate communications professionals at 50 Fortune 500 companies. Whether you are a department head or a telecommuter, it's valuable to know how corporate America's writers approach writing.

The 33-question survey asked respondents a range of questions about style and usage at their organizations as well as their own preferences for writing. The results of that survey, spelled out in Chapter 1, provide an overview of the state of writing at some of the world's leading corporations. The findings confirm that guidance is in short supply for most employees who write on the job—even though every professional surveyed relies on one stylebook or more to write.

Say It "Simply, Pointedly and Quickly"

Chapters 2 through 5 cover other aspects of writing on the job. This includes a discussion of why style matters, recommendations for writing more effectively and suggestions for writing e-mail and using e-mail systems to maximum advantage.

Walter Kirn, an author and the literary editor of *GQ* magazine, wrote, ". . . the American genius for language lies in understatement, in saying things simply, pointedly and quickly, and in making new and clean and swift what otherwise might be ponderous, round and slow." These chapters are designed to help writers approximate that standard.

Go with the Flow

Language is constantly changing—nowadays at an accelerated pace and thanks in part to the influence of technology. Every day we add new words to the business lexicon and abandon old ones. Language also changes in subtle ways. One day putting a preposition at the end of the sentence is wrong, and the next day it is acceptable.

Geoffrey Nunberg, a chairman on the Usage Panel of the third edition of *The American Heritage Dictionary,* said: "Usage doctrines must change with the times, of course. The fundamental linguistic virtues—order, clarity and conciseness—are unassailable, yet they must be constantly reinterpreted against an evolving social background."

While grammarians and language pundits can afford to deliberate on changes in usage principles, people who write on the job cannot. Employees need to write in the language of the marketplace, which means using new words and using existing words in new ways. The trick is to do this without compromising writing standards.

"Countless careers rise or fall on the ability or the inability of employees to state a set of facts, summarize a meeting or present an idea coherently," said William Zinsser in the book *On Writing Well*. We agree. Communication skills are a primary consideration when hiring and promoting people at most major corporations.

We provide direction about new words and usage to help you strike a balance between the grammar lessons you learned in the past and the abandonment of standards prevalent in so much business writing. Our aim is to make writing easier and the end products—whether they are letters, reports, e-mails, specifications, brochures, proposals or annual reports—stronger.

We hope our stylebook will become a well-worn resource that earns a place by your side whenever you turn on the computer to write.

1

FORTUNE 500
SURVEY RESULTS

SEVERAL YEARS AGO BOTH OF US WERE writing corporate material on deadline (a brochure and an annual report to be exact) when we found ourselves stumped by an array of style questions. Even though we had various stylebooks at our disposal, it was impossible to find definitive answers to many questions, especially those pertaining to technology, finance and new words. In an effort to look beyond stylebooks for guidance, we examined the style decisions made in the corporate material of the Fortune 500.

It was a time-consuming and often frustrating process. We realized that if we were struggling to find answers, then other people who write on the job must deal with the same issues. We at least had the advantage of access to stylebooks and backgrounds in publishing. But many employees lack the tools or training to help them write correctly and effectively in the workplace. That's when we decided to fill the gap.

We created a 33-question survey for corporate communications departments at the Fortune 500 to gauge how major corporations approach writing. Professionals at 50 companies—Sprint, Nike, Prudential, Eli Lilly, Viacom, AT&T and Wal-Mart to name a few—participated in the survey, providing information on their standards, the standards within their departments and the writing style of their employees in general. All combined, these 50 companies represent more than 3.6 million employees. (For a complete list of the companies and respondents, see Acknowledgments.)

Their responses reveal some noteworthy trends.

Good Writing Matters

At most Fortune 500 companies, good writing matters—and it makes a difference in career advancement. When asked how important writing skills are to success at these organizations, only one professional responded not important. The other 29%* said very important, 22% said somewhat important, while 47% said that it depended on the position.

In addition, the overwhelming majority of survey participants are interested in benchmarking their style practices: 83% of those who responded said yes when asked whether they would like to know how other Fortune 500 companies formulate style guidelines. This reinforces the fact that people who write on the job are indeed looking for guidance.

Most Have Guidelines but Not for Everybody

Within the corporate communications departments, nearly three out of four companies surveyed—72% to be exact—follow style guidelines. The majority of these companies apply the guidelines to all printed materials; several respondents noted they also apply guidelines to online materials—including the Website, intranet and "official employee electronic bulletins." How extensive these guidelines are varies from industry to industry. While pharmaceutical companies tend to have voluminous guidelines, manufacturing companies often have minimal guidelines.

The issues that send professional communicators in search of a stylebook vary widely, too. When asked why they had most recently consulted a style manual, one person answered, "I use it too often to remember, but it probably involved hyphenation." Another needed to defend her correction of how the CEO used the word *comprise.*

Others said they resorted to stylebooks to resolve these questions: *altogether* versus *all together;* the word for people from the Philippines (*Filipinos);* how to abbreviate a state; capitalization and punctuation for bullets; whether to upper- or lowercase *Web;* how to write academic degrees; whether to capitalize *commonwealth* when writing *commonwealth of Kentucky;* use of quotation marks; use of commas; use of large numbers; *compared to* versus *compared with;* when a word is a collective noun; and capitalization.

Of the 37 companies that have guidelines, only 8 apply them company-wide. For the other companies the guidelines are used primarily in communications, media and marketing departments and in some cases in other areas of the company—including legal, investor relations, human resources and training.

This indicates that outside the departments where writing is an integral part of the job, employees at 84% of the companies surveyed are on their own when it comes to writing style. FedEx's senior communication specialist commented that the importance of good writing is sometimes discussed at her company but never reinforced because formal standards do not exist. Conseco's director of communications noted that creating company-wide guidelines would be overkill.

Rating the Rest of the Company's Writing

The near absence of company-wide guidelines may help explain why respondents gave their employees generally low marks for writing skills. On a scale of excellent/good/fair, only one company rated employees as excellent while 62% gave a fair rating and 36% good.

But seniority made a difference in this assessment, further confirming that good writing contributes to career growth. When asked to rate the writing skills of their senior executives, 13% of those who replied gave an excellent rating and 71% gave a good rating. Just 16% of senior executives received a fair rating.

In an effort to determine how to focus *The Business Style Handbook*, the questionnaire asked respondents to indicate the most glaring problems they encountered in employees' writing. The choices were clarity, spelling, grammar, punctuation and consistency.

Most respondents ticked off more than one category, and several ticked off all. But the two most frequently cited problem areas were clarity and consistency, followed by grammar. Punctuation and spelling were the least frequently cited. Comments written in the "other" category include the following: verbosity, structure, tone and faulty logic.

Few Guidelines for E-Mail, Though Most Favor Them

Of the companies surveyed, 86% had no style guidelines for e-mail. Senior vice president of external communications at GTE (now Verizon) noted that e-mail guidelines are unnecessary because e-mail is intended to be fast and informal.

Although only 14% of companies have e-mail guidelines, 60% of the corporate communications professionals at these companies adhere to guidelines for their own e-mail communication.

Moreover, when asked whether there should be writing standards for e-mail, 46% said yes. According to Praxair's associate director of communications, writing standards should be standards regardless of the medium. Eli Lilly's associate communications consultant agreed, noting that writing standards for e-mail regarding grammar, punctuation and spelling should be the same as for other written documents. Another respondent, Monsanto's manager of strategic communications, noted that most people would benefit from some *guidelines,* though *standards* would be difficult to implement.

Another 28% of respondents said that whether to apply standards to e-mail depends on factors including the audience, content, context and nature of the e-mail. For messages to a limited audience, standards may not be needed, according to the executive director of employee communication for

Bell Atlantic (now Verizon). He also noted that for documents with widespread distribution, material should be short, to the point, written in plain English and should include references to an intranet site or some other source if more details are needed.

Only 26% of respondents said writing standards should not be applied to e-mail.

EVERYBODY USES A STYLEBOOK

Regardless of whether their departments or companies have guidelines, every one of the corporate communications professionals surveyed uses a stylebook. The most frequently used is *The Associated Press Stylebook and Libel Manual.* A total of 45 out of 50 professionals—or 90%—rely on it as their primary source. Some noted more than one source, such as in-house style guidelines, *The Chicago Manual of Style, The Elements of Style* and *Words into Type.* If the business is highly technical, other books—such as *Wired Style* or the *American Medical Association Manual of Style*—are also used.

The prevalence of *The Associated Press Stylebook* can be attributed to factors including its alphabetical format and accessibility. At the same time many corporate communications professionals have journalistic backgrounds. One survey participant noted that since *The Associated Press Stylebook* is the industry standard at newspapers, some corporate communications professionals may be partial to this book because of its familiarity. Dana's marketing communications manager made another point. He believes that when press releases conform to Associated Press style, newspaper editors may be less inclined to edit them.

LIMITATIONS OF THE STYLEBOOKS

Of the stylebooks cited by the professionals surveyed—as both primary and secondary sources—none are written specifically for people who write on the job. According to the *Ragan Report, The Weekly Survey of Ideas and Methods for Communication Executives,* stylebooks are "put together not with the corporate situation in mind, but rather for journalism or academe."

Some survey participants have addressed this resource gap by creating their own internal style manual. International Paper developed an employee stylebook based on Associated Press style and *The American Heritage Dictionary.* The *International Paper Stylebook* includes some general information about grammar and punctuation, a trademark listing and a list of frequently used terms and capitalization. The manager of corporate communications/publications at International Paper wrote in the "Introduction" that the purpose of the stylebook is to provide "guidance and a basis of consistency for our written correspondence—both internal and external." The *International Paper Stylebook* is also noteworthy in that it addresses the needs of all employees who write on the job, not just the professional communicators or senior executives.

R.R. Donnelley & Sons also has developed style manuals, used for its newsletter and annual report, as well as by freelance editors, according to its director of corporate communication. In addition Eli Lilly has an in-house stylebook, and Ingersoll-Rand and Ameritech were in the process of developing their own guidelines at the time of the survey.

The questionnaire asked respondents what they would like *The Business Style Handbook* to focus on. Choices included concise guidelines for executives, issues related to new technology, grammar and punctuation, and standardization. Several respondents answered "all of the above," and most ticked off at least two categories. All tallied, each of the four categories received a similar number of votes, with concise guidelines at the top of the list, followed by grammar and punctuation, standardization and technology. Several professionals wrote that plain English should be another priority.

COPING WITH LAG TIME

The language of business and its usage have raced ahead of most stylebooks, creating another gap for people who write on the job. Most reference books don't have entries for many writing issues that arise in today's workplace.

Examples include whether to write *Nasdaq* or *NASDAQ;* whether to use a singular or plural verb with *ergonomics;* when to use *and* versus *&;* whether to use a singular or plural verb with *human resources;* the correct abbreviations for foreign currencies; how to write *B2B;* when *buyback* is one word versus two; how to alphabetize Spanish surnames; whether to capitalize or lowercase *digital age;* whether to use the word *access* as a verb and whether the word *data* can take a singular verb. The list goes on.

At the same time, new words, phrases and usage rules constantly enter the workplace. When the survey asked respondents to name a new word or phrase that has become mainstream, answers included *online, go-live, bricks and mortar, clicks and mortar, Y2K, impact* (as a verb), *cyberspace, proactive, at the end of the day, value-added, going forward, FedEx it, best practices, synergies, e-tail, globalize, dot-com* and *e-mail.* (All but four respondents said their companies write *e-mail* with a hyphen. One professional hyphenates it, except when feeling "lazy"; then he writes *email.)*

When asked how they establish standards for words and phrases that have not yet made their way into stylebooks and dictionaries, respondents indicated a range of resources. Many companies rely on usage in large national newspapers. Three respondents, Georgia-Pacific's senior manager of corporate communications, Nike's senior communications manager and Safeway's vice president of communications, go to the *New York Times* when a new word or phrase crops up. Dana's manager of marketing communications turns to the *Wall Street Journal* if it's not in *The Associated Press Stylebook.* UnitedHealth Group's manager of corporate communications also uses the *Wall Street Journal.* An editor at AT&T relies on both the *New York Times* and the *Wall Street Journal.* Home Depot's internal communication director turns to *USA Today.*

The creative director at Quantum checks with the International Association of Business Communicators. Viacom's manager of editorial services uses his own judgment while Intel's media relations manager seeks the opinion of the legal department. USAA's specialist for public affairs noted that "corporate consensus" determines standards for new words while Mead's vice president of corporate communications said "group consensus" carries the day. Newell Rubbermaid's director of corporate communications said he too relies on consensus.

Wired Style is the source used for new technology terms by R.R. Donnelley's director of corporate communication, as well as United Technologies' manager of publications.

Ameritech's manager of communications quality has various sources, including the Federal Communications Commission Website. CompUSA's director of public relations cited the trade press as one of her sources. Pharmacia & Upjohn's director of corporate internal communications said when *The Associated Press Stylebook* doesn't have the answer, he relies on historical preference.

STRONG VIEWS ON BUZZWORDS

About half the communications professionals at the Fortune 500 do not like buzzwords, and the mere mention of them evokes ire. When asked if they had a favorite buzzword, a number of respondents emphatically stated that they dislike, detest, hate or try to avoid buzzwords. This was also a question that brought out the exclamation points. Eli Lilly's associate communications consultant noted that not only did she *not* have a favorite buzzword, but she also tried to avoid them. CompUSA's director of public relations concurred, noting that this was a pet peeve. AFLAC's manager of editorial services took it a step further, noting that he hated buzzwords, including the word *buzzword*.

For the respondents who don't share the aversion to buzzwords, a few that get the thumbs-up include *value-added, input, impact* (as a verb), *broadband, synergies, bottom line, paradigm shift, robust, leverage, proactive, incentivize* and *corporatespeak*.

MIXED REVIEWS FOR IMPACT OF TECHNOLOGY

Asked whether computer technology has affected writing in a positive or negative way, just 20% of the respondents replied in the negative. The majority sees benefits. Verizon's executive director of employee communication said the technology is positive for those who constantly edit, revise and update material. Others shared a similar view, noting that the real benefit of computers comes in the rewriting and editing stages. Williams Communications' senior manager of corporate communications said technology is beneficial for continually improving and changing documents. St. Paul's manager of communications noted that, on the positive side, people are writing more because of the technology, but on the negative side, they often become careless because of the need to write and respond quickly.

This view was shared by others when asked whether the general business population is writing better because of computers: the response was 3-to-1 in favor of no. WellPoint's senior consultant for corporate communications noted that employees are writing more but not necessarily better. Quantum's creative director concurred, noting that technology gives publishing power to poor writers but does not necessarily improve grammar and spelling.

Write a Company's Name the Way the Company Does

A point on which there was near unanimity was how to write a company's name. When asked how they would write the name of a company that writes its name in all capitals, the overwhelming majority said they follow the company's style exactly. Take, for instance, *CIGNA*. Survey participants will use all capitals even if it does not conform to their own style guidelines. Only eight respondents would follow their in-house style.

Preferred Dictionaries and Word Processing Programs

Most companies surveyed have a standard dictionary, two of which stood out: 35 respondents use various editions of *Merriam-Webster's* while 12 use the latest edition of *The American Heritage Dictionary.* Three use the *Oxford English Dictionary* and one uses *Newton's Telecom Dictionary* to supplement *Webster's.* Consensus also exists on the word processing program used by survey participants: 48 out of 50 use Microsoft Word. This provides for a certain uniformity of style within organizations.

WITHOUT STYLE GUIDANCE

In companies without internal writing guidelines, some communications professionals seek outside guidance and suggest other employees do the same. Viacom's manager of editorial services said his writing improved after reading Richard Lanham's *Revising Prose.* Sempra Energy's manager of publications said writing seminars are useful. The newsletter editor in the publications department at SCI Systems said a review of grammar would help some employees.

HOW IT ALL ADDS UP

When creating the questionnaire, our goal was to obtain an overall idea of large organizations' priorities and preferences for effective communication as well as the kind of standards they adhere to. We had no preconceived notions about corporate America's style practices.

As varied as the responses were, they overwhelmingly confirm one trend: Although good writing matters at large organizations, the majority of employees receive no direction to help them write more effectively at a time when the language of business is evolving rapidly. This suggests that all parties— the organization, its customers, its vendors and all its employees—need and would benefit from guidance.

The good news is that this challenge is not necessarily difficult to address. According to the survey, the eight companies that give employees style guidelines and standards also give their employees better ratings as communicators.

In fact, five of the eight that have company-wide guidelines gave their employees a good or excellent rating on writing skills. When a company values these skills and provides direction, employees respond.

U.S. businesses spent more than $2 trillion on computers, software and other technology products during the 1990s. If companies are willing to expend such enormous sums on providing the tools to communicate, then it only makes sense to give employees the know-how to produce clear and effective communication.

*NOTE: All percentages are based on the number of respondents who answered that particular question. The respondents' participation in this survey does not necessarily indicate an endorsement of this stylebook.

2

WHY STYLE MATTERS

You may wonder what all the details of style covered in this book
have to do with communicating well. You are, after all, a businessperson—
not a grammarian. Your customers are going to buy the new equipment,
regardless of where you place your commas or whether you capitalize every
word in a sentence, so why should you take the extra time to improve your
writing skills when you could be on the telephone making more sales?

The answer is simple: credibility.

To get your message across to readers—whether they are customers,
employees, vendors, clients or colleagues—you must have credibility. When
inaccuracy, error, inconsistency, jargon and carelessness riddle a written document, you put your credibility on the line. Business relationships thrive on
trust, of which credibility is a key factor. Communication that is undisci-
plined, unfocused and unreliable sends a message about your organization that
could result in lost opportunities.

Fortune magazine has written about the "culture of discipline" that sepa-
rates "so-so companies" from "great" companies. These "inner directed" companies build cumulatively instead of reacting to the whimsy of the next big
thing. Good communication skills are part of the discipline of the corporate

culture of "great" companies—because companies cannot be great unless they are credible.

How Style Can Work Against You

To reach your readers—which is the primary aim of written communication—you need to adhere to certain conventions of style. These conventions are part of the discipline of language. They exist to promote understanding, not to thwart your creative energies. A simple paragraph, however, may contain enough questions about language to stump even a seasoned writer.

That's why stylebooks were created. They reinforce principles of grammar and punctuation. They keep the vernacular current and fresh. They clear away the discrepancies of conflicting information. Overall a good stylebook keeps you alert and thoughtful, helping you to think more clearly about the best way to communicate effectively.

But writing style is also multilayered. According to *The Oxford Essential Guide to Writing,* there is grammar; usage (how you are supposed to write as a member of a certain community); mechanics (how certain conventions make writing consistent and clear); and approach (how you convey the message to readers). All these layers can conspire to slow the writing process. In fact, they can be real hurdles. Not only can you get tangled up in the mechanics of a complex sentence, but you may also struggle with the tone or approach your document should take.

To make matters more difficult, language is dynamic. It evolves continually to reflect the environment from which it springs. Keeping up with all the change can be daunting. Take, for instance, what has occurred with the technology boom. Suddenly many words have an *e-* prefix, or *Website* may appear three different ways within a single document. People who write on the job don't know how to proceed. Companies that have style guidelines in place can address these changes. Companies without guidelines leave employees to fend for themselves.

This is why you can never assume you have all the skills you need to communicate well. You have to take into account that language is dynamic and your objectives will change from one project to the next. In fact, writing habits developed in high school and college may not be appropriate for your current job. You need to continually assess the way you use language—to make sure you achieve your aim, which, in the world of business, is to reach your readers.

How Style Can Work for You

One of the reasons people who write on the job fall into jargon and corp-speak is that they have no one steering them away. And the rationale for such language exists.

Your business is a dark science. It is so complicated, so dense, so incomprehensible to the average mind that only you and a select few are privy to its secrets and mysterious beauty. That is why you need to write in a language no one understands.

This approach can be counterproductive. Imagine going on a sales call with rumpled hair and in your weekend sweat suit. What's the likelihood of making a sale? Ignoring the way you present material to the reader is like dressing inappropriately. It undermines you, sends the wrong message about your company and defeats your purpose.

Writing, at its best, is a balancing act between you and your readers. It is tempting to fall into the jargon of your business, but you should always ask yourself if your writing gets the job done when you use it. This doesn't mean that technical language isn't useful. The span of business covers everything from nuts and bolts to metaworlds and packet-switching. It is a complicated world, but it is still your job to make it look simple.

So aim for simplicity, and realize time is not on your side. Readers are bombarded with information. If you cannot catch their attention quickly, chances are good you will lose them. Your mother may struggle to understand you, but readers will not. While there is no guarantee that you will hook each reader every time, you can improve your chances immensely if you aim for writing that is clear and concise. Remember, it is impossible to influence people if your thinking is fuzzy, your objectives are camouflaged and your language confounds.

That's why it's important to develop a style that is accessible, functional and simple. Your writing style, ultimately, tells your readers what you think of them. When you take the time to write clear sentences—with the proper punctuation, correct grammar and spelling, and consistent organization—you tell readers you value them and you are capable. You also make their job, which is to read your document, easier.

Flannery O'Connor, the renowned short story writer, once said, "The writer is only free when he can tell the reader to go jump in the lake." This notion may appeal to students, but it will not serve you well when you write the annual report. Business writing style is more craft than art. Your primary objective is to influence readers—and you cannot do this if you ignore, belittle or confuse them. A simple, clear style is a courtesy to the reader. And, like most courtesies in business, it is a requirement.

Take Charge

The price seasoned writers pay for stellar prose is heavy—and most people who write for the job have neither the time nor the inclination to pursue this level of writing—but that does not mean you cannot improve the skills you already have. All you need is willingness and guidance.

Writing is a process. Each individual project starts with a first draft and ends with the final review. As you work through this process, you need to be willing to be simple rather than complex, clear rather than fuzzy, accurate rather than sloppy and brief rather than long-winded.

In your everyday life you probably write as you speak. You will say and write *I enjoy a cup of hot chocolate after shoveling snow because it takes the chill out of my bones.* You write this way because it seems natural and appropriate.

The minute you walk into the office, though, your tone changes. You write instead *It is beneficial to consume eight ounces of hot chocolate after removing frozen precipitation from the earth's surface because it raises body temperature to an agreeable level.*

You distance your readers almost unconsciously by choosing unsuitable words to get your message across. It is unnecessary but inescapable—unless you pay attention to how your style works for or against you. If you want to get the job done, your best bet is a direct, simple, clear style.

In the past decade the push to use plain language has gathered momentum because it is good for business. An article in the *New York Times* said, "The Veterans Benefits Administration . . . said it expected to save about $500,000 a year because, after training employees in its life insurance division how to write more clearly, the response rate on one of its letters shot up to 62 percent, from about 35 percent."

The same article listed other initiatives that organizations have made to emphasize simplicity. In 1997 the Securities and Exchange Commission ordered mutual fund companies to rewrite their prospectuses in plain language. In 1999 President Bill Clinton urged government agencies to rewrite all material the public sees. The Food and Drug Administration mandated that drug labels be easier to read by 2005.

Put All the Pieces Together

You also have to adhere to the grammar, usage and mechanics that will promote clear writing. Clarity, consistency and accuracy are essential for writing to be authoritative and persuasive. If your reports are full of errors and inconsistencies, your readers will lose patience and fail to take your message seriously. It also can hurt the bottom line.

Exact figures on how much inaccuracies and errors cost companies are impossible to tally, but the prevalence of mistakes in corporate communication is well documented. "Many organizations distribute spreadsheet macros to manage budgets and allocate resources. . . . Raymond Panko, a professor at the University of Hawaii, reviewed decades' worth of studies on spreadsheets and found that an average of 30% have errors built into their rules. We're talking misplaced decimal points, transposed digits, and wrong signs. A 1996 study by the British arm of Coopers & Lybrand found that 90% of spreadsheets contained errors," according to an article in *Fortune.*

To further complicate matters, on any given day a writer may be challenged by the placement of a comma, the correct punctuation of quotations or the intricacies of the semicolon. Who cares? If meaning is not jeopardized, what's the big deal if you forget to put in a comma or spell *Website* as one word or two? Why get tangled up in minutiae, especially when the deadline is an hour away?

The fact is that attention to detail is not up for grabs in business. Good form, accuracy and consistency are the hallmarks of authoritative writing. A careless style—or even an idiosyncratic style—can undermine a project. The details matter.

It has been reported that the founder of J. Crew once stormed out of a meeting because someone wrote "SPR 94" on a report instead of "SP 94," which was how he wanted to see the word *spring* abbreviated. This illustrates not only how a boss's expectations can be rigorous but also that many style decisions are subjective. Some style choices are merely preferences, but, for the sake of coherence and consistency, you need to adhere to them. A growing number of organizations expect employees to be on the same page when it comes to style and usage.

Content is paramount in communication, but writers cannot afford to downplay style, either. In this age of information, writing skills are on full display. The expectation at most companies is that writing be clear, concise, simple and direct, and " 'the people who get ahead in business are the ones with good presentation skills,' of which good grammar is a critical component," according to an executive at a major corporation, who was quoted in an article in the *Wall Street Journal.*

Language is dynamic, not neat and tidy. To harness this unruly process, people who write on the job need guidance. Without becoming rigid or pedantic, this stylebook should help to provide the direction you need.

3

THE CASE FOR STANDARDS

LARGE ORGANIZATIONS INCREASINGLY recognize the importance of investing in their employees as a source of competitive advantage. In this enlightened environment, strengthening writing skills is an obvious contender for some investment, particularly now that computers have made everyone a writer.

Yet most employees continue to struggle when writing on the job. According to the *Journal of Communication Management,* "The modern corporate environment places an unprecedented expectation upon employees to communicate. The range of communications mechanisms available in modern working life tends to generate a wealth of communication activity without necessarily producing quality communication."

Employees can hardly be blamed for inadequate writing skills. According to our survey of the Fortune 500, only 8 of the 50 companies polled have a company-wide writing standard. This is a considerable disservice to employees who are required to write, particularly since every one of the corporate communications professionals surveyed uses one or more stylebooks. Why deprive an organization's nonwriters of a writing tool the organization's writers can't do without!

Time for Companies to Invest in the Users

During the 1990s companies focused on upgrading the computer workstation (which, according to Jeremy Rifkin in *The Age of Access,* has a life span of less than 24 months). In this decade companies need to invest in employees' know-how—including their writing skills. This can start by creating standards, which will help an organization to:

- **Improve the quality of communication.** Ultimately the goal of standards is to promote clear, concise writing, which is what everyone in business wants to read. When an organization puts all employees—from the programmers to the engineers to the accountants—on the same page for writing style and usage, it raises the bar on written communication. It sends a message that good writing matters.

- **Increase competitiveness.** Good communication skills have never been as important as they are today. Employees who communicate effectively will give companies a competitive edge in the 21st century. It is fundamental to good business. Successful companies not only recruit the best people; they also develop them.

- **Empower employees.** The introduction of standards gives employees a tool to improve their writing skills. It's one thing to tell people they should write better; it's another to give them guidelines to get there. CEOs may be able to rely on the corporate communications department to write, edit and proof their memos, but most employees don't have the same luxury. A reference guide that reinforces the fundamentals of grammar, punctuation and style empowers employees.

- **Increase efficiency.** Standards make life easier for the writer—which translates into efficiency. When writing and editing documents, employees don't need to waste time deciding how to write, punctuate or abbreviate a word. Instead they can spend their time on content and the challenge of writing quickly and effectively.

- **Ensure consistency.** Standards introduce consistency across all the organization's materials and audiences. Take the example of two employees at a pharmaceutical company. Laura Kelly in corporate communications refers to a stylebook to write the client newsletter while Vincent Uibel in human resources relies on instinct to write an employee benefits package. Kelly writes *healthcare* while Uibel writes *health care.* Who's right? They both are, but within one company everybody should write it the same way.

People Welcome Guidance

The Fortune 500 survey respondents gave their employees generally low marks for writing skills. And, after sampling some of the material that has crossed our desks in the last few years, we believe the situation may be even worse at smaller companies.

The good news is that people generally want guidance. When Purdue University created an online writing lab, OWL—reportedly the first of its kind— the site received 885,930 visitors in its first five months. That's 7,000 hits a day from writers looking for online assistance with grammar and punctuation (http://owl.english.purdue.edu).

"It's baffling how important this resource has become," said Muriel Harris, professor of English and director of the writing lab. "We needed something to serve our students, but now we help businessmen around the world who have English as a second language, teachers in rural communities who use our handouts because they don't have books, and other universities that are establishing their own OWLs."

Create a Standard

Instituting a standard need not be complicated. The first step is to raise awareness that the quality of written communication is important. This may involve a memo from a senior executive or an entry in the company handbook. At a bare minimum, employees should be encouraged to run their documents through the grammar and spell checker.

Taking the concept to the next level entails giving all employees a reference guide for grammar, usage and spelling. Although all professional communicators use such guides, the notion remains foreign to most employees who have not worked in communications fields. The relevant department (e.g., corporate communications, media, training) can choose a stylebook that addresses the company's needs or spearhead the creation of in-house guidelines. An alternative is the hybrid approach in which the company selects a stylebook and then supplements it with additional guidelines that are particular to the company and industry.

WIN EMPLOYEE BUY-IN

Convincing employees that standards are in their best interest may take some work. Initially they may react by wondering how they can be expected to spend time honing writing skills when they already eat lunch at their desks every day.

That's precisely the point. Standards free everyone from the time-consuming preoccupation of deciding what's standard and what's not. Even though the highest standards are not foolproof, they still can liberate the busy employee from making decisions about the hundreds of details that trip up even the seasoned writer. Rather than impose on employees, standards provide a service to them.

Another issue is that old habits are hard to break. When we asked colleagues to review our manuscript to ensure it included frequently used business terms, one became indignant at the notion that the word *data* could be used with a singular verb. This is hardly surprising since style can vary from one stylebook to the next.

Even we could not reach agreement on certain style customs. The commonplace business practice of turning nouns into verbs, as in *Let's fast-track this project,* turned into a lively debate—with one of us resisting fervently while the other claimed the practice is useful, colorful and ubiquitous in the workplace. In the end, because of their obvious usefulness in business, we opted to include some words and phrases that may be considered nonstandard. We do, however, realize that strict grammarians may object.

Language is a powerful tool. And employees should use it to the maximum advantage. Applying standards to the way language is used at the workplace has never made better sense.

4

WRITE WITH PURPOSE

To communicate effectively in the business world, you need to convey your message in language that is clear, direct and simple—and you need to do it fast. Everyone is busy today, operating under information overload. "Anything you write is competing for influence with hundreds of other documents on your readers' desks—or e-mail systems," said Stuart Z. Goldstein, managing director of corporate communications at The Depository Trust & Clearing Corporation. "If you don't grab your readers' attention quickly, you risk losing them."

Don't waste people's time by making them struggle to decipher your message. Have a strategy when you write. Approach writing as a process and break this process into steps.

Have a Goal

Think it through. Ask yourself why you are writing and what you expect to achieve. Are you writing to inform, to make a request, to make a recommendation, to solicit feedback, to initiate discussion, to convince, to complain?

According to a senior manager of corporate communications at Williams Communications, writers should determine what they want the audience to do and then write in a way that persuades them.

Be clear about your subject matter. In business, the subject of your communication is often predetermined. You want Lorna Milbauer to attend the conference in Atlanta next month. That's the subject of your e-mail. Or you want to increase your department's budget for software. That's the subject of your memo. Think critically about your subject. Gather the facts and ask yourself if they warrant your effort and your readers' attention. If senior management has asked all departments to cut expenses by 5%, this is probably not the time to ask for a budget increase.

Anticipate questions to ensure you achieve the desired outcome. If you are mapping out a product-launch strategy, provide a timetable. If you are requesting a response, give a deadline. If you are lobbying for a budget allocation, put a number on it. If you are asking someone to call or e-mail you, list your direct telephone number and e-mail address. If you are referencing a Website, include the Web address.

Know Your Audience

Communications professionals at the Fortune 500 emphasized over and over again how important it is to write with your readers in mind.

Understand what your readers know about the subject and the level of detail they will want. The vice chairman may ask for a memo on how foreign exchange rates are affecting profitability, but chances are he does not want details about currency fluctuations in every market. Customers want to know how a new online service will help them, not how the technology operates. The mailroom needs to know when the annual report will be sent out, not that the printer had a mechanical problem and is running behind schedule. If a prospective client asks for information on your firm's experience in healthcare mergers and acquisitions, it's overkill to include your accomplishments in entertainment M&A as well.

Write and Think at the Same Time

Often the hardest part of writing is sitting down in front of a blank screen. A director of public relations at CompUSA observed that writers should just get started, rather than worry about getting it right on the first try.

Also remember that, as you write, the thought process continues to evolve. "Writing is thinking on paper. Anyone who thinks clearly can write clearly, about anything at all," according to William Zinsser, author of *On Writing Well.* The many decisions you make as you write will shape your message and influence your audience's response.

Use the Right Language

Choose words that convey your meaning in the simplest terms. It may be tempting to write in the idiom of your business or specialty. It's familiar, saves time and sends the signal that you are an insider. But is it appropriate? Again, be guided by your audience. For a memo to readers versed in technology and systems, technical language works. If you are sending the same memo to the entire organization, write in plain English so that everyone understands.

Write as you speak. Readers are confused, not impressed, by legalistic or esoteric vocabularies. Write simply because simplicity is a product of careful thought and choice, not because you underestimate your audience.

Make clarity a priority when selecting words. Shoot for the specific and concrete, not the ambiguous and abstract. "If you do not choose words wisely, words will, in effect, choose you, saying things about the topic you do not intend and affecting readers in ways you do not want," said Thomas S. Kane in *The Oxford Essential Guide to Writing*.

Keep It Short—Most of the Time

The senior manager of marketing communications at Nabisco offered some concise advice to those who write on the job: Be brief. Write short sentences and paragraphs and put the most important information up front.

Use strong, well-chosen words to make an impact: *The consumer foods division increased revenues by a record 22% in the third quarter.* Wordy, roundabout sentences dilute the message and take up more space: *During the third quarter of the year, revenues in the consumer foods division were up by 22%, which is the highest quarterly increase ever in the company's history.* Direct sentences start with a noun and follow closely with the verb. Don't tax the reader with sentences that are loaded down with adjectives and adverbs.

Does that mean a short sentence is always preferable to a long one? Not necessarily. A paragraph of short sentences can sound choppy. And a long sentence can be well written and concise, provided every word counts. To create balance, mix up sentence length—but always remember that space is at a premium. Don't throw everything into the mixture for the sake of filling up a page.

Make Longer Documents User-Friendly

If the document must be lengthy, lead with an executive summary and include a table of contents. Good organization promotes economy and emphasis in your writing, and your documents will be easier to read as a result. *Fortune* magazine reported on a good model set forth by one corporate titan: "Procter & Gamble is, of course, famous for insisting upon one-page memos to ensure crisp, rigorous, and focused analyses. Two-page memos don't get read."

Sample Memo to All Employees

SUBJECT: PROTECTING THE CORPORATE IDENTITY

In preparing any type of communication—whether letters, PowerPoint presentations, marketing materials or memos—all employees should remember to follow our standards governing corporate identity. It is everyone's responsibility to ensure that we use our corporate symbols consistently.

Why the Brand Matters

A brand establishes a company's image in the marketplace and differentiates it from competitors. It communicates the company's vision, philosophy and approach. It also conveys the relationship a company has with customers and employees.

How to Protect Our Logo

The logo is the visual depiction of our brand, and employees are the front line in protecting this logo. In our commitment to communicate quality in all that we do, proper use of the logo is essential. Here are some guidelines to follow:

- **Keep the symbol and name together.** Our logo consists of the green compass symbol and either the initials *AAD* or the company's full name, *Aegean's Architecture & Design*. Don't separate these two elements.

- **Use & when you write our name.** Write *Aegean's Architecture & Design*, not *Aegean's Architecture **and** Design*.

- **Use the templates.** Our graphics department has created templates for internal memos, letterhead, fax cover sheets and PowerPoint presentations.

- **Check the online manual.** If you have questions about our policies, refer to the Corporate Identity Manual on the intranet or contact Karen Gregory, by e-mail at kgregory@aad.com, or by telephone at 421-1876.

For material that is more than one page, write headings that succinctly state what each section discusses. This helps you focus in the writing process and also guides readers, telling them what the document covers. In addition, it allows your audience to read selectively and find what they're looking for easily.

Write headings that say something and can stand on their own. For example, the heading *Longer Documents* is vague, whereas *Make Longer Documents User-Friendly* is a recommendation and also tells the reader what to expect in this section.

Bullets are another way to make documents more readable and more concise, which in turn makes your message clearer. They are visually appealing as well. You could write *Fortune 500 companies are strong candidates to buy this product. U.S. government organizations are also potential customers, as are multilateral institutions,* but it's more effective to write:

The market for this product is broad-based and includes:

- Fortune 500 companies
- U.S. government organizations
- Multilateral institutions

Another advantage of bullet points is their flexibility. You can write them as single words or phrases (as in the preceding example); with a concise introductory phrase, followed by an explanation (see the next section, Get Right to the Point); or as a complete thought, as in the following example:

The three action steps are:

- Form an e-business group.
- Develop an internal Internet culture.
- Create virtual communities.

Be consistent in how you start each bullet point. This will be determined by the lead-in sentence, which unifies the entire section. In the preceding examples, notice how the first example has no verbs or period while in the second each bullet is a complete sentence and ends with a period.

Get Right to the Point

Start with your conclusion—it's possible your entire document will not be read—and then make your case in order of importance. Take the same approach with each paragraph, putting the main point in the first sentence. For many documents it is useful to begin by synthesizing key points into a bulleted phrase, followed by a brief summary of the point. Whenever possible use concrete numbers, examples and reliable sources to persuade. The following three examples illustrate this.

1. I recommend we open a Brazil office in 2003. Reasons include:

   - **Cost savings.** It will cut our cost of doing business in the Brazilian market by 15% over the next three years.

   - **Higher regional sales.** Demand for our products is growing 10% p.a. in Latin America. We can use our Brazilian operation to source other Latin markets and to further increase brand awareness throughout the region.

2. You should switch to our service for the following reasons:

   - **24/7 customer service.** Someone will be available whenever you have a question.

   - **A strong global network.** We have offices in more than 80 cities around the world, so you can contact us even when you travel.

3. I am pleased to announce Andrei Savin will join us as CFO, effective June 22. His credentials include:

   - **Outstanding experience.** Andrei has worked in global finance for more than 25 years at three multinational companies.

   - **Excellent references.** The CFOs at Andrei's former employers uniformly commend his talent and dedication.

If you need to develop each point in more detail, do so later in the document. If you need to include extensive background information or documentation, do so with an attachment or appendix.

Take the Credit

Use language to convey that your department, your company or you are in control. For example, *The European division grew market share in France to 40% in 2002* credits the division with growing share—it didn't just happen. It is much stronger than *Market share in France grew to 40% in 2002.* (This suggests that market share grew itself without any effort from the European division.)

In general, write in the active, not passive, voice. It is stronger and puts the subject in command. *The company delivered the new product on schedule* emphasizes that the company met its commitment. The active voice is much stronger than this construction: *The new product was delivered on schedule.* (This leaves the company out of the picture entirely, which is usually not what you want to do.)

Writing in the active voice does not always come naturally. You may need to go back and rework some sentences. Look for *is/was/are/were* followed by a past-participle verb (*is delivered/was written/are produced/were positioned).* For example, change *The memo **was written** by Clara* to *Clara **wrote** the memo.* Remember that the most vital word in every sentence is the verb, so use it to full advantage.

Shift the Emphasis

For all its merits the active voice is not always the best choice. When you need to be tactful or to emphasize what is happening to the object rather than the subject, the passive voice is more effective. In *Plain Style: Techniques for Simple, Concise, Emphatic Business Writing,* Richard Lauchman says, "The passive is often necessary and writers who believe it is 'bad' or 'weak' will often emphasize the wrong idea."

Say you want to be imprecise about who is responsible for an action to avoid allocating blame. In this case the passive voice works: *The white paper was not completed on schedule.* (It's unclear who missed the deadline.) *The investor relations department did not complete the white paper on schedule.* (In this sentence the responsibility lies squarely with investor relations.)

Here is another example of the passive: *The quarterly earnings projections were missed.* The numbers were off, but the phrasing is vague about who's at fault. Compare that with *The software division missed its quarterly earnings projections.* (Here the software division is accountable.)

In a sentence about a study and its authors, a passive construction allows you to emphasize the study (the object), as in *A groundbreaking study on the treatment of migraines was written by researchers in Sweden.* Compare that with the active construction, which gives the authors top billing: *Researchers in Sweden wrote a groundbreaking study on the treatment of migraines.*

Take a Stand

Sometimes you need to state a position. It is often best to do so with conviction. Strip out phrases that weaken your thought. Use language that conveys confidence: *I recommend we end the joint-venture talks immediately.* Compare that with *In my opinion, it would be worth considering whether or not we should contemplate putting an end to the joint-venture talks as soon as possible.* The preceding sentence is full of hedges.

Take out words that sound soft. *I believe we can correct this problem by Tuesday.* If it is something you really believe, write *We will correct this problem by Tuesday* or *I am confident we will correct this problem by Tuesday.* Note that in writing about the future, *will* is stronger than *can.*

Other words that weaken your position include *feel* and *think. We feel we need to issue a memo about the compensation study.* If you're committing it to writing, presumably it is what you feel, so it is better to write *We need to issue a memo about the compensation study.*

Remember, *can* is more decisive than *could,* and *will* is more decisive than *would.*

THINK ABOUT POINT OF VIEW

Be deliberate about your choice of *I, we* and *you* (pronouns). These words change your relationship to the reader, making a difference in tone as well as results. At the same time, maintaining a consistent point of view unifies and strengthens a document.

A memo to the CEO could read: *I will ask all employees to submit ideas for developing Internet technologies.* This suggests it is your initiative. Alternatively you could write *We will ask all employees to submit ideas for developing Internet technologies.* The *we* indicates that your group or division is asking. It is often advisable to use *we* in business writing when more than one person is involved in a decision or initiative, which is generally the case.

We can also be used to speak on behalf of the organization. A letter to clients might read *We appreciate the opportunity to serve you.* This is friendlier than *The company appreciates the opportunity to serve you,* although you'll probably need to switch between the two in most documents of that sort.

Many business writers avoid writing *I* or *we,* but remember that these words can be effective when your identity and opinion count.

The use of *you* speaks directly to your readers: *We invite you to complete the attached questionnaire.* Compare that with *The company invites all employees to complete the attached questionnaire.* The *we/you* sentence is personal, direct and cordial. It pulls readers into the initiative.

When the facts have to speak for themselves, use the third person: *The company will accept applications for the new customer service department.* This is the voice of *just the facts, please.* It is also the preferred form in scientific, legal and academic writing, in which the writer remains transparent because objectivity takes precedence. But avoid taking the third person to the extreme. *The writer believes* instead of *I* can sound awkward, even in a report on hydroponics. This construction can also sound pretentious. The same is true for *one.* In business writing try to avoid sentences such as *One will benefit from buying the complete insurance package.* Instead write *You will benefit* or *Customers will benefit.* Whatever your choice of pronoun, select one that will dominate.

Keep a Tight Time Frame

Pay attention to the verb tense you use and try to be as consistent as possible throughout the document. Avoid switching back and forth among past, present and future, even though you may need more than one tense to deal with time factors.

Unify your writing by tense to ensure clarity. For instance, the time sequence is confusing in the following two sentences: *The timetable was unrealistic. Quality assurance is at risk, and our schedule was already tight.* Compare that with the use of *is* throughout: *The timetable is unrealistic. Quality assurance is at risk and our schedule is already tight.*

Confusing and inconsistent verb tenses make the reader work too hard, which is not what you want your document to do. Whenever possible, write in the simple present or past tense, unless you are trying to convey a specific time sequence.

Also minimize use of the *-ing* form of verbs (called the perfect tense). It is more decisive and cleaner to write *The company plans to roll out the new product in March* than *The company is planning to roll out the new product in March.* Another example: *The CEO will discuss the fourth-quarter financials at the meeting* is stronger than *The CEO will be discussing the fourth-quarter financials at the meeting.*

Review Everything

After you finalize a document or an important e-mail, spell check it. Then review it on hard copy for content and clarity. Allocate enough time for this part of the process and follow the advice of a communications specialist at Southern Company: Put yourself in the reader's place. If time permits, also ask a colleague to read it over for you.

Be sure your document covers all your points and is clear. Check that it flows logically and has smooth transitions. Then review your document, looking for ways to cut it, to make it more concise. Take out words, phrases or paragraphs that are repetitive or add no value. Tighter language conveys focus and is more likely to be read attentively. A shorter document also saves the reader time.

Go back and verify all the facts. Check to make sure that numbers and calculations are correct, quotes are exact and sources cited are accurate. If you're listing a Web address, for example, go to the Internet and make sure your reference will take the reader to the right site. Verify the spelling of all proper names, including people, organizations and places. Check that titles are correct. Also make sure names and titles are correct on distribution lists.

Next put your document through a rigorous review for grammar, spelling, punctuation and style. Errors and inconsistencies are distractions that compromise your message and subtly undermine your credibility—"the written equivalent of a misbuttoned shirt," said Michael Sinsky, senior deputy prosecuting attorney for King County in the state of Washington. Once you've gone through the trouble of composing a well-written document, don't undermine yourself with mistakes of this nature.

Finally, if you're sending a letter or using a courier service, double-check addresses and phone numbers on the letter and on the envelope; if it's an e-mail, be sure the right person or persons are in the To and *cc* lines; if it's a fax, double-check fax numbers.

Make It Look Good

Don't underestimate the power of visual elements; also review the document for its look. Readers notice the overall design of a document, and a busy or haphazard layout will discourage them from continuing.

Font styles (bold and italics) are one way to make documents user-friendly, but don't overuse them; otherwise they lose their impact and documents start to look busy. Also be aware that when applied to more than a few words, bold and italics render text more difficult to read. Make sure the punctuation following italic or bold type is in the same font. Observe how magazines use bold and italics selectively and make that a guide.

Put headings and subheadings in bold to make them stand out. It reinforces the written break in the text with a visual differentiation. Also use bold to emphasize words in text that provide critical information, as in **January 12 is the deadline.** But, in general, minimize the use of bold within the body of your text. Try to convey the emphasis in your writing instead.

For bulleted information, it is sometimes effective to set off introductory words in bold to guide the reader. But don't go overboard and bold the entire thought; then you lose the emphasis and weaken the document visually. See the following example:

The quality initiative will institute a culture of learning, in which employees learn from:

- **Customers,** by actively seeking their feedback to understand their needs, issues and points of view
- **Each other,** by sharing information across the entire company to build knowledge
- **The marketplace,** by benchmarking against similar organizations and the competition, and adopting best practices
- **The experts,** by attending training seminars and by staying abreast of developments in the field

Compare that with the following example, in which the whole point of bolding is lost:

The quality initiative will institute a culture of learning, in which employees learn from:

- Customers, by actively seeking their feedback to understand their needs, issues and points of view
- Each other, by sharing information across the entire company to build knowledge
- The marketplace, by benchmarking against similar organizations and the competition, and adopting best practices
- The experts, by attending training seminars and by staying abreast of developments in the field

A few more guidelines for fonts:

- Use italics when you want to differentiate text but with a less pronounced visual impact than bold. Italics are often a better choice within blocks of text.

- Don't use bold and italics together for more than a few words; it's difficult to read.

- Avoid underlining to emphasize text; it makes a document look less polished, and many people find it difficult to read. Avoid combining underlining with either bold or italics.

- Use different font sizes sparingly; otherwise your document begins to look chaotic. For example, in long documents a larger type size can be useful to create title pages and section titles. But, in general, keep the alternate type sizes fairly close in size to the rest of the text. It's excessive, for example, to create 36-point section headings for a document written in 12-point type. A better choice would be 14-point type, which is clearly distinguishable without being overwhelming.

  If using different font sizes, be consistent. If a document contains titles and you put the first title in 14-point type, make sure each subsequent title is also in 14-point type.

- Avoid mixing fonts within a document. If you start out with Times New Roman, use it throughout. **Don't switch to Bookman midstream.**

Choose the Best Medium

Know your readers' preferences about receiving written material. If you don't know their preference, you can ask. In some companies nearly everything is done by e-mail, but in others hard copy takes precedence for memos, reports and so on. Some clients prefer regular mail, courier or fax while others will insist on e-mail only. Depending on the content and the recipient, you may need to send material both electronically and on hard copy. Within organizations, you may encounter some executives who are averse to either e-mail or hard copy. Take their preferences into account.

Budget Your Time

Finally, give yourself enough time to put all the pieces together. Omitting the last page of your report is as serious as having incorrect numbers. To create accurate and professional documents, budget your time so that you can complete the task.

5

E-MAIL:
BEFORE YOU HIT SEND

ANYTHING YOU WRITE ON THE JOB reflects on you, so even with e-mail, be mindful of writing style. And before hitting the Send button, be sure to think through every aspect of communicating electronically to ensure you use e-mail to its best advantage.

Most organizations have e-mail policies that focus on the proper use of the e-mail system. But few have guidelines for how to write e-mail and use e-mail systems effectively. Of the Fortune 500 companies surveyed for this book, just 14% have e-mail style guidelines (one was in the process of writing them). That leaves it up to you.

CHOOSE THE RIGHT STYLE

In deciding how to write an e-mail, be guided by who's receiving it and the nature of the correspondence, always keeping in mind that e-mails are easily forwarded to third parties. If you're sending a message to the general counsel, make sure your grammar, spelling, punctuation and capitalization are in order. If you're writing to a client, also make it error-free and treat it as formal correspondence. If you're writing to wish a colleague a happy birthday, relax your style and take an informal approach.

Also be guided by the e-mails you receive. If you're dealing with a client company in which everyone takes an informal approach, follow that lead. While conducting research for *The Business Style Handbook,* we sent Amazon.com's CEO, Jeff Bezos, an e-mail to ask his preference for writing *Amazon* since it appears as both *amazon* and *Amazon* in the company's own materials. The response was a good indication of Amazon's corporate style. "Feel free to capitalize or to not capitalize our name. I've seen it done both ways as well. Since we're an Internet company, we're not too caught up in convention and formal procedures," replied Ryan Kipple. This suggests that a relaxed style could actually further your cause with Internet companies, though it is always a good idea to proofread all e-mails.

If, on the other hand, you are dealing with a company where tradition and Brooks Brothers' suits prevail, conduct your correspondence with an eye toward the "convention and formal procedures" that Amazon shrugs off.

BE CAUTIOUS WITH CONTENT

There is no such thing as privacy in e-mail. "Write an e-mail as though it could end up on the front page of the *New York Times,*" said Ida Lowe, director, user support services, Thomson Financial—Operations, who has taught courses on e-mail at the City University of New York. Always err on the side of caution regarding content. Don't send confidential or classified information via e-mail—and don't put anything into an e-mail that could offend others, embarrass you or come back to haunt you.

Be aware that every time you send and receive e-mail, copies are made on servers, where they can be retrieved by anyone—from an employee (at your company or at your Internet service provider) to a hacker.

Also remember that all e-mail sent through the system at work is the property of your organization. You risk being fired for using the system to send or forward messages that are sexist, racist, pornographic or homophobic. And even after e-mail is deleted from your computer, it's still in the system and can be retrieved easily. Lawyers today regularly subpoena e-mail for court cases. Other reasons for caution with e-mail include:

- **You don't control distribution.** Once you hit the Send function, you never know who will end up receiving your message—inside and outside the organization. An e-mail you write to internal audit about a problem in your department could end up being forwarded FYI to your boss. In fact the Forward function makes it incredibly easy to disseminate information quickly and widely. With a few keystrokes someone can forward your e-mail to the entire organization and beyond.

- **All or part of your message can be forwarded.** Words taken out of context can be misconstrued.

- **You can inadvertently send messages to the wrong person.** If your company has two people named Price, for example, they probably get e-mail for each other on a regular basis. Also, if you're replying to an e-mail message, you could inadvertently reply to everyone on the *cc* distribution, when you intended to respond only to the original sender.

- **With the *bcc* feature, you never know who's included in correspondence.** (In most systems *bcc* recipients are not included in Reply to All responses.)

- **Many organizations monitor incoming and outgoing e-mail.** This includes both business and personal messages. Always remember that someone in your organization may be reading your correspondence.

When to Use E-Mail

Deciding when to use e-mail is often a question of corporate culture and policy. In general the decision will take into account the individuals you need to communicate with, the nature of the information and the degree of urgency.

ONLINE SHORTHAND: ABBREVIATIONS

Note that many people write these in lowercase.

2L8	Too late	IRL	In real life
AAMOF	As a matter of fact	KISS	Keep it simple stupid
AFAIK	As far as I know		or Keep it super simple
AKA	Also known as	LOL	Laughing out loud
B4N	Bye for now	LTNS	Long time no see
BCNU	Be seeing you	NBD	No big deal
BTW	By the way	NBIF	No basis in fact
CUL	See you later	OTOH	On the other hand
FYI	For your information	SOS	Same old stuff
FWIW	For what it's worth	THX	Thanks (also TNX)
FYA	For your amusement	TIA	Thanks in advance
IAC	In any case	TIC	Tongue in cheek
IMHO	In my humble opinion	TNX	Thanks (also THX)
IMO	In my opinion	TPTB	The powers that be
IOW	In other words	WTG	Way to go

It's also useful to inquire about people's preferences for correspondence. This includes people inside as well as outside your organization. Some prefer e-mail only, some prefer hard copies of everything and some may want both. Some may prefer the telephone. If you are uncertain whether e-mail is appropriate for a particular document, ask either the recipient or someone else who is in a position to know. If you're dealing with senior executives, ask their assistants for guidance. In many cases, you'll find it is best to copy the assistants on your e-mail to executives.

Unless it has been stipulated otherwise, use e-mail to send formal communications, such as memos, letters, reports and proposals. Also use e-mail to forward documents or information; for semiformal messages that provide information, ask questions or respond to them; to send for-the-record messages (the electronic version of paper trails); for quick messages that may be no more than a line or two; and for any informal correspondence.

You can use e-mail for messages of congratulations or thanks. But in the case of condolences, a personal note is more appropriate.

Another consideration is that although e-mail transmission is swift, not everyone reads incoming mail immediately. While some people monitor their e-mail regularly, others check for messages only once or twice a day, and some don't even open most e-mail.

WHEN NOT TO USE E-MAIL

E-mail is not always the best way to communicate. Sometimes a face-to-face visit, a phone call, a voice mail, interoffice mail or regular mail is preferable. Again, be guided by the circumstances. The manager of corporate public information at PPG Industries noted that e-mail too often takes the place of a more efficient phone call.

In addition, the ease of the *cc/bcc* function can lead to a great deal of unnecessary e-mail, clogging people's inboxes as well as e-mail systems. Each situation and work environment will differ, but, in general, don't copy bosses on all e-mail correspondence. It's better to obtain an understanding of what they want to be copied on than to err through overinclusion. Moreover, if a message or an attachment is really important for a boss to see, perhaps it's better to send it directly rather than via a *cc*. The same goes for colleagues.

Also avoid e-mails that merely say *thank you* or *OK,* even though you would normally make such a comment verbally. You're saving a busy person the trouble of opening (and deleting) another e-mail. This also avoids unnecessary traffic on the e-mail system.

In sending replies, use the Reply to All feature sparingly for the same reasons. Just because the sender copied 25 people on an e-mail doesn't mean the same 25 people need to see your reply. In some cases they will, but think it through before you automatically hit the Reply to All function.

In addition, refrain from using your office system to send nonbusiness material to everyone in your company, to forward chain e-mail messages, or to push political, social or other causes.

Make It Easy on Your Reader

Make your e-mail easy to read and file.

- **Use the Subject line.** Tell the recipient what your e-mail is about in the Subject line. Keep it informative, clear and concise. If you're forwarding an e-mail and the existing Subject line is unclear, then write a new Subject line for your recipient. A clearly written Subject line has the added value of making it easier for the person on the other end to save the e-mail to a folder, if necessary, and find it quickly in the future.

- **Break paragraphs with a line of space.** This makes e-mail messages easier to read.

- **Avoid special formatting in messages.** Not all e-mail systems have features such as bold, underline, bullets, tabs and some symbols (e.g., F, £, ¥). If you rely on these features to make your message user-friendly, they may be lost in transmission, leaving your document difficult to read or confusing.

- **Use attachments for formatted documents.** Because formatting may be lost or garbled in e-mail, use attachments when material is specially formatted. This includes tables, charts, outlines with tabs, and text with bullets.

- **Label attachments.** If attachments are necessary, label them clearly, particularly if you're attaching more than one file per e-mail. This will enable the recipient to distinguish among the documents and file them easily.

- **Avoid attachments when possible.** For short messages (that aren't formatted), place the text directly into your e-mail. This is faster and easier for the reader, who won't have to open an attachment after opening your e-mail. For example, if you are sending a three-sentence notice to all employees that the office will close early Friday, it is unnecessary to write a memo on a separate document and then attach that file to your e-mail. It's far more user-friendly and straightforward to put the information in your e-mail message. It is also less taxing on the e-mail system.

- **Limit messages to a screen.** If people will have to scroll down, use an attachment instead.

- **Minimize replies that include previous messages.** Don't automatically send back an entire message with your reply. It puts unnecessary demands on e-mail systems and storage capacity. Do so only if it's necessary for your message to be understood clearly or if you want to respond to specific points without rewriting those points yourself. In this case, rather than return the entire e-mail, consider copying only the relevant sections from the sender's e-mail, preceded by a symbol (usually >) that marks the beginning of the original text. Then answer that specific point directly beneath. (Most e-mail systems have an Edit feature at the top of the screen to facilitate this.)

- **Clean up messages before forwarding.** If you're forwarding a message or string of messages, delete any miscellaneous material that your recipient doesn't need to see, such as the original sender's letterhead; To, From, Subject and date lines; or any disclaimer language that appears at the end. This makes your message easier to read.

- **Use the Out of Office notification.** If your system has a feature that can notify people who send you e-mail that you are out of the office, use it. If necessary, specify the person to contact in your absence, including a full name, e-mail address and telephone number.

- **Use abbreviations judiciously.** Be sure readers will recognize any abbreviations you use. In many organizations this will reflect the corporate culture. Some standard abbreviations include *FYI, ASAP, cob* (close of business), *info, w/o* (or *w/out), docs* (documents).

- **Avoid emoticons.** These are symbols intended to help communicate the tone of a message, such as ;-), which means wink, or :-o, which means shocked. Most emoticons are some variation on the smiley symbol. In business, don't assume other people recognize or respond well to emoticons. This will depend in part on corporate culture, but when in doubt, don't use them. (*Emoticon* is derived from the words *emotional icon.*) See page 50 for some other frequently used emoticons you might need to recognize.

Be Formal in Formal E-Mail

If you are using e-mail for formal correspondence, both within and outside your organization, apply the same standards you would to a memo, report, letter or fax. Quantum's creative director noted that guidelines should also be followed for corporate messages going out to a broad audience. Always assume your e-mail will be printed out on the other end.

If you're using the message area for formal correspondence with people outside your organization, it's not necessary to start with full addresses (street, city, state, country) for the recipient or yourself. You also don't need to include the date at the top since e-mail systems incorporate this.

If your formal correspondence is in the attachment, write the attachment as if you were sending it via interoffice or regular mail. Reference the attachment in your message, using the same greeting, closing and degree of formality you use in the attached document. See the following example:

Dear Mr. Kelleher:

Attached please find a letter outlining the pricing information you requested. I look forward to hearing from you.

Sincerely,

Stephen Letzler
Director of Internet Business Solutions
Telephone: 415-656-2190

BE APPROPRIATE WITH GREETINGS

Err on the side of formality if you're uncertain.

As with a letter, the greeting will depend on how well you know the person and the situation. For external correspondence, use *Dear Mr. Graham:* or *Dear Ms. Williams:* (which is always safe). Avoid *Mr. Graham:* (without the *Dear)*; it's too abrupt. But if you're on a first-name basis, either *Dear Steve:* or *Steve:* is appropriate. Note that business correspondence takes a colon (*:)* rather than a comma after the name.

In general, avoid the *Hi Steve* or *Hello Steve* greeting in business unless you have a personal relationship with the recipient. It conveys a level of familiarity and informality that many people consider unprofessional.

Also avoid starting business e-mail messages without any greeting, even though the recipient's name is in the To line; it could be construed as impolite. If you don't know the recipient's name, go with a standard letter greeting, such as *To Whom It May Concern:*.

For correspondence within an organization, you can generally drop the *Dear* and just write the person's first name or *Mr./Ms.* with the last name, followed by a colon. But if the corporate culture has different norms, follow them.

SIGN OFF

Even though e-mail systems include the sender's name on the e-mail, sign off with your name in business correspondence. Also include a closing, which should mirror your greeting in tone. Formal closings include *Sincerely, Yours truly, Very truly yours, Best regards, Regards, Cordially,*.

Be sure your sign-off gives recipients the information they need about you, including the name of your organization, your full name, title, e-mail address, telephone number and regular address if necessary. Include the Web address for your organization's Website if it's useful to the person on the other end. Many systems have e-mail signatures that automatically tack on your contact information. If you use this feature, don't repeat your name by also typing it at the end of your message.

ONLINE SHORTHAND: EMOTICONS

:-)	Happy	:-!	Foot in mouth
;-)	Wink (mild sarcasm)	:-T	Keeping a straight face
:-D	Laughing, shock or surprise	:*)	Clowning
:-/	Perplexed	^5	High five
:-(	Frown (displeasure)	^	Thumbs up
:-@	Screaming	:-[	Pouting
:-O	Yell	:-,	Smirk
:-o	Shocked, surprised, wow	:-X	My lips are sealed
:-&	Tongue-tied	:-*	Oops

For correspondence within organizations, closings are optional and can be informal, as in *Feel free to contact me with questions or comments, All the best, Thanks, Talk to you later,*. If you don't use the e-mail signature feature, include your name at the end. If you know or have dealt with the person, just write your first name or your initials (first and last). Otherwise, use your full name.

Avoid ending e-mails and other business correspondence with a *PS*. It's preferable just to include that thought within the body of the text. Likewise avoid *PPS* (post postscript).

BE SMART ABOUT E-MAIL

Treat e-mail as an opportunity to put your best foot forward. Your boss could forward your memo to a senior executive, giving you unexpected visibility. A client in one division of a company could forward your e-mail to a different division that is considering hiring you for a project. Your note of thanks to a colleague, copied to her boss, could end up with the head of human resources, saying as much about you as it does about the colleague.

Take the extra steps to be sure your correspondence works for and not against you.

- **Spell check.** If your e-mail system has a spell checker, use it. But remember that you can't rely on the spell checker to catch all errors. For example, if you typed *you* instead of *your,* the spell checker will miss it because both are words.

- **Proof it.** If the e-mail is sufficiently important, in addition to spell checking, also take the time to proof it carefully—printing it out if necessary.

- **Avoid emotional e-mails.** The speed of e-mail can sometimes backfire on you. Messages written in anger and haste often convey a harsh tone that is rarely well received and can exacerbate a tense situation. When time permits, draft difficult e-mails and review them again several hours later.

- **Don't shout.** Writing in all capitals is considered shouting in Netiquette, a term for network etiquette.

- **Use receipt notification.** Some systems can notify you when your e-mail has been opened and also if your message is deleted without being opened. These tools are useful, especially when you're waiting for replies.

- **Respond promptly.** As with all business communication, respond as quickly as possible, especially when senders indicate they are on a deadline. And remember, if someone requests information from you via e-mail, he or she has a record of when the request was made.

- **Print it out.** If an e-mail is important, print it out just in case your systems go down. This includes e-mails you send and receive.

- **Refrain from using the exclamation point!** It's rarely appropriate in business writing. If you need to express emotion, let your words carry it. Save the exclamations for friends and family.

USE *CC* AND *BCC* APPROPRIATELY

The purpose of a *cc* is twofold. It allows people other than the primary recipient to see an e-mail or document. It also allows everyone on the routing to know who else received it. Blind copying (*bcc*) allows the sender to share information with the *bcc* recipient, unbeknownst to the other people on the routing.

As a sender, remember that the *bcc* is exclusionary and can alienate some people. As an e-mail recipient, remember that with *bcc* you can never be sure who else received an e-mail message.

Another use of *bcc* is to send a distribution in which everyone gets a blind copy. This levels the playing field because no one knows who else is on the routing. When handling distributions this way, senders generally put their own address in the To line. In most work situations this type of distribution is best avoided.

WEB SOURCES FOR ABBREVIATIONS, EMOTICONS AND OTHER E-MAIL CONVENTIONS

www.squareonetech.com

www.anrecs.msu.edu/technology (See E-mail Etiquette Guide.)

www.everythingemail.net

www.windweaver.com/emoticon.htm

Watch Out for Viruses

Be careful about opening e-mails or attachments that may contain viruses. If you don't recognize the sender and the message line is cryptic, don't automatically open it. A virus can wreak havoc on your system.

A-TO-Z ENTRIES

Key to Entries

H. L. Mencken said, "A living language is like a man suffering incessantly from small haemorrhages, and what it needs above all else is constant transactions of new blood from other tongues. The day the gates go up, that day it begins to die."

Many of the entries in *The Business Style Handbook* reflect the "new blood" in the language of business. Our intent is to promote consistency and clarity in all written materials while taking into account how language is used in the workplace. Using *access* and *contact* as verbs may cause some grammarians to lose sleep, but on the job, this usage is common practice.

In addition, while some writing conventions are inflexible, much of the language we use is a matter of personal preference. This book strives to make distinctions between the hard-fast rules and individual preferences.

This key defines terminology and also spells out the thinking that informs many of the style choices in *The Business Style Handbook*.

- **First reference:** When a term is introduced for the first time in text, it is called a *first reference*. The usual practice in a first reference is to write the complete name (with an explanation if necessary). Then in the subsequent references, the shortened form or abbreviation is sufficient. For example: The new head of *human resources* called a meeting with the entire *HR* department. The *Federal Reserve Board* lowered interest rates; the *Fed* meets again in two weeks.

- **The language of grammar:** In general, *The Business Style Handbook* avoids grammatical terms that may be unfamiliar to nonprofessional writers. For instance, instead of *when used as a compound modifier,* this book writes *when used as an adjective* or *when used as an adverb.* Plain English is the priority.

- **Keystroke guideline:** The fewer keystrokes it takes to form a word, the better. *The Business Style Handbook* adopts this approach when possible, but only as long as it does not jeopardize comprehension. Also, punctuation is minimized so that abbreviations without periods are preferred, though there will always be exceptions. Writing *FYI* (for your information), *IPO* (initial public offering) or *OK* (okay) without periods is not confusing. But *US* (for U.S.) and *am* (for a.m.) may not work as well, so in these and some other instances, this book recommends using periods.

- **Consistency:** In business writing, consistency is a priority. Writing *Website* three different ways in a single document makes it look unprofessional. It's not that one version is right and the other is wrong; it's a question of consistency. So if *The Business Style Handbook* suggests *Website* and everyone in your organization writes *Web site,* your goal is to make sure it doesn't appear both ways in a single document.

- **Capitalization:** The instruction to capitalize a word or phrase means to capitalize just the first letter of the word or main words, not the entire word or all words. When the guideline says to capitalize and italicize movie titles, for instance, it means to follow this style: *The Garden of the Finzi-Continis.*

- **Numbers:** Entries that begin with numbers, such as *24/7* or *360-degree review,* are listed before letter entries, so that both *24/7* and *360-degree review* appear at the beginning of the *T* Chapter.

- **Alphabetization:** Entries that are acronyms or abbreviations are alphabetized by the letters in the abbreviated form, so that *FYI* is alphabetized using *Y* as the second letter. This means *FYI* appears after the entry *further* rather than after the entry *forward.*

  Alphanumeric entries come after entries that are all numbers, so that *3D* comes after *24/7.* Alphanumeric entries, such as *401(k), 3D, Y2K,* come before words that are all letters. They are alphabetized as though the numbers were spelled out: *401(k)* (four), *3D* (three), *Y2K* (starts with a letter, so it follows entries that start with numbers). Phrases formed from two or more words are alphabetized as though they were a single word, so that *today* comes before *to-do; serviceable* comes before *service mark; minuscule* comes before *minus sign; question mark* comes before *questionnaire; real-time* comes after *really; y-axis* comes after *yard.* This applies for phrases with and without hyphens.

- **Examples:** In the entries most examples are set in italics to differentiate them from the explanations (not because the words should be in italics).

- **Formal versus informal:** Audience determines whether the writing is formal or informal. Formal writing is expected in an annual report; informal writing is the norm for e-mails among colleagues.

- **Accents:** *The Business Style Handbook* recommends using diacritical marks whenever possible, so write *résumé* instead of *resume* if your word processing program can produce accents.

- **Nonstandard usage:** Because this stylebook focuses on business writing, we favor the use of some words and phrases that may be considered nonstandard (such as *fast-track, FedEx* and *impact* as verbs) because of their obvious usefulness. Strict grammarians may disagree.

- **Names of periodicals:** Style varies here, too. Some stylebooks include the *The* in newspaper and magazine names; others do not. This stylebook does not, writing the *Wall Street Journal,* not *The Wall Street Journal.*

- **Names of books:** In book names, however, *the* is capitalized, as in *The American Heritage Dictionary.*

- **Ephemeral words:** Most of the entries cover style issues that have plagued writers for a long time; however, we may have included one or two ephemeral words (words that will never make it into the dictionary because they will be superseded by other words). Language is dynamic, but it still is helpful to know how to deal with those ephemeral words during their life span.

The rest of the material in the entries should need no further explanation. Language is inherently logical. As long as you strive for consistency, value brevity and aim for clarity, most sentences will fall neatly into place. *The Business Style Handbook* is a tool to help you achieve these goals.

·A·

a, an Use *a* before consonant **sounds:** *a briefcase, a history of debt, a letter, a one-time deal* (the *o* sounds like *w*), *a United Way campaign* (the *u* sounds like *y*). Use *an* before vowel **sounds:** *an even match, an NYSE stock* (the *n* sounds like *en*), *an MRI* (the *M* sounds like *em*). This guideline is rooted in phonetics (sound).

abbreviations Use abbreviations sparingly. They are a shortcut for writers but may confuse readers.

- To check if a company uses abbreviations in its full name, visit the company's Website, check its marketing or other branded materials (such as letterhead, business cards) or use *Standard & Poor's Register of Corporations, Directors and Executives.* Hoover's Online is another useful source (www.hoovers.com). According to communications executives at the Fortune 500, a particular company's style (in punctuation, abbreviations) should be followed. Use the full name of the company in an address. Also use the full name in the first reference to the company in a document, as in *I recommend we buy the products from Intel Corporation. Intel has the best technology for our needs.* Always check the spelling, capitalization, punctuation and abbreviations in company names. See **company names** entry.

- Abbreviate the following titles when used before a full name: *Mr., Ms., Mrs., Dr.*

- For medical doctors, write *Dr. Heidi Waldorf* or *Heidi Waldorf, M.D.* (with a comma). Do not write *Dr. Heidi Waldorf, M.D.*

- For dentists, write *Dr. Nancy Coughlin* or *Nancy Coughlin, D.D.S.* (with a comma). Do not write *Dr. Nancy Coughlin, D.D.S.*

- For nonmedical doctors, write *Raymond Murray, Ph.D.* (with a comma), or *Dr. Raymond Murray.* Do not write *Dr. Raymond Murray, Ph.D.*

- For the esquire title used by lawyers, write *Virginia Melvin, Esq.* (with a comma). Do not write *Ms. Virginia Melvin, Esq.*

- Abbreviate and capitalize *junior* or *senior* after an individual's name: *Michael Brown, Jr.* (with a comma).

- For the abbreviations of states, use standard state abbreviations in text as long as the town or city is included: *John lives in Ponte Vedra, Fla.* Do not abbreviate state names when they stand alone in text: *John lives in Florida.* Use the two-letter Postal Service abbreviations with full addresses, including ZIP codes. For a list of the state abbreviations, see **state abbreviations** entry.

- Do not abbreviate job descriptions (which are different from titles), even if they precede the name, as in *technologist Alex Sexton.*

- Use abbreviations in tabular material, slide shows and bibliographies.

- Do not abbreviate the days of the week, unless they appear in tabular material or slide shows. See **days of the week** entry.

- For months, abbreviate *Jan., Feb., Mar., Apr., Aug., Sept., Oct., Nov., Dec.* in text as long as they are followed by numerals: *Dec. 27, Jan. 29, Sept. 15.*

Do not abbreviate *May, June* or *July,* even if followed by a figure: *June 22.* (Always spell out the month if it appears alone or with just the year: *December, October 1984.)*

- With the word *number,* abbreviate to *No.* (with a capital *N)* only with figures: *Mr. Friedman will stay in room No. 23. The company is Spain's No. 1 Internet service provider.*

- When lowercased phrases are abbreviated, such as *a.k.a.,* which stands for *also known as,* use periods if the abbreviation would look like an error or create confusion (for instance, *a.m.* could be mistaken for the word *am; c.o.d.* for the word *cod).*

- In text, spell out *Avenue, Boulevard, Street* when figures are not present: *Corporate offices are on Maple Avenue.* Use the abbreviated form when the number is present in the address: *Corporate offices are at 1200 Maple Ave.* (No comma is used in the number *1200* because it is an address.) Spell out and lowercase with more than one street name: *The office is between Maple and Elm avenues.*

- For compass points, abbreviate and capitalize when they appear after street names, as in *The doctor's office is at 100 Boyer Ave. E.* Spell out and capitalize when they come before street names: *The doctor's office is at 100 East Boyer Ave.*

- When using abbreviations, replace *and* with *&,* so that *research and development* becomes *R&D, profit and loss* becomes *P&L.* (Do not use an ampersand in place of the word *and* in text. Write *Jim **and** Edwin will handle the request,* not *Jim & Edwin will handle the request.)*

ABCs No apostrophe is needed.

above Avoid using the word *above* to refer to preceding material, except in business forms where it is certain the reference will appear on the same page: *The prices above are in effect until Dec. 31, 2003.* (The same guideline applies to the word *below.*) Usually the words *previously* or *following* can be substituted for *above* or *below*. The use of *above* or *below* as a noun is best avoided in formal documents. Avoid writing *See the above for the new phone number.*

accents Use accents in printed material since most word processing programs have symbol-inserts for them, as in *Your résumé did not arrive.* Common diacritical marks are: acute accent (é), grave accent (è), diaeresis or umlaut (ü), circumflex (ê), tilde (ñ), cedilla (ç).

access Using *access* as a verb is considered nonstandard, but this usage is so widespread that business writers generally ignore the rule. This stylebook uses the verb form: *You can access the white paper from the company's Website.*

accommodate Often misspelled. Remember two *c*'s and two *m*'s.

accounting, bookkeeping There is a difference between these two terms. Accounting requires judgment when recording debits and credits—and in the preparation of statements concerning the assets, liabilities and operating results of a business. Bookkeeping is the uncritical recording of the accounts and transactions of a business.

Achilles' heel Write with an apostrophe because it is a possessive. The reference is from Homer's *Iliad.* Note that for the possessive, classical names often follow a different form from other names, so it is not written *Achilles's heel.* An *Achilles' heel* in a business context is a weakness that can have a negative effect.

acknowledgment This is the preferred spelling (not *acknowledgement).*

acronym An acronym is a word formed from the first letter or letters of a series of words. Acronyms are pronounced as single words, as in *NASA, NATO, NOW.* If the acronym is longer than four letters, capitalize the first letter and lowercase the remaining letters, as in *Nasdaq, Nafta.* Company names are an exception to this guideline. Follow a company's style, as in *AFLAC* (not *Aflac).* Most acronyms do not require periods. When acronyms cross over and become generic terms, lowercase them, as in *radar, modem, abend* (abnormal end of task).

Initialisms do not form words and are pronounced by letter, as in *IRS* (for *Internal Revenue Service* and pronounced *I-R-S)* or *CBOE* (for *Chicago Board Options Exchange* and pronounced *C-B-O-E).* Most initialisms are capitalized without periods.

To write acronyms or initialisms, follow this guideline: Spell out the entire phrase in the first reference; use just the acronym/initialism afterward. *John Andrews is employed by the Brotherhood of Locomotive Engineers. He works at BLE headquarters in Cleveland.* If an acronym or initialism is widely recognizable, however, it's not necessary to spell out in first reference, as in *Nasdaq.*

active voice Write in the active voice whenever possible rather than the passive voice. In the active voice, the subject acts. *The sales manager corrected the account executive.* In the passive voice, the action is done to the subject, as in *The account executive was corrected by the sales manager.* The emphasis changes. The active voice is stronger and more direct.

While the active voice is preferred in most business writing, there are instances where the passive voice is necessary. See Chapter 4 for more information on active and passive voice.

AD, BC *AD* stands for *anno Domini:* in the year of our Lord. *BC* indicates a calendar year before Christ. Use abbreviations in all references. The year goes after *AD,* as in *AD 76.* Do not write *the second century AD.* It is redundant. The *second century* is sufficient. For *BC,* the year goes before: *Chapters 11 to 50 in Genesis date back to 1445 BC.*

addresses Follow these guidelines:

- In text, spell out *Avenue, Boulevard, Street* when figures are not present: *Corporate offices are on Maple Avenue.* Use the abbreviated form when the number is present in the address: *Corporate offices are at 1200 Maple Ave.* (No comma is used in the number *1200* because it is an address.) Spell out and lowercase with more than one street name: *The offices are between Maple and Elm avenues.*

- When compass points are in an address, abbreviate and capitalize when they appear after street names, as in *The CEO's office is at 100 Boyer Ave. E.* Spell out and capitalize when they come before street names: *The CEO's office is at 100 East Boyer Ave.*

- For states, use the two-letter Postal Service abbreviations (e.g., *CO, TX)* with full addresses, including ZIP code. No comma is needed between the state abbreviation and the ZIP code. The Postal Service requests that the two-letter state abbreviations be used on all mail. Note that the four-digit add-on ZIP codes take a hyphen, as in *80452-2511.* When writing a letter, the inside address should duplicate the address on the envelope. See **state abbreviations** entry.

- For state names in text, use the standard state abbreviations instead of the two-letter state abbreviations (e.g., *Calif.* instead of *CA)* when the name of a city is included. If the state name stands alone, spell it out. See **state abbreviations** entry.

ad hoc   Italics are not needed for this familiar Latin phrase, which means for a specific purpose or situation at hand. *The ad hoc committee disbanded after the project's completion.*

adjective   It is a word that describes or limits (modifies) the meaning of a noun or pronoun: *strategic* plan, *demanding* boss. When two or more words preceding a noun act together to form an adjective (called a unit [or compound] modifier), the words are hyphenated, as in *two-year* plan, *full-time* job, *billion-dollar-a-year* software maker, *cubicle-to-office* ratio, *2-for-1* stock split. See **hyphen** entry.

ADR See **American Depositary Receipt** entry.

adverb It is a word that describes or limits a verb, an adjective or another adverb. It answers the question where, how or how much, or when: walk *slowly, very* short, do it *now,* run *up.* Do not hyphenate phrases containing adverbs when they precede a noun, as in *fully vested* employee, *completely renovated* office, *highly complex* contract. See **hyphen** entry.

adviser This is the preferred spelling (not *advisor,* the British spelling).

affect, effect *Affect* as a verb means to influence: *How will interest rates affect the economy?* Usually *affect* is a verb. *Affect* as a noun refers to various psychological states and the corresponding emotional responses (such as interest-excitement, enjoyment-joy, surprise-startle, fear-terror, distress-anguish, anger-rage). Most business writers will not have many opportunities to use *affect* as a noun.

Effect as a noun means result: *The delay had a negative effect on the production schedule.* Usually *effect* is a noun. *Effect* as a verb means to cause or bring about a specific result: *The new head of finance will effect major change in that department.*

African-American Use a hyphen and capitalize both *A*'s. The term *African-American* is preferred to *black.*

after- Most *after-* words are one word, as in *aftertax, afterhours, aftershock, aftermath, afterthought, afternoon.*

after all Spell as two words.

afterward This form is preferable to *afterwards.*

Age Capitalize an age with a specific date: *Stone Age, Bronze Age, Age of Reason, Gilded Age, Dark Ages.* When the time period does not have a fixed date, lowercase *age: space age, digital age, nuclear age.*

age Always express with figures: *The 21-year-old student did not participate in the internship. The man, 65, is eligible for retirement. The NYSE delisted the 1-year-old company's stock.* Note that the rule to spell out numbers under 10 does not apply to age. See **numbers** entry.

agreement A common mistake in writing is a mishap in subject/verb/pronoun agreement. The best way to avoid this is to identify the subject of the sentence; then check the verb and pronouns to make sure they agree. If the subject is singular, it must take a singular verb and singular pronouns; if the subject is plural, it must take a plural verb and plural pronouns. *The two departments,* which *have a healthy rivalry, were comparing their sales figures for August. The department, which is responsible for sales, was reviewing its figures for August.*

Remember that collective nouns take a singular verb and pronoun, even though they refer to more than one person or thing.

> CORRECT: *A flood at the **company** shut down **its** business for a day.*
> INCORRECT: *A flood at the **company** shut down **their** business for a day.*
> CORRECT: ***Members** of the sales team **meet** each Friday to discuss **their** progress.* (The subject is *members,* not *team.*)
> CORRECT: *The sales **team meets** each Friday to discuss **its** progress.* (The subject is *team.*)

a.k.a. Use *a.k.a.* with periods in all references. It stands for *also known as.*

Alaska Do not abbreviate in text, but use *AK* with full addresses, including ZIP code. *AK* is the two-letter Postal Service abbreviation. Seven other states are not abbreviated in text: Hawaii, Idaho, Iowa, Maine, Ohio, Texas, Utah. See **state abbreviations** entry.

all ready, already *All ready* means everybody and everything ready: *They were all ready to board the plane. Already* means previously: *They have already arrived at the convention.*

all right Two words (not *alright*).

all-time Use a hyphen, as in *The U.S. dollar hit an all-time high against the yen.*

all together, altogether *All together* means everybody and/or everything together, a group. *The administrative assistants sat all together at the luncheon. Altogether* means completely or utterly: *She gave up the project altogether. Altogether* also means all told or all counted: *Altogether 12 people attended the meeting.*

a lot The only acceptable form for *a lot* is two words (not *alot*).

alpha Lowercase *alpha* in this construction: *The company is alpha-testing the new customer-relationship software.* Software often goes through two stages of release testing: *alpha* (in-house) and *beta* (outgoing). *Beta* releases are generally made to a group of trusted customers; the program is mostly working but still under test.

alphabetization Follow these guidelines:

- For phrases formed from two or more words, alphabetize as though they were a single word, so that *today* comes before *to-do; serviceable* comes before *service mark; minuscule* comes before *minus sign; question mark* comes before *questionnaire; real-time* comes after *really; y-axis* comes after *yard.* Note that this applies for phrases with and without hyphens.

- When alphabetizing words beginning with *Mac/Mc,* do so as though all letters were lowercased: *MacDougal, Mackey, McDonald.*

- If alphabetizing by last names, put *Jr., Sr.* or a Roman numeral (e.g., *III)* last, as in *Bond, Michael, Jr.* (not *Bond, Jr., Michael).*

- When alphabetizing Spanish last names in which both the mother's and father's family names are used, such as *Vicente Fox Quesada (Fox* is the father's name and *Quesada* is the mother's name), always put the father's surname first, as in *Fox Quesada, Vicente* (not *Fox, Vicente Quesada).*

- Alphabetize acronyms or abbreviations by the letters in the abbreviated form, so that *FYI* is alphabetized using *Y* as the second letter rather than alphabetizing it where *for your information* would go.

- For numbers that form words or phrases, such as *24/7* and *20/20,* alphabetize before letter entries, so that both *24/7* and *20/20* appear before all *T* words. Alphabetize as though the numbers were spelled out, so that *24/7* (twenty-four) comes before *20/20* (twenty-twenty).

- For alphanumeric words or abbreviations, such as *401(k), 360-degree review, 3D, Y2K,* alphabetize after numbers and before words that are all letters. Alphabetize as though the numbers were spelled out: *401(k)* (four), *3D* (three), *Y2K* (starts with a letter, so it follows words that start with numbers).

- For titles of works of art, alphabetize by the first principal word so that *The Canterbury Tales* is listed under *C.*

alumna, alumnae, alumnus, alumni *Alumna* refers to a woman who graduated from the school; *alumnae* is plural for women. *Alumnus* refers to a man who graduated from the school; *alumni* is plural for men. *Alumni* is the plural for the men and women who graduated from the school.

AM/FM Capitalize and use a slash.

a.m., p.m. Lowercase with periods. Use figures, as in *We will meet at 9 a.m. in the conference room* (not *nine a.m.*). Note the space between the number and *a.m.* If the time is on the hour, it is not necessary to include a colon and two zeros. Just write *9 a.m.* Use the colon for fractions of hours, as in *9:15 a.m.* It is better to specify *a.m.* or *p.m.* than use the *o'clock* form. If the *o'clock* form is used, spell out the number, as in *nine o'clock,* not *9 o'clock.*

Amazon.com The company logo lowercases *amazon,* but in marketing materials it is written with a capital *A.* When we contacted the company about its preference, the reply was: "Feel free to capitalize or to not capitalize our name. . . . Since we're an Internet company, we're not too caught up in convention or formal procedures." So use the capital *A* all the time. Spell out *Amazon.com* in the first reference; use *Amazon* afterward.

American Depositary Receipt Spell out in the first reference; use *ADR* afterward. The plural is *ADRs.* Note the spelling of *Depositary* (not *Depository).*

American English Many differences exist between American English and British English, especially in spelling and punctuation. In the United States, American English takes precedence over British forms.

American Stock Exchange Spell out in the first reference; use *AMEX* or *the exchange* afterward. (Note that it is written as *Amex* and *AMEX* in the AMEX Website; whichever you choose, use it consistently.) *AmEx* is also used to refer to *American Express.* In most cases context will ensure there is no confusion.

amid Preferred to *amidst.*

among *Among* is preferred to *amongst.* Use *among* with more than two persons or things: *She divided the tasks among the four departments. Between* is used with two persons or things: *She divided the tasks between the finance and marketing departments. Between you and me, there is not a lot of room for flex-*

ibility at this organization. (Note it is *between you and **me**,* not *between you and I*.)

amount, number Use *amount* for things that cannot be counted one by one, as in *The amount of time spent on the reports varies each quarter.* Use *number* for things that can be counted one by one, as in *The number of days spent on the reports varies each quarter* or *She put a number of coins on the counter.*

ampersand Use the ampersand (*&*) in an organization's formal name if that is what the organization uses, as in *Barnes & Noble* (do not write *Barnes **and** Noble*). But do not use *&* in place of *and* in text. Write *Trinidad and Tobago,* not *Trinidad & Tobago.* When using abbreviations, replace *and* with *&,* so that *research and development* becomes *R&D, profit and loss* becomes *P&L.*

analog This is defined as "data in a stream of continuous physical variables" in *Wired Style.* The opposite is *digital,* which "refers to the way information is stored on a string of separate bits that represent on/off states."

and Do not replace the word *and* with an ampersand (&). Write *Trinidad and Tobago,* not *Trinidad & Tobago.* But if an organization uses an ampersand in its name, as in *Pharmacia & Upjohn Inc.,* do not write *Pharmacia **and** Upjohn Inc.* When using abbreviations, replace *and* with *&,* so that *research and development* becomes *R&D, profit and loss* becomes *P&L.*

And, But It is acceptable to begin sentences with either of these words.

angry, mad These two words are not interchangeable. Use *angry* when the meaning is irritation, *mad* when the meaning is insane.

annual Do not write *first annual event.* It does not become an annual (yearly) event until it is held for two consecutive years.

antitrust One word.

anxious It means worried, full of anxiety: *He was anxious about the product launch.* Do not use *anxious* in place of *eager,* which means desirous: *She was eager to complete her degree.*

anybody, anyone, any one The one-word forms are used to mean any person. *Anybody who speaks Spanish can take the call. Anyone* and *anybody* always take a singular verb. Use two words when singling out someone within a group: *Any one of the managers can go to the meeting.*

anymore Use the one-word form in all references.

apostrophe Follow these guidelines for the apostrophe:

- Use it to indicate possession. The singular possessive is formed by adding an *'s: the manager's chair, the managing director's parking space.* The plural possessive is formed by adding just an apostrophe: *the vice presidents' budgets, businesses' operations.* For a plural that does not end in *s,* form the possessive with an *'s: the children's nursery, women's rights, the men's room.*

- A difference of opinion exists about whether nouns ending in *s* require a second *s* as well as the apostrophe to form the possessive: *the hostess's dinner party, James's umbrella.* **Most** stylebooks, including *The Business Style Handbook,* advocate using the second *s.* But if the next word begins with *s,* drop the *s* after the apostrophe, as in *the hostess' salad, for goodness' sake.*

- Classical names often **do not** take the second *s* to form the possessive, as in *Achilles' heel, Moses' commandments* (not *Achilles's heel, Moses's commandments).*

- Joint possession is formed by placing an *'s* on the last element of a series: *Smith and Johnson's proposal* or *Andrea and Bart's apartment.*

- Use an apostrophe in a contraction. Place the apostrophe where the letter is omitted: *have not = haven't, let us = let's, we are = we're, do not = don't.* **One of the most common mistakes in print** is to confuse the possessive pronoun *its* (belongs to it) with the contraction *it's* (it is). *The department always meets **its** deadlines but **It's** a deadline that must be met.*

- For decades, use this style: *1990s* or *'90s* (whichever form you choose, use it consistently).

- Use an apostrophe to indicate missing letters, as in *ne'er do well.*

appraise, apprise Do not confuse these terms. *Appraise* means evaluate, as in *Mary Ward will appraise the recently acquired art before we buy insurance. Apprise* means inform, as in *I will apprise Coleen of all developments.*

Argentine This is American English and is preferred to *Argentinian,* which is British English. *The Argentine government pegged its currency to the U.S. dollar in 1991.*

ASAP This is informal for *as soon as possible.* Use all capitals for business correspondence. Spell out the entire phrase in formal documents.

as per It is preferable to use *according to* or *in accordance with.* Also avoid *as to whether;* just use *whether.*

asterisk A star-like figure (*) used in writing to indicate either an omission or a reference to a footnote. It is also used in searches as a wildcard.

at Avoid *at* unless it contributes to the meaning: *Where is it?* Do not write *Where is it at?* Also avoid *We will meet at about 9 a.m.* Instead write *We will meet about 9 a.m.*

at sign Use the symbol @ in e-mail addresses and for URLs, but in text write it as the *at sign.*

attorneys general Add an *s* to the first word to form the plural of most compound nouns. Another example is *mothers-in-law.*

attribution Attribute all material, with the exception of general knowledge, to the appropriate individual or source. Most readers want to know, "Who says so?" and telling them gives the statement more credibility. *Ergonomics reduces repetitive stress injuries* is an assertion that needs backing up. When the writer states that *OSHA's study claims ergonomics reduces repetitive stress injuries,* the assertion has more authority.

autumn Lowercase *autumn,* which is interchangeable with *fall.* Lowercase all seasons.

average This means conforming to norm or standards: *The average increase was 6%.* Do not confuse it with *ordinary,* which means usual, without distinction. It is better to write *It was an ordinary day on the floor of the exchange* than to write *It was an average day on the floor of the exchange. Average of* takes a plural verb in a construction such as this: *An average of 1,000 jobs per plant* ***were*** *lost when gas prices rose to a new high.* The verb agrees with *jobs (jobs were lost),* not *average.*

awhile, a while When written as one word, *awhile* is an adverb: *She will stay with him awhile.* The two-word form is preceded by a preposition: *She plans to stay for a while.*

·B·

"Be brief. Be precise. Be accurate."

—Paul Dickard, director, public relations

Ingersoll-Rand Company

B.A., B.S. See **bachelor of arts** entry.

baby boom, baby boomers These phrases refer to the population surge after WWII and the people born during that period (1946–64). Note they are not capitalized. The shortened form for the people is *boomers.*

bachelor of arts, bachelor of science Use the abbreviations in the first reference: *B.A.* for *bachelor of arts* and *B.S.* for *bachelor of science.* It is also correct, but less specific, to write *a bachelor's degree* (which applies to both the *B.A.* and the *B.S.).* If spelled out, lowercase *bachelor of arts* and *bachelor of science.* Also lowercase terms designating academic years: *freshman, sophomore, junior, senior.*

backslash One word.

backward Use *backward* in all cases. Even though *backward* and *backwards* are interchangeable in some instances, only *backward* works as an adjective: *The misprint in the advertisement was a backward letter.*

bad, badly *Bad* is an adjective (describing what someone or something is like); *badly* is an adverb (how something is done). Confusion on which word to use occurs with some verbs. Use *bad* when the verb explains how someone or something feels, smells, tastes or looks: *Marie feels bad because she did not submit the proposal on time. Marie feels badly . . .* suggests that Marie's sense of touch is poor.

banner This refers to the advertisements that appear on Web pages. Banners encourage users to click on them, which then takes users to the advertiser's Website.

B-band See **broadband** entry.

BC, AD *BC* indicates a calendar year before Christ, as in *Chapters 11 to 50 in Genesis date back to 1445 BC.* Note the year goes before *BC. AD* stands for *anno Domini:* in the year of our Lord. Use abbreviations in all references. The year goes after *AD,* as in *The vase was dated AD 76.* Do not write *the second century AD.* It is redundant. *The second century* is sufficient.

bcc, blind carbon copy Use *bcc* in all references. But if the abbreviation could create confusion, write *blind copy* instead (you don't need the *carbon).* Changing *blind copy* or *bcc* into a verb is common practice. *Jim blind-copied his boss on the memo* (note the hyphen in the verb form) or *Jim bcc'd his boss on the memo.* When referring to the *bcc* function on e-mail, lowercase and put *bcc* in italics as in, Be sure to *bcc* Tracy Lam on your e-mail. (This and *cc* are exceptions to the guideline that computer and e-mail functions should be set capitalized, as in *the Send button.)*

bear, bull Both *bear* and *bull* are lowercased and can be used to describe people. A *bear* feels generally cautious about the stock market or is bearish. A *bull* feels generally positive about the market or is bullish. *The bulls on Wall Street predict the market can only get better while the bears caution that the bubble is* *about to burst.* A *bear market* exists when stock prices are declining or when stock prices are expected to decline. A *bull market* exists when stock prices are rising.

behemoth Lowercase this word when referring to a large organization and meaning something enormous in size or power. In the Old Testament of the Bible, a *Behemoth* was a large and powerful animal.

bellwether Use the term *bellwether* to indicate a trend. *Absenteeism is a bellwether for employee morale.* Note the spelling of *bellwether.* Originally this term applied to a sheep (wether) with a bell around its neck. The sheep was the leader of the flock.

below Avoid using the word *below* to refer to material that follows, except in business forms where it is certain the reference will appear on the same page: *The prices below are in effect until Dec. 31, 2003.* (The same guideline applies to the word *above.*) Usually the words *following* or *previously* can be substituted for *below* or *above.* The use of *below* or *above* as a noun is best avoided in formal documents.

belt-tightening Use a hyphen, as in *The COO wrote a memo on the need for belt-tightening* or *The COO announced a series of belt-tightening measures.*

beside, besides Use *beside* when the meaning is next to: *Lenny's desk is beside the window.* Use *besides* when the meaning is in addition to or except for: *Who besides Lenny sits in this area?*

best seller Do not hyphenate this phrase. *Jack Welch's biography was a best seller* or *Jack Welch's book rose to the top of the best seller list.* Even though *best seller* acts like an adjective in the second sentence, no hyphen is needed because the meaning is clear. If the meaning of a phrase is clear without the hyphen (*best seller list, real estate agent, income tax form, word processing program*), don't use one.

beta Lowercase *beta* in this construction: *The company is beta-testing the new customer-relationship software.* Software often goes through two stages of release testing: *alpha* (in house) and *beta* (outgoing). *Beta* releases are generally made to a group of trusted customers; the program is mostly working but still under test.

better, well *Better* means still in the process of recovering. *Well* means completely recovered. *Mary Ann is feeling better. The doctor expects her to be well after she takes the antibiotic for 10 days.*

between, among *Between* is used with two persons or things. *She divided the tasks between the finance and marketing departments. Between you and me, there is not a lot of room for flexibility at this organization.* (Note it is *between you and me,* not *between you and I.*)

Use *among* with more than two persons or things. *She divided the tasks among the four departments. Among* is preferred to *amongst.*

biannual, biennial *Biannual* means twice a year. *Biennial* means once every two years. *Bimonthly* means every other month, while *semimonthly* means twice a month. Using these terms occasionally confuses readers. In most cases it is better to write *twice a month, every two months. The periodical is published every other month.* The same applies to *biweekly* and *semiweekly.*

bibliography Some business writing needs to include a bibliography, which is an alphabetical list of the sources used, whether footnotes are included in the text or not. The list, which appears at the end of the work (after endnotes), can also be called Works Cited or References. If a bibliography is extensive, many thorny issues can arise. A good source for a bibliography, especially for formal writing, is *The Chicago Manual of Style.* If the citation is simple and straightforward, follow this style: **author, title, place of publication, publisher, date.** Use standard state abbreviations, not the two-letter postal abbreviations. Citing an Internet source can also be troublesome. For academic and scientific writing, a good source for a bibliography of Internet references is

Online! A Reference Guide to Using Internet Sources, by Andrew Harnack and Eugene Kleppinger (www.bedfordstmartins.com). Otherwise providing a URL in the text should be sufficient.

Use these examples as guidelines:

For a book by a single author:
Rifkin, Jeremy. *The Age of Access.* New York: The Putnam Publishing
  Group, 2001.

For multiple authors:
Varney, Charles Edward, and Abdullah F. Akbar. *The Jewel Carriers.*
  Balboa Island, Calif.: Creative Ink, 1999.

For a book by editors:
Hairston, Maxine, and John J. Ruszkiewicz, eds. *The Scott, Foresman
  Handbook for Writers.* Glenview, Ill.: Scott, Foresman and
  Company, 1988.

For a book with an edition number:
American Heritage Dictionary. 4th ed. Boston/New York: Houghton
  Mifflin Company, 2000.
(Note that the reference to *edition* uses the ordinal number and has a lowercased *ed.*)

For an article from a periodical:
Leonhardt, David. "In Language You Can Understand." *New York
  Times,* 8 Dec. 1999, sec. C: 1+.
(The plus sign indicates the article continues beyond the first page, but not necessarily on consecutive pages.)

For a corporation, institution or association:
American Medical Association. *The American Medical Association
  Encyclopedia of Medicine.* New York: Random House, 1989.

For a paper:
Horton, Sabina. "Preventing Workplace Injuries." Paper presented at
  the annual meeting of the International Society of Widgetmakers,
  Hilton Head Island, S.C.: April 2000.

For the Internet:

National Association of Investors Corporation, NAIC Online, 20
    September 1999 <http://www.better-investing.org> (1 October
    1999).

For the sciences:

Sagar, A. 2001. J2EE design patterns: The next frontier. *Java
    Developer's Journal,* Aug.: 10+.
(The sciences use a different style for bibliographies. The primary differences are that an initial, instead of the full first **name**, is used; the **date**
follows the author's name [instead of coming at the end]; all the words in
the **titles,** except the first word [and the first word of any subtitle], are
lowercased; and article titles do not take quotation marks.)

Big Board Spell out *New York Stock Exchange* in first reference; use *Big Board*
(capitalize both *B's*), *NYSE* or *the exchange* afterward.

Big Brother Capitalize both *B's* in this term, which comes from the book
1984 by George Orwell. The ever-present figure representing control over individuals (and exerted by authoritarian government in the book) also refers to
the invasive aspect of telecommunications, where issues of privacy are at stake.
If the term *big brother* refers to an older sibling, lowercase it.

big money Lowercase this informal expression.

Big Three automakers General Motors, Ford, Chrysler. Note that *Big Three*
is capitalized, but *automakers* is not. Chrysler is now the American car division of DaimlerChrysler. Note there is no space between *Daimler* and *Chrysler.*

billion, million Use the word *billion* or *million* instead of writing out the
zeros. A billion is equal to a thousand million. (FYI: a billion in British usage
is equal to a million million). See **million, billion** entry.

biofuel Do not use a hyphen. Biofuel is a renewable alternative to fossil fuel, as in *Ethanol, a biofuel, reportedly will be the gasoline of the 21st century.*

biotech, biotechnology Use these interchangeably.

black Lowercase racial descriptions that are derived from skin color. *African-American,* with a hyphen, is the preferred term.

bloc, block A bloc is a grouping of countries, people or interest groups with a shared purpose or goal, as in *Divergent economic policies hampered efforts to form a regional trade bloc.* Write *block* with a *k* for other references.

board of directors Lowercase and spell out in the first reference. Shorten to *the board* afterward. Use the abbreviation *BOD* in informal writing. Note the verb. *The board of directors **meets** Thursday.* It agrees with *board* (the board *meets*), not with *directors* (the directors *meet*). *Boards of directors* is the plural.

boldface Reserve the use of boldface for headlines, headings, subheads, etc. When emphasis is needed, use boldface sparingly in text; otherwise it can look muddy. Put the punctuation following a font in the same font. For example, if you have a bold word at the end of the sentence, then put the period in bold also. *Charlie is adept at C++ but not at **COBOL.*** (Note the bold period.)

bondholders One word.

bot Spell out *computer robot* in the first reference; use *bot* afterward.

bottom line Two words.

brackets Do not use brackets *[ ]* and parentheses *( )* interchangeably. Use brackets:

- When it is necessary to use parentheses within parentheses. *The actuary table was not included in the monthly report (the statistics, however, are included in the new annual report [due to be published in March]).*

- To insert comments or explanations into direct quotations. *Newman said, "Charlie Sommers [director of marketing] will be the first person promoted to vice president since 2001."*

- To acknowledge errors that originate in quoted material: *Mark Smith said, "The moral [sic] of the company is at an all-time low."* Note *[sic]* is italicized. The *[sic]* tells your reader that the word *moral,* which should be *morale,* is not an error on the writer's part but is actually faithful to the original material.

brainstorm One word.

brand name *Brand name* is a nonlegal term for a service mark or trademark. When brand names are used, capitalize them. *Marie needed a Band-Aid for her knee.* Some words, originally brand names, have become generic terms and are no longer capitalized, as in *petri dish, zeppelin.*

Brazilian names See **Portuguese names** entry.

breakup Write as one word when used as a noun, as in *The Justice Department ruling will force a breakup of the company.*

bricks and mortar This term is used to refer to businesses that have physical structures as opposed to e-tailers or virtual companies. *Clicks and mortar* refers to companies that have integrated a Website with existing fulfillment, logistics and marketing. Both phrases often are used as adjectives (in which case hyphens are used and the *s* is dropped), as in *The company is making the transition from successful brick-and-mortar retailing to a click-and-mortar business.*

bring, take *Bring* means to carry toward the speaker. *Take* means to carry away from the speaker. *Bring me the file on the cabinet. Take this file and put it away.*

Britain See **Great Britain** entry.

broadband Spell out in the first reference; use *B-band* afterward. It is a wider-than-normal telephone line. In a general sense it means a network that can send more information than the narrowband network.

broadcast As a verb the past tense is *broadcast* (not *broadcasted*): *CBS broadcast the news bulletin this morning.* As an adjective: *The CEO sent a broadcast e-mail about the acquisition.* As a noun: *Millions viewed the live broadcast.*

broker/dealer This can be written with a slash (*/*) or with a hyphen (*-*), but Nasdaq uses a slash, so that is the preference in this stylebook. The plural is *broker/dealers.*

browser It is software used to surf the World Wide Web (as in Netscape Navigator or Internet Explorer).

building Do not abbreviate if it is a part of the proper name. *The Empire State Building was lit up in green for St. Patrick's Day.* Note that *Building* is capitalized because it is part of the formal name. In all other instances, lowercase it.

bullet Use bullets to make documents more readable. Business writers generally prefer bullets to outline style (with numbers and letters), but don't overuse bullets. If the text following a bullet is a complete sentence, use a period. If the text following a bullet is not a complete sentence, do not use a period.

- Use a period here.
- No period here

This stylebook favors using *bullet* as a verb, even though it may be considered nonstandard. *He bulleted the year's accomplishments in the executive summary.*

bulletproof One word. *Helenmarie assured management the new systems had bulletproof security and reliability.*

bullion Gold or silver in bar form. Do not confuse with *bouillon,* a clear broth with seasonings.

bureau Capitalize when it is part of the formal name of an organization or agency; lowercase when used alone or to designate a corporate subdivision: *The Bureau of Labor Statistics reported the unemployment rate dropped to 3% in the last quarter. The* Financial Times *is expanding its Paris bureau.*

burn out, burnout This is two words when used as a verb, as in *The project leader warned management that the programmers would burn out if they continued working 24/7.* Write as one word when used as a noun, as in *The project leader warned management that burnout among the programmers was a concern.*

business casual Lowercase this term for less formal business attire. *Our dress code is business casual every day.*

businesses This is the plural of *business.* Form the plural possessive by adding just an apostrophe, as in *businesses' operations.*

businesslike One word.

business model This refers to the way a company makes its money. Its model is either sustainable (can continue making money) or unsustainable (cannot continue making money).

businessperson One word. This can be useful since it avoids reference to gender. If it sounds stilted, rewrite the sentence. *A group of businesspersons will accompany the senator to Vietnam* can be changed to *A group of business executives will accompany.* . . .

business school Spell out in the first reference; use *B-school* afterward.

business-to-business Spell out in the first reference; use *B2B* afterward. *The head of the company's business-to-business division announced three new B2B initiatives.* This refers to communications and transactions conducted between businesses as opposed to between businesses and consumers.

business-to-consumer Spell out in the first reference; use *B2C* afterward. This refers to communications and transactions conducted between businesses and consumers.

business-to-distributor Spell out in the first reference; use *B2D* afterward. This refers to communications and transactions conducted between a business and the distributors it uses to sell its products to consumers.

business-to-government Spell out in the first reference; use *B2G* afterward. This refers to communications and transactions conducted between businesses and government.

busywork One word. *The intern spent most of the summer doing busywork.*

but It is acceptable to begin sentences with *But* (and *And*). Do not use *but* after the expression *cannot help.* Instead of *The purchasing manager cannot help but see the difference in quality,* write *The purchasing manager cannot help seeing the difference in quality.*

buy back, buyback This is two words when used as a verb. *The company will buy back up to $2 billion of its stock.* Write as one word when used as a noun, as in *The buyback is set for the third quarter.*

buzzword The Fortune 500 communications professionals surveyed for this stylebook are split down the middle when it comes to the use of buzzwords in business writing. Approximately half disdain buzzwords of any kind while the other half think some buzzwords are effective (for instance, *bottom line, globalize, incentivize, leverage, paradigm shift, proactive, robust, synergy* and *value-added).* As a general rule, use buzzwords judiciously, always keeping the readers in mind. If a buzzword is lively and capable of injecting some spunk into a dull sentence (and it does not alienate the readers), then use it.

byline A byline is a notation at the beginning or end of an article carrying the writer's name. For internal and external publications, establish a style for bylines and use it consistently throughout the publication, as in *by Lisa Argento, By Lisa Argento, BY LISA ARGENTO* or just *—Lisa Argento.* It is also useful to establish a policy on which material gets a byline. Generally all front-page material and feature articles get bylines. Short news items generally do not (although initials preceded by a dash [—] are sometimes given as a courtesy to the writer).

byproduct One word.

bytes, bits Note the spelling of *bytes.* According to *Wired Style,* "While it takes 8 *bits*—each designated either a 1 or a 0—to make up a *byte, bits* are generally used to describe transmission speeds; *bytes* are used to describe storage capacity."

·C·

"Never assume. Check everything."

—Clara Degen, manager and editor, employee communications
McKesson HBOC, Inc.

callback When used as an adjective or a noun, use the one-word form. *The company receives thousands of callback requests each week.* Use two words for the verb: *call back.*

can, may These two words are not interchangeable. *Can* means able: *Charlie DePhillips can write the memo. May* means permission is implied: *Lori Feldman may leave work early to attend her daughter's basketball game.*

cancel, canceled, canceling, cancellation These are the preferred spellings.

can hardly Do not use *can't hardly;* it is a double negative. Instead write *After working the night shift, the manager can hardly keep her eyes open.*

cannot One word—always.

capital, capitol *Capital* is the term for a town or city that serves as a seat of government. *Capital* also means money or wealth. A *capital* letter is an uppercase letter. *Capitol* is a term for the building in which a legislative assembly meets.

capitalization Always think twice about capitalizing a word. Many business writers, especially in the field of technology, tend to use capitals where they are not necessary. Some general rules follow. Consult a dictionary for specific questions.

- Capitalize all proper nouns: *Robert Rubin, Carnegie Hall.*

- Capitalize the names of companies, organizations and schools following their style in the first reference. In subsequent references substitute the full name for a shortened form (e.g., Nike, FedEx, the Fed, Rutgers) or a lowercased shortened form (company, corporation, commission, university), as in *Accenture Ltd. will cut 1,500 jobs. Accenture announced the decision last week. The company also placed some staff members on leave with reduced pay.*

- Capitalize the first word of a complete sentence. *The office is open.*

- Capitalize the first word of quoted material that is a full sentence: *Maureen Moore said, "The accountant can't believe the audit is finished."* Do not capitalize the first letter of a quote if it does not begin a complete sentence. *Andrew said that to finish the project late would mean "sudden death."*

- Capitalize the letter *I* when it stands alone: *I eat, I sleep, I work.*

- Capitalize the first letter of the main words in a title (book, play, headline, etc.): *Officials Question the Numbers in the Reports.* See **headline** entry.

- Capitalize the professional title of an individual when it precedes a proper noun: *Federal Reserve Board Chairman Alan Greenspan.* (Job descriptions are rarely capitalized, as in *copyeditor Matia Beirne.)*

- In correspondence, capitalize all titles in the address.

- Capitalize only the first letter in a complimentary closing: *Yours truly.*

- Capitalize days of the week, months: *Thursday, April 9.*

- Capitalize all holidays—official, unofficial, religious, secular—including the word *Day,* as in *Martin Luther King Day.*

- For résumés, school subjects are not capitalized unless they are languages: *English, Latin, biology, chemistry.* Only specific place names modifying a noun are capitalized: *European history.*

- Capitalize a noun not usually capitalized (*uncle*) when it is part of the proper noun: *Uncle Nick, Auntie Ro.*

- Capitalize *North, South, East, West* only if it is a region, not a direction. *They are planning to move to the South. Go south on Harpeth Street to find the office.* Capitalize directions if they are part of a proper noun, as in *the Lower East Side, South Street.* In an address, spell out and capitalize *North, South, East, West* when they appear before the street; abbreviate and capitalize when they appear after the street: *1200 South Maple Street* versus *1200 Maple Street S.*

- Capitalize words that precede numbers, as in *Page 12, Section 4, Version 3.*

- Capitalize words that are e-mail or computer functions, as in *Hit the Send button.* The exceptions to this guideline are *cc* and *bcc.* When referring to the *cc* or *bcc* function on e-mail, lowercase and put *cc* and *bcc* in italics, as in, Be sure to *cc* Tracy Lam on your e-mail or Sha-keisha *cc'd* the entire department on the memo.

caption A caption is the blurb under (or next to) a photograph. Write a caption for most photographs. It should describe what the reader cannot see by looking at the photograph. Try to keep it to one or two sentences. Write it in the present tense. Sometimes it makes sense to give some background to the photograph. Identify individuals pictured (*from left to right* or *clockwise).* A common error is that the spelling of proper nouns in the caption does not match the spelling in the text. Take extra time to check this. Stand-alone photos (photographs that are not part of an article or text) usually have longer captions, but brevity should still be a consideration. Avoid irrelevant captions, as in *A man at work on the factory floor* or *An employee uses the company gym* or *A woman beams approval at her co-workers.* An informative caption reads: *Douglas Eich, a foreman at the Detroit plant, examines the new ergonomic adjustments made to the assembly line in May 2002.* Don't assume the reader will see the connection between the photograph and the text. Writing a good caption takes skill.

carat This is a unit of weight for gemstones. Do not confuse this with *karat,* which measures the fineness of gold. *Her future husband gave her a 14-karat gold ring with a 2-carat diamond.* A *caret* (^) is a mark used by editors and proofreaders.

carbon copy, cc Use *cc* in all references unless the abbreviation could create confusion. If spelling out, write *copy* (you don't need the *carbon): Sha-keisha copied the entire department on the memo. Sha-keisha cc'd the entire department on the memo.* When referring to the *cc* function on e-mail, lowercase and put *cc* in italics, as in, Be sure to *cc* Tracy Lam on your e-mail. (This and *bcc* are the exceptions to the guideline that computer and e-mail functions should be capitalized, as in *the Send button.)*

carriers, shippers *Carriers* transport or convey goods. *Shippers* are the owners of the goods or receive goods for transport.

case-sensitive This takes a hyphen and means that it makes a difference whether letters are upper- or lowercase. Many passwords and some Web addresses are case-sensitive.

cash flow, cash-flow This is two words when used as a noun, as in *The company has difficulties with cash flow.* Write with a hyphen when used as an adjective, as in *The company has cash-flow difficulties.*

cash on delivery Use *c.o.d.* with periods for all references. Without periods it could be confused with the word *cod,* as in fish.

catalog This is the preferred spelling (not *catalogue*).

Catch-22 Capitalize the *C* and use a hyphen. This phrase, from the Joseph Heller novel of the same name, means an inherently illogical condition in a law, regulation or circumstance that creates a no-win situation. *The company is in a Catch-22: It cannot become profitable without investing more capital, but it cannot raise capital because it is unprofitable.*

cc See **carbon copy, cc** entry.

CD Use *CD* in all references. It stands for *compact disc* or *certificate of deposit. CDs* is the plural.

CD-ROM Use *CD-ROM* in all references. Note the hyphen. It stands for compact disc–read-only memory. The plural is *CD-ROMs.*

cellphone One word.

Celsius This is the temperature scale used in the metric system. If using this scale, specify *32 °C* (with a capital *C,* without a space before or after the degree symbol and without a period after the *C).* Use figures and the degree symbol. Use a word, not a minus sign, for temperatures below zero, as in *The pipes froze because it was minus 10 °C.*

Fahrenheit is the temperature scale used in the United States. Note that *Fahrenheit* and *Celsius* are capitalized. To convert Celsius or centigrade temperature to Fahrenheit, multiply by 9, divide by 5 and add 32.

Also note that everyone has a temperature, usually 98.6°, so do not write that *Mark has a temperature.* Instead write *Mark has a high temperature* or *Mark has a fever.*

center on Use *center on,* as in *Marie's presentation centered on the upcoming RFP.* Do not use *center around.*

cents Spell out and lowercase *cents,* using numerals for amounts less than a dollar, such as *59 cents.* For slide shows, tables or other material using decimals, write *$0.59.* Use the currency symbol and a decimal for amounts greater than a dollar, as in *$62.39.* When exact figures are not essential, round numbers to avoid using decimals. See **foreign currency** entry.

century Spell out the words *first* through *ninth* if they precede *century,* as in *ninth century.* Use numerals for higher numbers, as in *20th century.* Lowercase *century* unless it is part of a proper noun.

certainly, very Use *certainly* and *very* sparingly. Always aim to be concise. These words add little meaning to a sentence.

cesarean section Lowercase both words.

cession Something that is yielded or surrendered; not to be confused with *session,* which is a meeting.

chaebol This is a Korean word for that country's business conglomerates, such as Hyundai and Daewoo. The word *chaebol* is both singular and plural, so don't put an *s* on it. *According to some analysts, the sluggishness of reform at many of the chaebol is worrisome.* This term is familiar to an international audience, so no italics are necessary.

chairman, chairperson, chairwoman These terms are lowercased unless written as an official title preceding a name; then capitalize: *Chairman John Lukas.* Do not use the term *chairlady,* unless it is an organization's formal title for an office. Some women prefer *chairman* to *chairwoman.*

Chanukah This holiday has three spellings. *Hanukkah* (not *Chanukah* or *Hanukah)* is the preferred spelling. Capitalize all holidays—official, unofficial, religious, secular.

Chapter 11 Capitalize the *C* when referring to *Chapter 11* bankruptcy protection.

charts, graphs Because space is at a premium in charts and graphs, use abbreviations you would not normally use in text, such as *bn* for *billion.* Develop style preferences that lend themselves to visuals and use them consistently (e.g., write *2003–08* instead of *2003–2008).* Write titles that are concise and convey as much information as possible, as in *2003–08: Income by Region ($bn).*

    If you have a series of related charts in a slide show or other material, check all the elements for consistency, including type size and font; size, shape and punctuation for bullets; use of colors; size of graphics; use of decimal points; and spellings and use of names (e.g., Lehman, Lehman Brothers or Lehman Brothers Holding Inc.—go with the shortest if possible).

chief executive officer Whether to use the abbreviation *CEO* in the first reference depends on the audience. Capitalize all three letters. The plural is *CEOs.* An alternative is *chief executive.*

chief financial officer Whether to use the abbreviation *CFO* in the first reference depends on the audience. Capitalize all three letters. The plural is *CFOs.*

chief information officer Whether to use the abbreviation *CIO* in the first reference depends on the audience. Capitalize all three letters. The plural is *CIOs.*

chief operating officer Whether to use the abbreviation *COO* in the first reference depends on the audience. Capitalize all three letters. The plural is *COOs.*

chief privacy officer Whether to use the abbreviation *CPO* in the first reference depends on the audience. Capitalize all three letters. The plural is *CPOs.*

chief technology officer Whether to use the abbreviation *CTO* in the first reference depends on the audience. Capitalize all three letters. The plural is *CTOs.*

childcare One word.

Chinese names In Chinese, names are written with the family name first, followed by the given name: *Sun* (family name) *Xiao* (given name). Although many English-language publications follow that style and would write *Sun Xiao,* this creates confusion about first and last names. To avoid such confusion when writing for business, put Chinese names in the same order as names written in English: given name first, followed by the family name: *Xiao Sun* or *Mr. Sun.*

chutzpah Often misspelled; it is another word for audacity.

Cincinnati Often misspelled.

citation Unless it is a scientific or academic report, parenthetical documentation (instead of footnotes and bibliography) may work best for citing sources. Follow this style for parenthetical documentation: *Humorist Dave Barry cited a headline that read "Search for Woman in Fertilized Egg Suit Goes Nationwide" in his Sunday column* ("Grammar Just Loves a Good Infarction," *Bergen Record,* Feb. 25, 2001).

cite, site *Cite* means to quote: *He cited his source in the bibliography. Site* means a place for a building: *They gathered at the building site for the inspection. Site* also means a location on the Web: *The URL for this site is not accurate.*

cities If the city is synonymous with the state or is widely recognizable, then the city can stand alone in text. The following list of cities can stand alone (based on the style used by *The Associated Press Stylebook* for domestic cities and *The New York Times Manual of Style and Usage* for international cities).

If a place name is not identifiable in context, then for clarification include the state or country.

United States:

Atlanta	Detroit	Milwaukee	St. Louis
Baltimore	Honolulu	Minneapolis	Salt Lake City
Boston	Houston	New Orleans	San Antonio
Chicago	Indianapolis	New York	San Diego
Cincinnati	Jersey City	Oklahoma City	San Francisco
Cleveland	Las Vegas	Philadelphia	Seattle
Dallas	Los Angeles	Phoenix	Washington
Denver	Miami	Pittsburgh	

International:

Algiers	Dublin	Luxembourg	Quebec
Amsterdam	Edinburgh	Macao**	Rio de Janeiro
Athens	Frankfurt	Madrid	Rome
Bangkok	Geneva	Manila	San Marino
Beijing	Gibraltar	Mexico City	San Salvador
Berlin	Glasgow	Milan	Shanghai
Bombay	Guatemala City	Monaco	Singapore
Bonn	The Hague	Montreal	Stockholm
Brasilia	Havana	Moscow	Tel Aviv
Brussels	Hong Kong	Munich	Tokyo
Budapest	Istanbul	New Delhi	Toronto
Buenos Aires	Jerusalem	Oslo	Tunis
Cairo	Johannesburg	Ottawa	Venice
Calcutta	Kuwait	Panama	Vienna
Cape Town	Lisbon	Paris	Warsaw
Copenhagen	London	Prague	Zurich
Djibouti*			

*__Djibouti__ is also the name of the country.

**__Macao__ is also written __Macau__.

civil rights movement Lowercase names of political or quasi-historical movements if specific dates are not assigned (e.g., *cold war, westward movement, gold rush).*

class action, class-action No hyphen is needed for the noun, as in *Shareholders filed a class action alleging the company failed to disclose information about its foreign exchange hedging practices.* When used as an adjective, write it with a hyphen, as in *Shareholders filed a class-action lawsuit alleging the company....*

clause This is a group of related words within a sentence that has both a subject and a predicate (a verb and all its auxiliaries, modifiers and complements). An independent (or main) clause is a complete statement (if it stood alone, it would be a simple sentence). A dependent clause is not a complete statement and cannot stand alone.

cliché Note the accent. This is an expression or truism that has lost its originality through overuse. Try to avoid using clichés. If it is necessary to use one, don't put quotation marks around it.

clickability It is one word and means that a Website has many links.

clicks and mortar This term is used to refer to brick-and-mortar companies that have integrated a Website with existing fulfillment, logistics and marketing. (*Bricks and mortar* refers to businesses that have physical structures as opposed to e-tailers or virtual companies.) Both phrases often are used as adjectives (in which case hyphens are used and the *s* is dropped), as in *The company is making the transition from successful brick-and-mortar retailing to a click-and-mortar business.*

clock time Use figures, as in *We will meet at 9 a.m. in the conference room* (not *nine a.m.).* It is better to specify *a.m.* or *p.m.* than to use *o'clock.* Note the space between the number and *a.m.* If the time is on the hour, it is not necessary to include a colon and two zeros. Just write *9 a.m.* Use the colon for fractions of hours, as in *9:15 a.m.* If the *o'clock* form is used, spell out the number, as in *nine o'clock,* not *9 o'clock.*

co(-) Keep the hyphen when forming nouns, adjectives and verbs that indicate occupation or status. *The co-chairman of the annual fund-raiser was Michael Greene.* For other *co-* words, some are hyphenated and others aren't: *cooperate, coordinate, co-owner, co-worker.* Check in the dictionary if you are uncertain.

c.o.d. Use *c.o.d.* with periods for all references. It stands for *cash on delivery.* Without periods it could be confused with the word *cod,* as in fish.

collectibles Often misspelled (not *collectables).*

collective nouns A noun that denotes a unit (or collection) takes a singular verb and pronoun. *The committee is meeting to discuss its technology proposal. Headquarters is located on Elm Street.* Usually collective nouns take a singular verb.

Colombia, Columbia Often confused. *Colombia* is a country in northwestern South America. *Columbia* is the university or its undergraduate college and also the name of many U.S. cities.

colon A colon (*:)* is a strong pause used to introduce related statements, quotations or lists. If the statement following the colon is a complete sentence, a proper noun or a quotation, begin it with a capital letter: *Sheila Nadata is rising rapidly in the company: She will be promoted to vice president next year.* Otherwise use a lowercase letter: *Three positions will open up next month: account executive, administrative assistant, manager.*

comma A comma (*,*) is a signal to pause in a sentence. Do not overuse commas. They are there to clarify meaning. Too many commas can make a sentence unwieldy. Follow these guidelines:

- When two long clauses are linked by a conjunction (e.g., *and, but, for)* and each clause can stand alone as a separate sentence, use a comma before the conjunction in most cases: *Bill will go to the meeting, but he must finish the proposal first. Mary likes her new job, and she plans to stay until she retires.* (For a comma to be used here, the subject must be included. Do not use a comma if the sentence reads *Mary likes her new job and plans to stay until she retires* [the *she* is missing]). If the two clauses are short, there is no need for a comma: *Andrei called in the trade and Nikolai executed it.*

- If the word or phrase is essential (restrictive) to the meaning of the sentence, then do not use commas around it: *Martin Scorsese's film* Kundun *is playing at the theater.* (He has directed more than one film.) When the word or phrase is not essential to the meaning of the sentence (an appositive), it is placed **between** commas: *Mary's sister, who started her own business, lives next door.* (Appositives expand on the information provided, but they are not essential to the meaning of the sentence.)

- The salutation of a **personal** letter takes a comma, as in *Dear Mary,.* (A **business** letter salutation takes a colon, as in *Dear Ms. Lesnikowski:.)*

- The complimentary close of a letter is followed by a comma: *Sincerely,.*

- Use commas to set off parenthetical words: *I believe, therefore, we should hire an accounting company to conduct the audit. If, however, this is not agreeable to you, you should seek the counsel of some other law firm.*

- An introductory phrase of **five or more words** is usually set off by a comma to show that it is subordinate to the main clause: *Because the manager had placed the proposal on the stage after the speech, he forgot to bring it back to the office.* After a short introductory phrase, use a comma only if it is needed for clarity: *To Marie, Elizabeth seemed to be overwhelmed.* It is not necessary to place a comma in this construction: *After an hour we* *left the cafeteria.* (Many writers use commas after **all** introductory phrases. It is not incorrect, but the **five-or-more-words** guideline is a good standard.)

- Use commas in a series (called the *serial comma): Pens, pencils, stapler, ruler, etc. are in the desk drawer* (note there is no comma after the word *etc.).* No comma is necessary before the *and* in a simple series (single items): *France's flag is red, white and blue.* (Note that it is not incorrect to write *red, white, and blue* with two commas; it's just not necessary to use the serial comma. Whichever style you choose, the key to use of the serial comma is consistency.) The majority of business writers do not use the serial comma unless it is needed for clarity: *Jim spoke about the tax liability, Ed spoke about taxes and tariffs, and Stuart covered pricing and financing.*

- A comma marks off a date when it appears in text: *She currently works in Chicago, but on September 6, 2002, she will relocate to Paris* (note the comma after the year). Do not insert a comma before the month and the year if it appears without the day: *In December 2005 I will retire.*

- Use a comma before a direct quotation to set the attribution off from the rest of the sentence: *Allen Markowitz said, "I will never hire an intern again."* Also: *"I will never hire an intern again," said Allen Markowitz.* However, do not use a comma if the quoted statement ends with a question mark or an exclamation point: *"When does the London Stock Exchange close?" he asked.*

- Use a comma when the quotation does not end the sentence. *If you want to be known as a "player," join the M&A group. The best chapters of the book are "Romancing the Inspectors," "Getting Tough with Contractors" and "The Zoning Board Shuffle."*

- Do not use a comma at the start of a partial quotation: *Yuri Fridman said we needed "to start from scratch."*

- Use a comma in direct address: *Thomas, it was a pleasure meeting you at the conference Wednesday.*

- Use a comma to set off interjections: *Yes, I will go to the meeting with you.*

- Use a comma to set off a city or town: *Nancy Rine, Baltimore, and Luisa Beltrán, Barcelona, Spain, represented the company at the meeting.* (Some cities can stand alone without a state or country. See **cities** entry.)

- Separate ages with two commas: *Bill Eckert, 59, plans to take early retirement.*

- Do not use a comma before parentheses, as in *Vinny will take the plane to New York (and the subway to Brooklyn).*

- Use commas to separate two or more adjectives if each equally modifies the noun alone: *He was the only short, slim participant in the study.* However, if the first adjective modifies the second adjective and noun, no comma is necessary: *The facilities manager asked the janitor to cut down the tall blue spruce.*

- Use a comma when the first and last names are reversed: *Byrne, Myles.* Use a comma to separate a name from a title: *Myles Byrne, president.* Use a comma for a personal name suffix: *Myles Byrne, Jr.*

- Use a comma after the company name with *Inc.,* if a comma precedes *Inc.,* as in *We will visit SCI Systems, Inc., on our next trip.* Do not use a comma if the company name does not use a comma before *Inc.,* as in *Marissa applied for a job at Safeway Inc. last month.*

Commonwealth of Independent States Spell out in the first reference; then use *CIS.* This refers to 12 of the former republics of the Soviet Union.

communiqué Note the accent.

company, companies If the words *company* or *companies* appear alone in a second reference, always spell out and lowercase. *The Bank of New York Co. will release the annual earnings report in a few weeks. The company did not specify the reason for the delay.* Use *it/its* when referring to a single *company* (not *they/their). The company launched **its** new Web service* (not ***their** new Web service). **It** announced the news in March* (not ***They** announced).*

company names The Fortune 500 communications executives surveyed for this stylebook overwhelmingly agree on how to write company names: Spell out and punctuate the name exactly the way the company does in correspondence and in the first reference (including *Inc., Ltd., S.A., P.L.C.* and other equivalents); use the shortened form afterward. *Nike, Inc., is a Fortune 500 company. Nike participated in the survey.* (Note the commas and the abbreviated form of *Inc.* in the first reference.)

To verify the correct spelling and punctuation, visit the company's Website, check its marketing or other branded material (such as letterhead, business cards) or consult *Standard & Poor's Register of Corporations, Directors and Executives.* Hoover's Online is another useful source (www.hoovers.com). Spend the extra time to make sure that the spelling and punctuation of company names are correct.

company-wide Use a hyphen for *company-wide, enterprise-wide, firm-wide, industry-wide. Nationwide, worldwide* are one word.

compare to, compare with Use *compare to* when describing resemblances between unlike things, as in *JoElyn compared the concert to an exercise in meditation.* Use *compare with* when examining similar things to determine their similarities or differences. *The staff compared the new software with the previous version.*

compass points In text, lowercase *east, west, north, south,* except when they designate regions, as in *the South,* or when they are part of a proper name, as in *the Lower East Side, South Street.* In an address, spell out and capitalize *North, South, East, West* when they appear before the street, but abbreviate and capitalize when they come after the street, as in *1200 South Maple Street* versus *1200 Maple Street S.*

complement, compliment *Complement* has noun, verb and adjective forms. It means a part that completes the whole. *The manager's writing skill complements his assistant's ability to calculate numbers. Their skills are complementary.* *Compliment* also has noun, verb and adjective forms, but it means either flattery or free. *He complimented her writing style. The magazine sent a complimentary tote bag to all new subscribers.*

complimentary close Words that appear at the end of correspondence and just before the writer's name are used as a polite ending. Capitalize the first letter of the close, but lowercase all other words, as in *Very truly yours,.* Put a comma after the close. In choosing a close, take into account the degree of formality and familiarity. In an e-mail to a colleague, for example, use *All the best, Best, Cheers,;* for a letter to a client, use a more formal close, such as *Sincerely,* or *Yours truly,.*

comprise, compose *Comprise* means to include. The whole comprises the parts, but the parts compose the whole. The distinction between *comprise* and *compose* is losing ground, but many grammarians still insist on it. To use these verbs correctly, follow these examples: *The IS department comprises 50 people.* (A common error is to write *The IS department* ***is comprised of*** *50 people.* Do not use the *is* form with *comprise.) The IS department is composed of 50 people.*

comptroller, controller Government financial officers are *comptrollers*. Financial officers in businesses are *controllers*. Both words are pronounced the same way.

computer code Punctuation in computer code is idiosyncratic. It can deviate from punctuation style in regular text. Do not change code.

computer functions Write computer or e-mail functions with a capital letter. It is not necessary to use quotation marks as well. *I hit the Send button.* This guideline applies to other functions, as in *Nancy hit the Submit button after she finished the order* and *Make sure you hit Print just once.*

confab This is informal. It is a shortened form of *confabulation,* a chat.

conjunction It is a word that joins words, phrases or clauses, such as *and, but, not, since, although, when.*

connoisseur Often misspelled.

connote, denote *Connote* means to suggest; *denote* means to mean explicitly.

consumer price index Spell out and lowercase in the first reference; use *CPI* afterward. The CPI measures price changes, excluding taxes. There is a difference between the CPI and the cost of living index (COL), which is the amount of money needed to pay taxes and buy goods and services necessary for a certain standard of living. Do not capitalize indexes.

contact Writing *contact* as a verb is now considered standard.

continual, continuous *Continual* means over and over again; *continuous* means uninterrupted. They are not interchangeable. *The flu outbreak has caused **continual** absences among the employees. The **continuous** din of the copy machine gave her a headache.*

continued line In publications, when an article jumps to another page, set the *continued line* in smaller italicized type, as in *continued on Page 180.* It can be written as a footer in the white space below the bottom margin of a page. It can also be placed in brackets in running text (but do not put into a smaller typeface in this case). Always make sure that the page numbers are correct for the *continued on* and *continued from* lines. The abbreviation is *cont.*

> **Example:**
> . . . Patty Leonard executed the trade on [*continued on Page 180*]
> Remember to include a *continued from* line in the pickup.

Example:
[*continued from Page 10*] December 28, 2002. Leonard did not. . . .

contractions Contractions (e.g., *isn't)* are considered informal in speech and writing, but for most business writing contractions are acceptable.

cookie This refers to a file stored on a hard drive by a Website the user has visited, so that the Website will recognize users who return to the site. Cookies hold information about users' browsing habits, such as sites visited.

coopetition No hyphen. This refers to partnering with a competitor while simultaneously trying to put it out of business. It is a blending of the words *cooperation* and *competition.*

copacetic, copasetic Both spellings are correct. The origin of this word is unknown. It means satisfactory or acceptable.

copyright This refers to the protection given to the author of a work, such as an article, book, painting, music, photograph. The symbol for a work protected by copyright is ©. *Copyright* is a noun; it is also a verb in the past tense, as in *Lorna copyrighted the cantata she wrote last year.*

corporate affairs Lowercase the names of departments within companies, unless it is already established practice to capitalize. Note that *corporate affairs* takes a singular verb because the phrase refers to the department. *Corporate affairs is responsible for community relations.* If that sounds awkward, rewrite the sentence, as in *The corporate affairs department is responsible for community relations.*

corporate America Do not use a capital *C* in *corporate.*

corporate communication(s) Lowercase the names of departments within companies, unless it is already established practice to capitalize. Note that *cor-*

porate communications takes a singular verb because the phrase refers to the department. *Corporate communications is responsible for the annual report.* If that sounds awkward, rewrite the sentence, as in *The corporate communications department is responsible for the annual report.*

corporatespeak, corp-speak   These terms are informal and refer to business jargon. Write *corporatespeak* as one word; use a hyphen with *corp-speak.*

cost of living, cost-of-living   Spell out and lowercase in the first reference; use *COL* afterward. Hyphenate when the phrase is an adjective, as in *The company gave all employees a 2% cost-of-living adjustment.* The COL is the amount of money needed to pay taxes and buy goods and services necessary for a certain standard of living. There is a difference between the COL and the consumer price index (CPI), which measures price changes, excluding taxes. Do not capitalize indexes.

could have   Do not use *could of, should of, must of, would of.* These constructions are incorrect but common in speech. Write *could have,* etc.

country   Use *it/its* when referring to a *country* (not *they/their*). *Brazil devalued its currency* (not *their currency*). *It will also increase interest rates* (not *They will also increase*).

couple   This word takes a plural verb and pronoun if it is used in the sense of two people. *The couple were reunited at their alma mater.*

court cases   Use either *v.* or *vs.* for *versus* in court cases. (Whichever abbreviation you choose for *versus,* use it consistently.) The *v.* or *vs.* is set in a different font from the names, as in *Hirsch* v. *3Com* or Anderson *vs.* McKiernan. If used in a headline, lowercase the abbreviation: Roe v. Wade Battle Begins. When not referring to court cases, spell out *versus* in text, as in *At the company softball game, it was the Titans versus the Bullets.*

courtesy titles In text, do not include *Mr., Mrs., Ms.* in the first reference to an individual, because the full name should be used, as in *Andrea Sholler will join the company March 5* (not *Ms. Andrea Sholler*). Afterward, the title can be used, as in *Ms. **Sholler** has extensive experience in business development.* Other options for subsequent references are to use the first or last name only, as in ***Andrea** has extensive experience* or ***Sholler** has extensive experience.* . . . Many newspapers use only the last name in subsequent references, but many companies use a courtesy title.

For women, use *Ms.* unless *Mrs.* is someone's preference.

In addresses, use *Mr.* or *Ms.* When sending a direct mailing, it simplifies matters to refer to all women as *Ms.*

The plural of *Mr.* is *Messrs.* The plural of *Ms.* is *Mss.* The plural of *Mrs.* is *Mmes.*

credit Give credits for photographs or illustrations in printed material. Usually the credit is positioned underneath or beside the graphic in small capitals (in 8-point or a smaller typeface, as in SUZANN ANDERSON).

criterion, criteria *Criterion,* which means rule or standard, is singular. *The main criterion for hiring Isabel is her B-school degree. Criteria is plural. For this job the criteria are a B-school degree and experience in the healthcare industry.* Make sure the verbs agree with the singular or plural form: *criterion **is*** and *criteria **are**.*

cross-border Write *cross-border* with a hyphen, as in *The company announced its third cross-border acquisition in a year.* In headings or headlines, capitalize the *b,* as in *Cross-Border Trading Explodes.*

culture cop This is a buzzword meaning that an individual within an organization has an accurate sense of the company's environment. The connotation can be positive or negative, depending on the context.

cup It is equal to eight fluid ounces. Do not abbreviate, unless it is tabular material, such as a recipe. The abbreviation is *c.* Use *cupful* and *cupfuls,* not *cupsful.*

currency See **foreign currency** entry.

curriculum, curriculums *Curriculum* is singular. For the plural, *curriculums* is preferred to *curricula.*

cut-and-dried Not *cut-and-dry.*

cut back, cutback This is two words when used as a verb, as in *The company cut back on spending to retain jobs.* Write as one word when used as a noun, as in *The company's spending cutbacks will enable it to retain jobs.*

cutthroat One word.

cutting-edge Use a hyphen with both the noun and adjective forms, as in *The new technology is cutting-edge* and *The company uses cutting-edge technology.*

cyber(-) Words beginning with *cyber* are usually one word, as in *cyberspace, cybercampaign, cybersquatters.*

czar This spelling is preferred to *tsar.* Since this is not a formal title (in the United States), do not capitalize when it precedes a name. This is also used to refer to a person with a great deal of power, as in *The president appointed a new drug czar to combat illegal drug trafficking.*

·D·

"Do your readers a service by anticipating their questions."
—Jeff Cole, manager, marketing communications
Dana Corporation

dangling phrases A phrase dangles when it cannot logically modify the noun or pronoun to which it refers. The following sentences are examples of dangling phrases:

> *To apply for a promotion, a review must be submitted by your manager* (a review cannot apply for a promotion).
> *With much effort the project was completed just before the deadline* (the project cannot exert effort).

To correct these, change the subject of the main clause:

> *To apply for a promotion, you must have your manager submit a review.*
> *With much effort we completed the project just before the deadline.*

dash There are two kinds of dashes, differing in length and usage.

- The most commonly used dash is the em dash. Use the em dash as a sudden break in thought (stronger than the comma). If the break comes in the middle of the sentence, put an em dash on either side of the phrase. Do not use more than two dashes per sentence. If the em dash is not a symbol-insert in the word processing program, it is typed by putting two hyphens together. It is not necessary to put a space on either side of the dash: *The diversity manager and the benefits manager—both from human resources—attended the meeting.* But the spacing is a matter of style. The *New York Times* puts a space between the text and the em dash — like this — but many business publications do not.

- The en dash is not as long as the em dash, but it is slightly longer than the hyphen. It has several uses. Use it for the minus sign or to indicate continuing numbers, such as date, time or reference numbers: *March–June 2003.* Use the en dash in place of a hyphen for a compound adjective consisting of two words or for a hyphenated word: *New York–born golfer, blue silk–papered bedroom.* Many business writers are not familiar with the en dash and use a hyphen instead. The en dash is a fine point.

data This noun, which is plural, has a singular (infrequently used) form— *datum.* In formal writing, the word *data* takes a plural verb to be grammatically correct. *The data are available online.* If this sounds awkward, revise the sentence. *Statistics are available online.*

Data often is used as a collective noun meaning information, especially in the technology industry. If used this way (which 60% of the Usage Panel of *The American Heritage Dictionary* found acceptable), use a singular verb. *The data was transmitted over the wires at 5 a.m.*

database One word.

dateline Many newspaper articles begin with datelines (specifying where and when the reporting took place). Generally a dateline appears when the article originates from a place other than where the newspaper is published or when a wire service has been used.

day care This is two words without a hyphen, even when used as an adjective: *He will drop his daughter off at the day care center before work.*

daylight-saving time Often misspelled (it is not *daylight-savings time*). Note the hyphen. In the United States the clock is set forward an hour on the first Sunday in April at 2 a.m. and set back one hour at 2 a.m. on the last Sunday in October.

daylong One word.

day sales outstanding Spell out in first reference; use *DSO* afterward. This means the average number of days that elapse between when a company books a sale and when it actually gets paid.

days of the week Spell out and capitalize the days of the week in text: *Sunday, Monday, Tuesday, Wednesday, Thursday, Friday, Saturday.* In tabular material, slide shows or charts and graphs, abbreviate days: *Sun., Mon., Tues., Wed., Thurs., Fri., Sat.* (or *S, M, T, W, T, F, S*, depending on space and order). See **month** entry.

deal Use *deal* interchangeably with *transaction.*

dealbreaker One word.

debuted This is the past tense for *debut,* as in *The new software debuted in the second quarter.*

decades You may use either form but do so consistently: *1990s* or *'90s.*

decimal Try to avoid using more than two decimal points in text. When exact figures are not necessary, round the numbers and avoid decimals altogether. Be consistent throughout the entire document.

decimalize It means to change to a decimal system. *Decimalization* is the noun. *Under decimalization stock prices are displayed in dollars and 1-cent increments.*

decision-maker, decision-making Use a hyphen.

degrees To indicate temperature, use figures and the degree symbol for all numbers except zero: *It is 76°* or *Do you think the temperature will rise above zero today?* Use a word, not a minus sign, for temperatures below zero, as in *The pipes froze because it was minus 10°.*

If a reference to the type of temperature scale is necessary, write *32°F* with a capital *F,* without a space before or after the degree symbol and without a period after the *F.* (Use the same style for the *C* in *Celsius.)* Fahrenheit is the temperature scale used in the United States. To convert Celsius or centigrade temperature to Fahrenheit, multiply by 9, divide by 5 and add 32.

degrees See **bachelor of arts, bachelor of science** entry; **master of arts, master of science** entry; **M.B.A.** entry; **Ph.D., Ph.D.s** entry; **L.L.B, L.L.D.** entries.

delist One word, no hyphen.

depart Always follow with a preposition: *He will depart after the weekend.* Avoid airline style: *He will depart Logan Airport.* Instead write *He will depart from Logan Airport.*

departments There is a great deal of inconsistency within companies on whether to upper- or lowercase department names. Unless it is established practice, lowercase department names, as in *human resources, finance, information systems, facilities, public relations.*

dependent Often misspelled (not *dependant).*

depression When the meaning is economic downturn, capitalize only when referring to the worldwide economic upheaval of the 1930s. In all other instances lowercase: *The central bank helped to avert a depression by lowering interest rates.*

desert (n.), desert (v.), dessert (n.) Misspellings often occur. The first noun means an arid area. *The Mojave Desert has two different spellings in the dictionary.* The verb means to abandon. *A soldier should not desert his troop. Dessert* is the final course of a meal. *We had apple pie for dessert.*

dialog, dialogue Use *dialog* when referring to the computer box; use *dialogue* in other instances.

different from Use the preposition *from.* It is preferred to *different than. These numbers are different from the preliminary estimates.*

digital age Lowercase references to this age because a specific date is not assigned to it. *Wired Style* offers several suggestions as to when this age began, 1984 being one of them since Apple Computer, Inc., produced the first personal computer that year.

digitize, digitized, digitizes, digitizing These forms are preferred to *digitalize, digitalized, digitalizes, digitalizing.* They mean to put into digital form.

dilemma Often used incorrectly. A dilemma is more than just a problem. It is the inability to choose between two or more difficult alternatives.

directions In text, lowercase *east, west, north, south,* except when they designate regions, as in *the South,* or if they are part of a proper noun, as in *the Lower East Side, South Street.* In an address, spell out and capitalize *North, South, East, West* when they appear before the street, but abbreviate and capitalize when they come after the street, as in *1200 South Maple Street* versus *1200 Maple Street S.*

disbursement Often misspelled.

disc, disk Often confused. Follow these guidelines from *The New York Times Manual of Style and Usage:* Use *disc* for brakes (*disc brake*), phonograph records (*disc jockey*), optical and laser-based devices (*compact disc*) and farm implements (*disc harrow*). Use *disk* for magnetic devices used with computers (*hard disk*) and the injury that occurs to the back (*slipped disk*).

disinterested This word has a different meaning from *uninterested. Disinterested* means neutral or impartial. *The companies signed an arbitration agreement to ensure that disinterested parties handle all disputes.* The word *uninterested* means not interested or indifferent.

disintermediate It means to eliminate the go-between person or company.

division Lowercase *division* when referring to parts of the government or corporations. *The food products division increased earnings by 12%.*

dollar Use figures with the *$* sign. Note there is no space between *$* and the number, as in *$4 million.*

- The rule to spell out numbers under 10 does not apply to money. *The binder costs $7.*

- Avoid redundancy. Write *$1 million,* not *$1 million dollars.*

- For amounts without a figure, always lowercase *dollars: The bond issue was denominated in dollars.*

- Use singular verbs with specified amounts. *More than $100,000 is expected when making the first payment.*

- For amounts less than $1 million, follow this style: *$9, $34, $500, $2,500, $50,000, $365,000.*

- For amounts more than $1 million, follow this style: *$2.3 million, $4.57 billion.*

- For documents with an international orientation or audience, put *US* before *$ (US$2.1 billion)*, since many other countries use dollars. Note that spaces are not needed on either side of *$* and periods are not used in *US*, which differs from the abbreviation for the United States, which is *U.S.* See **foreign currency** entry.

- Abbreviate *million* as *mn* and *billion* as *bn* for charts and graphs.

dollar-a-year, dollars a year Use hyphens and write *dollar* without an *s* when used as an adjective, as in *The million-dollar-a-year exhibit draws people from all over the world.* When used as a noun, write without hyphens, as in *The company spends millions of dollars a year on health benefits.* Note the *s* in *dollars.*

When using specific numbers, write *The $84 million-a-year exhibit draws people from all over the world.* Note that no hyphen is needed between the *$84* and *million*, although the rest of the phrase is hyphenated because it serves as an adjective. *He earns more than $250,000 a year.* No hyphens are needed in this case because the phrase is not an adjective. The same rules apply for other currencies and other uses of *dollar,* such as *dollars a month, dollars a week, dollars a day.*

domain This is the suffix in Web addresses that identifies the type of organization, as in *.com* (general use), *.edu* (educational institution), *.org* (organization), *.biz* (general use), *.pro* (professionals such as doctors and lawyers), *.name* (personal Website).

dot-com Use a hyphen, which is what most U.S. business publications use (instead of *dot.com* or *dotcom*). If this word follows the typical trail, it will end up as one word (as *e-mail* will become *email*). For now, use the hyphen. Dot-commers are people who work for dot-coms.

double-check Use a hyphen.

double digit(s) Write as two words when used as a noun, as in *The company expects revenue to grow in the double digits for the next three years.* Note the *s* in *digits.* Hyphenate when used as an adjective, as in *The company expects double-digit revenue growth for the next three years.* Note *digit* is without the *s* in the preceding sentence.

Dow Jones industrial average Spell out in the first reference, capitalizing only *Dow Jones;* use *the Dow* afterward.

download, upload *Download* means to copy an application or document from a network to a PC. *Upload* means to transfer a file from a PC to a server or onto the Net. *Upload* as a noun is a word for those transmitted files. Other forms are *downloadable* and *uploadable.*

downside One word. *Upside* is also one word.

downtime One word. *The site has not experienced any downtime. Uptime* is also one word.

Dr. When referring to physicians or dentists, put the title *Dr.* before the name: *Dr. Laura D'Annibale.* If you want to use the *M.D.* title, write *Laura D'Annibale, M.D.* Do not write *Dr. Laura D'Annibale, M.D.* It's redundant. The same holds for D.D.S. (dentist) and Ph.D.

DSL Use *DSL* in all references for *digital subscriber line. The company announced it was adding 2,000 DSLs a day.* Do not write *DSL lines,* which is redundant. DSL is a technology that allows users to gain access to the Internet over regular telephone lines at high speeds.

due to the fact that This is a wordy construction. Use *because* instead. Remember to be direct and keep writing short and simple.

Rudolf Flesch, the author of *The Art of Readable Writing,* says: "Avoid all prepositions and conjunctions that consist of more than one word. Aside from *inasmuch as*, this includes *with regard to, in association with, in connection with, with respect to, in the absence of, with a view to, in an effort to, in terms of, in order to, for the purpose of, for the reason that, in accordance with, in the neighborhood of, on the basis of* and so on. There's not a single one of these word combinations that can't be replaced by a simple word like *if, for, to, by, about* or *since.*"

· E ·

e- This prefix is short for *electronic* and now forms innumerable words: *e-initiative, e-business, e-company, e-finance, e-learning, e-tail.* Lowercase the *e* and note that most *e*-words use a hyphen. Capitalize at the beginning of a sentence, as in *E-learning is becoming the method of choice for middle managers who want to pursue their studies,* unless it is the name of a company, as in *eBay hired Laura Smith. Prior to joining eBay, she worked at an online bookseller.*

each When the subject of the sentence begins with *each,* it takes a singular verb. *Each of the investment bankers* **speaks** *Japanese.* When *each* follows a plural subject, however, it takes a plural verb: *They each* **want** *the same thing.*

each other, one another Use *each other* when referring to two people. *They looked at each other in disbelief.* Use *one another* when referring to more than two people. *Sandra, Christine and Alice will help one another with the project.* To form the possessive of *each other,* write *each other's. They read each other's reports and synthesized the findings into a single document.*

eager This means desirous. *Fran was eager to complete her degree.* Do not use *eager* in place of *anxious*, which means worried, full of anxiety. *He was anxious about the product launch.*

Earth Capitalize when written as a proper noun, such as *Earth, Venus, Mars* or *Earth Day.* Lowercase if it is not a proper noun, as in *The new CFO seems down to earth* or *The earth was dry from lack of rain.*

e-business Use *e-business* in all references. When this and other *e-* words begin a sentence, capitalize the first letter. *E-business executives sponsored the seminar.* This is another term for *e-commerce.*

e-commerce Use *e-commerce* in all references. It means electronic marketing, buying and selling on the Internet.

economic, economical *Economic* refers to the subject of economics. *Economical* means thrifty.

economic indicator Lowercase the names of indicators, as in *housing starts, consumer price index.* It is a statistic used, along with other indicators, to measure the state of general economic activity. Common leading indicators are building permits (suggesting the future volume of new construction), common stock prices, business inventories, consumer installment debt, unemployment claims and corporate profits. Other types of indicators move in line with the overall economy (coincident indicator) or change direction after the economy does (lagging indicator).

editorial An editorial is an opinion piece in a publication, which reflects the views of the publisher. An op-ed expresses the personal viewpoints of individual writers and is usually located opposite the editorial page.

e-dress   This term refers to an e-mail address.

e.g.   It means for example and stands for *exempli gratia* in Latin. This abbreviation is generally used for parenthetical material. It is lowercased, has two periods, is not italicized and is followed by a comma. *The design company has many European clients (e.g., ING, Equant, ABN Amro).* The abbreviation *e.g.* is not interchangeable with *i.e.,* which means that is and stands for *id est.*

either/or   Use *either/or* when referring to a choice between two things. *The company will list on either Nasdaq or the NYSE. Neither/nor* is the negative form. *Neither the CFO nor the CIO is authorized to speak to the media.* When all the elements in an *either/or* construction are singular, use a singular verb: *Either Coleen or Megan is expected to work on the project.* When all the elements in an *either/or* construction are plural, use a plural verb: *Either the desks or the file cabinets have to be moved.* When the construction mixes both singular and plural nouns, the verb should agree with the noun closest to it: *Either the receptionist or the secretaries have to come in Saturday.*

elder, eldest   Unlike *older* and *oldest,* these terms are generally reserved for persons (not things). Use principally with reference to seniority, as in *elder statesman, elder brother.*

eldercare   One word. This refers to care for the elderly, as in *Robin is researching eldercare options for her mother.*

ellipsis   The ellipsis (. . .) designates an omission of material. Use three periods where the omitted material occurs. If the material deleted includes a final period, type four periods (. . . .).

else   This word is often unnecessary, as in this construction: *No one else but Dylan is expected to arrive late.* Write instead *No one but Dylan is expected to arrive late.*

e-mail Use *e-mail* in all references. It is the short form for *electronic mail.* The hyphen will likely disappear at some point.

Most stylebooks maintain that *e-mail* is a system and an individual message should be referred to as an *e-mail message* (rather than an *e-mail),* although few in the workplace make such a distinction. This stylebook favors using *an e-mail* (singular) and *e-mails* (plural) instead of *e-mail message* and *e-mail messages* (plural). This stylebook also favors using *e-mail* as a verb, even though it may be considered nonstandard. *Please e-mail your documents to Nanette Graziano.*

Write e-mail or computer functions with a capital letter, as in *Christine hit the Reply to All button.* See Chapter 5 for more information on e-mail.

embargoed This is the past tense of the verb *embargo. The company embargoed the press release until Monday.*

embarrass Often misspelled.

emcee The word *emcee* is preferred to *MC.* It is short for *master of ceremonies.*

emeritus This designation implies that a person has retained a title after retiring. Place it after the formal title and lowercase. *Dr. Cathy Chiavetta, professor emeritus of chemistry at Lehigh, addressed the conference.*

emigrate When someone leaves a country, use *emigrate. His ancestors emigrated from Ireland.* When someone enters a country, use *immigrate. His ancestors immigrated to Brazil.*

emoticon Avoid using emoticons in most business correspondence. These are symbols intended to communicate tone or emotion in Internet communications, as in :-o, which means shocked, surprised or wow. *Emoticon* is derived from the words *emotional icon.* See Chapter 5 for more information.

endnote It is documentation that places information about the writer's sources outside the body of the text. This appears at the end of the text under the heading "Notes." Endnotes are placed before the bibliography. To type an endnote, type five spaces from the left margin and type the note number (without punctuation) slightly above the line. Leave a space and type the reference. Parenthetical documentation is an alternative to endnotes and footnotes: U.S. businesses spent more than $2 trillion in computers, software and other technology products during the 1990s ("Technology Spurs Economic Expansion," *Wall Street Journal,* Jan. 31, 2000).

enfant terrible Put this French phrase in italics. It means a person who causes trouble or embarrassment through imprudent remarks or action: Thomas prides himself on being the *enfant terrible* of the accounting department.

ensure, insure *Ensure* means to guarantee. *The airline canceled the flight to ensure passenger safety. Insure* refers to insurance. *The company insured its computer equipment for $2 million.*

enterprise-wide Use a hyphen for *enterprise-wide, company-wide, firm-wide, industry-wide. Nationwide* and *worldwide* are one word.

entrepreneur This is a person who organizes and manages a business, assuming the risk for the sake of profit.

envelop (v.), envelope (n.) The verb means to encase completely. *The police will envelop the plaza before former President Clinton speaks.* The noun refers to a flat, folded paper container, especially for letters.

Environmental Protection Agency Spell out in the first reference; use *EPA* afterward.

Equal Employment Opportunity Commission Spell out in the first reference; use *EEOC* afterward.

eras The names of eras or periods are uppercased, but not the words *era* and *period: Colonial era, Kennedy era, Cenozoic era, Romantic period.*

ergonomics This takes a singular verb, as in *Ergonomics is responsible for reducing repetitive stress injuries.* When it modifies or describes a noun, it should be written without the *s: an ergonomic chair, an ergonomic workstation.*

esquire This title used by lawyers comes after the name and is capitalized and abbreviated, as in *Richard Nesson, Esq.* Note the comma. It is never used when another title appears before or after the name. (It is incorrect to write *Mr. Richard Nesson, Esq.*) In most cases it's not necessary to use this title unless the individual lawyer prefers it.

essential clauses, nonessential clauses See **comma** entry.

et al. This abbreviated Latin phrase *(et alii)* means and others. Use it sparingly; many readers won't be sure of its meaning. No italics are necessary. This abbreviation is also used in bibliographies after an author's name if there are more than three authors.

etc. An abbreviation for *et cetera* meaning and so on and so forth. Use it sparingly. Do not place a comma **after** *etc.* when it occurs in the middle of a sentence: *She brought her laptop, cellphone, books, etc. to the conference.*

Ethernet Capitalize this term. It refers to a LAN that allows two or more stations to share connectivity. The Ethernet provides compatibility across many different platforms.

euphemism When mild, bland or indirect terms are substituted for harsh, direct or blunt words, euphemism occurs. *A series of technical infrastructure changes has resulted in modified product launch dates* is euphemism for *We missed the deadline.*

euro   Currency used by 11 of the 15 European Union nations. It is lowercased, just as *dollar, yen* and *pound* are lowercased. Do not put a space between the symbol and the number, as in *The shoes cost €200.* The symbol for the euro (€) is included in post-1999 word processing programs.

European Union   Spell out *European Union* when used as a noun, as in *The European Union was established in 1991.* When used as an adjective, spell out *European Union* in the first reference; use *E.U.* afterward. *The European Union countries issue an E.U. passport.*

every day, everyday   This is two words when referring to time. *He exercises every day.* Write as one word when describing something. *She wears her everyday clothes for gardening.*

every one, everyone   This is two words when referring to individual items or persons. *Every one of the computers crashed.* Write as one word when used as a pronoun referring to all persons. *Everyone met at noon for the teleconference.* Because *everyone* is singular, it should take singular verbs and pronouns, as in *Everyone must carry his or her own luggage* (not *Everyone must carry their own luggage).*

every time   Always two words.

exaggerate, exaggeration   Often misspelled. Connotative words that give little meaning to the text are terms of exaggeration, as in *wonderful, terrific, sensational, incredible, unbelievable.* Exercise restraint with these terms.

excerpt   An excerpt is always *from* a speech, essay, article, book. Do not use the preposition *of* with *excerpt. The excerpt from the book was provocative.*

exclamation point   Save the exclamation point for letters to the ex-! It is overused. But in sentences where an answer to a question is not expected, use the exclamation point instead of the question mark, as in *Wouldn't it be great if we received our bonuses early this year!* See **quotation marks** entry.

executive summary Lowercase. In a long document an executive summary is a brief synopsis of the key points, placed at the beginning of the document.

extranet Lowercase. This refers to a private network that uses Internet technology to link businesses with suppliers, customers and other businesses.

e-zine Note the hyphen. Italicize the names of e-zines (like newspapers and other periodicals), as in *Failure*. Also called *zines* or *Webzines,* these are online magazines.

. F .

*"Always ask, 'So what?' after you've written it, and don't send it
if you don't have a good answer."*

—Peter Thonis, senior vice president, external communications
GTE Corporation (now Verizon)

401(k) Lowercase the *k* and put into parentheses. Note there is no space
between the *401* and the *(k)*. Use *401(k)'s* for the possessive.

face to face, face-to-face This refers to communication that is not electronic.
Avoid the abbreviation *f2f* or *F2F,* which many readers will not recognize.
When using this phrase as an adverb, no hyphens are needed. *They met face
to face for the first time in Paris.* Write with hyphens when used as an adjective. *Face-to-face negotiations are not necessary to close the deal.*

facilities Use *facilities* when referring to a department within a corporation
responsible for the physical structures. Lowercase the names of departments
within companies, unless it is already established practice to capitalize.

Note that this usage of *facilities* takes a singular verb because it refers to
the department. *Facilities is overseeing the renovation.* If that sounds awkward,
rewrite the sentence, as in *The facilities department is overseeing the renovation.*

facsimile, fax Use *fax* when referring to the office equipment, the faxed document and the process. In fact, using the term *facsimile* instead of *fax* may
confuse readers.

factoid This means an invented fact believed to be true because of its appearance in print. It also means a brief or usually trivial news item.

Fahrenheit This is the temperature scale used in the United States. Use figures and the degree symbol for all numbers except zero: *It was 98° in Utah yesterday. Do you think the temperature will rise above zero today?* Use a word, not a minus sign, for temperatures below zero, as in *The pipes froze because it was minus 10°*. If a reference to the type of temperature scale is necessary, then write *32°F* (with a capital *F,* without a space before or after the degree symbol and without a period after the *F*). To convert Celsius or centigrade temperature to Fahrenheit, multiply by 9, divide by 5 and add 32.

fall Lowercase *fall,* which is interchangeable with *autumn.* Lowercase all seasons.

Fannie Mae Note the spelling of *Mae.* Spell out *Federal National Mortgage Association* in the first reference; use *Fannie Mae* afterward.

FAQ See **frequently asked question** entry.

farther, further Use *farther* when referring to concrete distance, as in *The farther he traveled from Beijing, the more he needed his translator.* Use *further* when the meaning is additional or continued, as in *The manager needs further education if she is to be promoted.*

fast track, fast-track Write *fast track* (no hyphen) when used as a noun, as in *The promotion puts Daniel Cregan on the fast track for the CIO position.* This stylebook favors using *fast-track* as a verb, even though it may be considered nonstandard. Use a hyphen with the verb form, as in *The director decided to fast-track development of the new software.*

father Lowercase *father* unless it substitutes for a proper noun. *His father used to work for IBM. Tell Father we cannot play golf today.* The same goes for *dad.*

fax, facsimile Use *fax* when referring to the office equipment, the faxed document and the process. In fact, using the term *facsimile* instead of *fax* could confuse readers.

fax numbers Follow these guidelines:

- For the United States and Canada, start with *1,* put the area code in parentheses and use a hyphen after the exchange, as in *1 (415) 474-4294.*

- If writing international fax numbers for a U.S. audience, give the U.S. international access code (011), followed by the country and city codes, as in *011 44 171 775 3400.* Use spaces instead of punctuation (such as hyphens) for international numbers. International numbers vary as far as punctuation goes and also in terms of how numbers are grouped. In addition not all countries use seven numbers.

- If writing international numbers for an international audience, do not include *011* since this is the international access code from the United States.

- Follow the same guidelines for telephone numbers.

faze Do not confuse this word with *phase.* Use *faze* when the meaning is to disturb or embarrass, as in *The setback did not faze the legal team.*

February Often misspelled.

federal Lowercase when referring to government (*federal agents),* unless it is part of a proper noun, as in *Federal Reserve Board.*

Federal Communications Commission Spell out in the first reference; use *FCC* or *the commission* afterward.

Federal Home Loan Mortgage Corporation Spell out in the first reference; use *Freddie Mac* afterward.

Federal Reserve Board Note it is *Board,* not *Bank.* Spell out in the first reference; afterward use *Federal Reserve, the Fed* (capital *F), the Reserve* (capital *R), the board* (lowercase *b).* The term *central bank* (lowercased) is another alternative, though it is used less frequently.

Federal Trade Commission Spell out in the first reference; use *FTC* afterward.

FedEx This stylebook favors using *FedEx* (the shortened form of Federal Express) as a verb, even though it may be considered nonstandard. *FedEx this package for me.*

female, male Use these terms as adjectives: *She was the only female CEO at the conference.* For nouns, use *woman* and *man* instead: *She was the only woman at the conference.*

fever, temperature Use *fever* to indicate an undue rise in temperature. *Three employees went to the nurse's office complaining of a fever. Temperature* refers to the degree of heat. Everyone has a temperature but not necessarily a fever. The terms are not interchangeable.

fewer, less Use *fewer* when referring to things or people that can be counted. *The OPEC countries are pumping fewer barrels of oil under the new quotas* (barrels can be counted). Use *less* for quantities that cannot be counted or can be considered as a whole. *The OPEC countries are pumping less oil under the new quotas* (oil cannot be counted). *I had less than $10,000 in my 401(k) account* (an amount). *The workstation has a life span of less than 24 months* (a block of time).

Filipino Use this term for people from the Philippines.

firefighter, fireman *Firefighter* is preferable as it avoids reference to gender.

firm-wide Use a hyphen for *firm-wide, company-wide, enterprise-wide, industry-wide. Nationwide* and *worldwide* are one word.

first, firstly Use *first* in an enumeration. *The first item on the agenda is the proposed acquisition; the second item is executive compensation.* Avoid *firstly, secondly, thirdly* and use *first, second, third* instead, as in *First we will discuss the proposed acquisition* (not *Firstly we will discuss*).

first-come-first-served Use hyphens and a *d* in all cases, as in *Breakfast is first-come-first-served.*

first in first out Spell out in the first reference; use *FIFO* afterward. Write *first in first out* with hyphens when used as an adjective, as in *The company changed to first-in-first-out accounting in 2001.* This is a method of inventory accounting.

fiscal, monetary Use *fiscal* when referring to budgetary matters: *The company's fiscal year begins in October.* The fiscal year is the 12-month period a company or the government uses for bookkeeping purposes. Use *monetary* when referring to the money supply. *The goal of the central bank's monetary policy is to keep a lid on inflation.*

five nines Either spell out *five nines* or write *99.999%* for this expression, which indicates reliability and uptime in a computer system, as in *The system is noted for its five nines.*

fixed income, fixed-income Use the hyphen when this phrase is an adjective, as in *fixed-income securities.*

flex-fuel vehicle Note the hyphen. This refers to any vehicle that can use more than one source for power, as in *It is a flex-fuel vehicle; the latest model runs on biofuel and gasoline.*

f.o.b. Lowercase and use periods. Use *f.o.b.,* which stands for *free on board,* in all references: *The goods from China were shipped f.o.b.*

following For clarity, use *after* instead of *following* in this construction: *After the meeting she went to the third floor.*

font Use alternative font styles (e.g., bold and italics) to make documents user-friendly, but don't overuse; otherwise they lose their impact and documents start to look busy. Also be aware that when applied to more than a few words, bold and italics render text more difficult to read.

Put punctuation following bold or italicized words in the same fonts, as in **January 12 is the deadline (no exceptions).**

food Usually lowercase food names (*bread, butter),* except when they are brand names or trade names, such as *Hot Pockets.* Capitalize proper nouns or adjectives when they distinguish a particular type of food, such as *Manhattan clam chowder, Muenster cheese.* If the proper noun in the food name does not depend on its distinction for its meaning, lowercase it: *french fries.*

Food and Drug Administration Spell out in the first reference; use *FDA* afterward.

foreign currency Spell out the full name of a currency if no value is cited, as in *The company invested hundreds of billions of yen in the project.* If quoting a value, either spell out the currency, as in *The company invested 400 billion yen* (the name of the currency comes after the value), or use the currency symbol: *The company invested ¥400 billion* (the symbol precedes the value).

Note that all countries have two currency symbols: a local code used primarily within the country and a three-letter international code. The International Organization for Standardization establishes these three-letter abbreviations, which are called *ISO 4217 codes.* For Japan's yen, the symbol is ¥ and the ISO code is *JPY.* The symbol for the U.S. dollar is $ (also written

US$) and the ISO code is *USD.* The abbreviations for the Australian dollar are *A$* and *AUD.* For the euro, they are € and *EUR.*

Decisions on how to write currencies depend on the audience, the context and the medium. If your audience will recognize the local symbols (and your word processor has them), use the symbols. Otherwise, spell out the full names of currencies.

If you are writing a document citing multiple currencies more than once, the three-letter ISO codes are an option. If your audience is financial and likely to know the codes, use them in the first reference. If your audience might be unfamiliar with the codes, spell out the currency in the first reference, followed by the ISO code in parentheses, then use the codes afterward.

Whichever approach you choose for writing currencies, use it consistently. Don't mix styles in a single document.

Also keep in mind that if you're writing an e-mail, currency symbols other than $ (e.g., £, ¥, *F)* may not transmit properly to the recipient, making the full names or the ISO codes a better choice.

If it is necessary to convert foreign currency into U.S. dollars, use the latest available exchange rate or, for historical data, the exchange rate prevailing at the relevant date. When you need to include both the local-currency value and the U.S. dollar value, put one of the two in parentheses, as in *The company issued a bond valued at €1 billion (US$900 million).* Note that no space goes between the symbol and the numerals.

The following list of countries and currencies includes in parentheses each currency's local symbol (when available), followed by the ISO code. Note that when countries change or redenominate their currencies, the symbols may change. Also note that in 2002 many European countries switched to the euro as their only currency. This list cites both legacy currencies and the euro for those countries.

Afghanistan: afghani (Af/AFA)

Albania: lek (L/ALL)

Algeria: dinar (DA/DZD)

Angola: kwanza (Kz/AOA)

Anguilla: dollar (EC$/XCD)

Antigua and Barbuda: dollar (EC$/XCD)

Argentina: peso ($/ARS)

Armenia: dram (AMD)

Aruba: guilder (also florin or gulden) (Af/AWG)

Australia: dollar (A$/AUD)

Austria: schilling (S/ATS), euro (€/EUR)

Azerbaijan: manat (AZM)

Bahamas: dollar (B$/BSD)

Bahrain: dinar (BD/BHD)

Bangladesh: taka (Tk/BDT)

Barbados: dollar (Bds$/BBD)

Belarus: ruble (BR/BYR)

Belgium: franc (BF/BEF), euro (€/EUR)

Bermuda: dollar (Bd$/BMD)

Bhutan: ngultrum (Nu/BTN)

Bolivia: boliviano (Bs/BOB)

Bosnia and Herzegovina: convertible mark (KM/BAM)

Brazil: real (R$/BRL)

Brunei: dollar (B$/BND)

Bulgaria: lev (Lv/BGL)

Burundi: franc (FBu/BIF)

Cambodia: riel (CR/KHR)

Cameroon: franc (CFAF/XAF)

Canada: dollar (Can$/CAD)

Cape Verde: escudo (CVEsc/CVE)

Cayman Islands: dollar (CI$/KYD)

Central African Republic: franc (CFAF/XAF)

Chad: franc (CFAF/XAF)

Chile: peso (Ch$/CLP)

China: yuan renminbi (Y/CNY)

Colombia: peso (Col$/COP)

Costa Rica: colón (CRC)

Croatia: kuna (HRK/HRK)

Cuba: peso (Cu$/CUP)

Cyprus: pound (£C/CYP)

Czech Republic: koruna (CZK)

Denmark: krone (Dkr/DKK)

Djibouti: franc (DF/DJF)

Dominica: dollar (EC$/XCD)

Dominican Republic: peso (RD$/DOP)

Ecuador: dollar ($/USD)

Egypt: pound (£E/EGP)

El Salvador: colón (SVC)

Eritrea: nakfa (Nfa/ERN)

Estonia: kroon (KR/EEK)

Ethiopia: birr (Br/ETB)

European Union: euro (€/EUR)

Falkland Islands: pound (£F/FKP)

Fiji: dollar (F$/FJD)

Finland: markka (mk/FIM), euro (€/EUR)

France: franc (F/FRF), euro (€/EUR)

French Polynesia: franc (CFPF/XPF)

Gabon: franc (CFAF/XAF)

Gambia: dalasi (D/GMD)

Georgia: lari (GEL)

Germany: deutsche mark (DM/DEM), euro (€/EUR)

Ghana: cedi (GHC)

Gibraltar: pound (£G/GIP)

Greece: drachma (Dr/GRD), euro (€/EUR)

Grenada: dollar (EC$/XCD)

Guatemala: quetzal (Q/GTQ)

Guyana: dollar (G$/GYD)

Haiti: gourde (G/HTG)

Honduras: lempira (L/HNL)

Hong Kong: dollar (HK$/HKD)

Hungary: forint (Ft/HUF)

Iceland: króna (IKr/ISK)

India: rupee (Rs/INR)

Indonesia: rupiah (Rp/IDR)

Iran: rial (Rls/IRR)

Iraq: dinar (ID/IQD)

Ireland: pound or punt (IR£/IEP), euro
(€/EUR)

Israel: shekel (NIS/ILS)

Italy: lira (Lit/ITL), euro (€/EUR)

Jamaica: dollar (J$/JMD)

Japan: yen (¥/JPY)

Jordan: dinar (JD/JOD)

Kazakhstan: tenge (KZT)

Kenya: shilling (KSh/KES)

Korea, North: won (Wn/KPW)

Korea, South: won (W/KRW)

Kuwait: dinar (KD/KWD)

Kyrgyzstan: som (KGS)

Lao (also written Laos): kip (KN/LAK)

Latvia: lat (Ls/LVL)

Lebanon: pound (£L/LBP)

Liberia: dollar ($/LRD)

Libya: dinar (LD/LYD)

Lithuania: litas (LTL)

Luxembourg: franc (LuxF/LUF), euro
(€/EUR)

Macao (also written Macau): pataca
(P/MOP)

Macedonia: denar (MKD/MKD)

Malawi: kwacha (MK/MWK)

Malaysia: ringgit (RM/MYR)

Maldives: rufiyaa (Rf/MVR)

Malta: lira (Lm/MTL)

Mauritania: ouguiya (UM/MRO)

Mauritius: rupee (MauRs/MUR)

Mexico: peso (Mex$/MXN)

Moldova: leu (MDL)

Monaco: franc (F/FRF), euro (€/EUR)

Mongolia: tugrik (Tug/MNT)

Montserrat: dollar (EC$/XCD)

Morocco: dirham (DH/MAD)

Mozambique: metical (Mt/MZM)

Myanmar: kyat (K/MMK)

Namibia: dollar (N$/NAD)

Nepal: rupee (NRs/NPR)

Netherlands: guilder (also florin or
gulden) (f./NLG), euro (€/EUR)

New Caledonia: franc (CFPF/XPF)

New Zealand: dollar (NZ$/NZD)

Nicaragua: gold córdoba (C$/NIO)

Nigeria: naira (NGN)

Norway: krone (NKr/NOK)

Oman: rial omani (RO/OMR)

Pakistan: rupee (Rs/PKR)

Panama: balboa (B/PAB)

Papua New Guinea: kina (K/PGK)

Paraguay: guaraní (G/PYG)

Peru: new sol (S/PEN)

Philippines: peso (PHP)

Poland: zloty (PLN)

Portugal: escudo (Esc/PTE), euro
  (€/EUR)

Puerto Rico: dollar ($/USD)

Qatar: rial (QR/QAR)

Romania: leu (L/ROL)

Russia: ruble (R/RUB)

Rwanda: franc (RF/RWF)

Saudi Arabia: riyal (SRls/SAR)

Senegal: franc (CFAF/XOF)

Seychelles: rupee (SR/SCR)

Sierra Leone: leone (Le/SLL)

Singapore: dollar (S$/SGD)

Slovakia: koruna (Sk/SKK)

Slovenia: tolar (SlT/SIT)

Somalia: shilling (SoSh/SOS)

South Africa: rand (R/ZAR)

Spain: peseta (Ptas/ESP), euro (€/EUR)

Sri Lanka: rupee (SLRs/LKR)

Suriname: guilder (also florin or gulden)
  (Sf./SRG)

Swaziland: lilangeni (L/SZL)

Sweden: krona (Sk/SEK)

Switzerland: franc (SwF/CHF)

Syria: pound (£S/SYP)

Taiwan: new dollar (NT$/TWD)

Tajikistan: somoni (TJS)

Tanzania: shilling (TSh/TZS)

Thailand: baht (Bht/THB)

Trinidad and Tobago: dollar (TT$/TTD)

Tunisia: dinar (TD/TND)

Turkey: lira (TL/TRL)

Turkmenistan: manat (TMM)

Ukraine: hryvnia (UAH)

United Arab Emirates: dirham
  (Dh/AED)

United Kingdom: pound (£/GBP)

United States: dollar ($/USD)

Uruguay: peso uruguayo ($U/UYU)

Uzbekistan: som (also written as sum)
  (UZS)

Vanuatu: vatu (VT/VUV)

Vatican City (also written as Holy See):
  Italian lira (Lit/ITL), euro (€/EUR)

Venezuela: bolívar (Bs/VEB)

Vietnam: dông (D/VND)

Yemen: rial (YRls/YER)

Yugoslavia: dinar (Din/YUM)

Zambia: kwacha (ZK/ZMK)

Zimbabwe: dollar (Z$/ZWD)

Sources:

http://pacific.commerce.ubc.ca (See Exchange Rate Service link.)

www.thefinancials.com/vortex/CurrencyFormatsTable.html

www.jhall.demon.co.uk/currency/index.html

www.bsi-global.com/Technical+Info.../Publications/_Publications/tig90.xalter

www.xe.net/gen/iso4217.htm

foreign exchange Spell out in formal documents, such as annual reports. In other documents, spell out in the first reference; use *FX* or *forex* afterward. Do not hyphenate *foreign exchange* even when used as an adjective, because the meaning is clear without the hyphen. *The company, which operates abroad, is exposed to fluctuations in foreign exchange rates. The finance department tracks FX rates for 60 markets. The Website has real-time forex quotations.*

foreign particles Lowercase *de, da, la, von* and other particles when they appear in foreign names. *The president of Argentina is Fernando de la Rúa.* Uppercase the particle only if it begins a sentence, as in **De** *la Rúa announced measures to strengthen the balance of payments.*

foreign words and phrases Use these judiciously and be sure they won't confuse readers. *The exchange of business cards is de rigueur when doing business in Japan.* If foreign words and phrases are widely recognizable, like *de rigueur,* don't italicize them. If they are not, then italicize. Be sure to place accents accurately in foreign words and phrases. Avoid using foreign words and phrases in a headline.

for example Use this phrase carefully. It should not be used to clarify an unclear statement that precedes it. Rather, use the example to reassert the preceding statement and deepen understanding. The Latin abbreviation for *for example* is *e.g.,* which stands for *exempli gratia.* In general, use this abbreviation for parenthetical material. It is lowercased, has two periods, is not italicized and is followed by a comma. *The design company has many European clients (e.g., ING, Equant, ABN Amro).* The abbreviation *e.g.* is not interchangeable with *i.e.,* which means that is and stands for *id est.*

former, latter *Former* means the first of two. *He interviewed the manager and the account executive and determined the former had more experience. Former* also means ex-. *The former mayor of Detroit was a Democrat. Latter* means the second of two. *Latter* also refers to nearer to the end. *He devoted the latter half of the meeting to a discussion of the budget.*

formulas Not *formulae.*

Fortune 500 companies For the most recent list, go to *www.fortune.com.*

forward Not *forwards.*

Fourth of July The other preferred forms are *July Fourth* and *Independence Day.*

fractions Follow these guidelines:

- When fractions in amounts less than 1 appear in text, spell out and hyphenate. *Approximately one-third of Americans have access to the Internet through work.*

- If fractions consist of whole numbers and fractions, use figures. *Wayne Anderson poured 2⅞ gallons into the mold.*

- For ages or pairs of dimensions, use numerals plus fractions, as in *Children must be at least 2½ years old to be admitted to the preschool in town* or *The supervisor used the 2¾"-by-5¼" plank to secure the shelf.*

- In tabular material, use figures, preferably expressing fractions with decimal points (*5.5* instead of *5½*). Use the multiplication symbol instead of the word *by* in tabular material (*5⅛ × 6⅞*) if decimals are not used.

free gift Avoid this expression, which is redundant. No one pays for a gift.

freelance One word without a hyphen is the preferred form. The noun is *freelancer,* as in *We are accepting bids from freelancers.*

frequent-flier miles Often misspelled. Note the hyphen.

frequently asked question Spell out in the first reference; use *FAQ* afterward. The plural is *FAQs,* with a small *s.*

Friday Capitalize days of the week.

fulfill, fulfilled, fulfilling Often misspelled.

full(-) Hyphenate when used as part of an adjective. *She is a full-time employee.* Do not hyphenate otherwise. *We would like you to work full time.*

further, farther Use *further* when the meaning is additional or continued, as in *The manager needs further education if she is to be promoted.* Use *farther* when referring to concrete distance, as in *The farther he traveled from Beijing, the more he needed his translator.*

FY 02 This is the abbreviation for *fiscal year 2002.*

FYI Capitalize all three letters. This is informal for *for your information.* Spell out in formal documents or in formal e-mails.

·G·

gallon There are four quarts or 3.8 liters to a gallon.

game plan Two words.

garnish, garnishee Garnish is a lien on property or wages to satisfy a debt. Garnishee is the person served with a legal garnishment. *Garnish* also can mean to decorate or adorn.

gay For sexual orientation the preferred usage when referring to homosexuals is *gay.* In specific references to lesbians, however, *lesbian* is preferred. Sexual orientation is not pertinent to most business writing. The same is true for age, race and gender.

GDP See **gross domestic product** entry.

gender Do not always assume maleness in writing. Revise sentences if necessary to address this issue. Rather than *Each executive must carry **his** own bag,* rewrite the sentence in the plural, as in *Executives must carry **their** own bags.*

General Accounting Office Spell out in the first reference and use *GAO* afterward.

Generation D, X, Y Note the capitalization in these three *Generation* terms. **Generation D:** This is used for the digital generation (which is lowercased); a similar term is *Millennial Generation* (capitalized), which describes students entering the work force as of 2000. **Generation X:** This is used for people born in the 1960s and the 1970s. The shortened version is *Gen Xers* or just *Xers,* but this is usually too informal for business writing. **Generation Y:** This is used for people born from 1979 until the present.

genus, species Usually, but not always, the genus name is uppercased and the species name is lowercased, as in *Esox lucius.* Both words are italicized. Always check the dictionary or use a stylebook (for instance, *Council of Biology Editors Style Manual).* If it is not a scientific document, use familiar names when writing for a general audience, as in *The roses are in bloom,* not *The* Rosa caroliniana *are in bloom.*

geographic names Follow these guidelines:

- For states, note the difference between standard state abbreviations and the two-letter Postal Service abbreviations (*Calif.* versus *CA).* See **state abbreviations** entry for list of both abbreviations.

- In text, use standard state abbreviations when cities or towns are included, as in *Needles, Calif.* If a city is synonymous with the state or is widely recognizable, then the city can stand alone in text. See **cities** entry.

- Use the Postal Service abbreviations only for full addresses. Capitalize both letters without periods. Do not use a comma between the state abbreviation and the ZIP code.

- Spell out the names of states and U.S. territories when used alone in text.

- If a non–U.S. place name is not identifiable in context, include the country as well.

- Do not abbreviate the names of countries, unless used as adjectives. *The U.S. sales manager will soon cover all North America. The U.K. office is located in London.*

get The principle parts of this verb are *get* (present), *got* (past), *got* or *gotten* (past participle). Both forms of the past participle are acceptable: *Mary had gotten the e-mail before she went to the meeting* and *Mary had got the e-mail before she went to the meeting.*

gibe It means to jeer or mock. Do not confuse with *jibe,* which means to conform to standard.

GIF Use *GIF* in all references. It stands for *graphics interchange format* and refers to the file format for Web-based images. GIF images, used mainly for icons or large images, are restricted to 256 colors.

globalization The American English spelling is with a *z.*

going forward No hyphen is needed. Do not write *going forwards.*

go-live Use a hyphen.

good, well Make the distinction between *good* and *well. Good* describes a noun, as in *He is a good manager.* Also use *good* with so-called linking verbs, such as *be, appears, seems,* as in *He is good at his job. Well* describes the verb, as in *He works well under pressure. (Well* describes how he works.) Also use *well* as an adjective, usually referring to a state of health, as in *The doctor expects her to be well after she takes the antibiotic for 10 days.*

　　Hyphenate *well-* phrases before a noun, as in *well-dressed executive, well-read student.*

goodbye One word, no hyphen.

go-to Use a hyphen. *Christopher is the go-to person for questions on the software rollout.*

government Lowercase, even when a specific government is meant: *U.S. government, Colombian government.*

grade, grader Hyphenate when used to form a noun (*third-grader*) and an adjective (*an 11th-grade student*).

No hyphen is needed with the phrase *grade level. Finance hired a new manager with a grade level of 42.*

graduate With the verb *graduate,* use the preposition *from,* as in *Tracey graduated from business school in 1990,* not *Tracey graduated business school in 1990.*

gram It is a basic unit of weight in the metric system. A gram is equivalent to one–twenty-eighth of an ounce.

gray, grey Use the American English *gray.* The British spelling is *grey.* Note, though, the dog is a *greyhound.*

great Avoid overusing this word. Like other words of exaggeration, *great* becomes meaningless when used too often in writing.

Great Britain Use this interchangeably with *Britain.* But note that *Great Britain* is not interchangeable with *England* or with the *United Kingdom.* Great Britain comprises England, Scotland and Wales. The United Kingdom comprises Great Britain and Northern Ireland.

Great Lakes There are five Great Lakes: *Lake Superior, Lake Huron, Lake Michigan, Lake Erie, Lake Ontario.* Always capitalize the full names of lakes.

greenback A one-word nickname for the U.S. dollar. Avoid using *greenback* in formal writing.

grisly, grizzly *Grisly* means horrifying, as in *The medical examiner made a grisly discovery when he opened the cadaver. Grizzly* means gray or grizzly bear. *The grizzly attacked the camper while he was sleeping.*

gross domestic product Spell out and lowercase in the first reference; use *GDP* afterward. It is the total of all goods and services produced by a nation.

gross national product Spell out and lowercase in the first reference; use *GNP* afterward. It is the total of all the goods and services produced by a nation, including citizens working abroad.

groundbreaking One word. *In a groundbreaking alliance, the two companies agreed to a joint marketing campaign in Asia.*

group Write with singular verbs and pronouns. *The group **meets** twice a month to review **its** schedule.*

guru This term commonly refers to a specialist or an expert.

·H·

"Write as you speak—if you speak clearly."
—David Mackey, manager, publications
United Technologies Corp.

hacker This term is used by some to mean a smart programmer and by others to refer to someone engaged in illegal or mischievous manipulation of computer software. In an age of computer viruses, refrain from using *hacker* when referring to an adept programmer. The verb is *hack,* as in *He couldn't hack into the company's systems because the security was so tight.* Another word for the negative connotation of *hacker* is *cracker.*

half, half(-) It is not necessary to use the preposition *of* with this word, although both constructions are correct: *half the battle, half of the battle.* Most phrases using *half* are hyphenated (*half-dozen, half-hour),* but exceptions exist (*halfway),* so it's a good idea to check the dictionary.

hangar, hanger Note the spelling. *Hangar* refers to the building; *hanger* is the device for hanging clothes.

hanged, hung A person is *hanged* (suicide or execution); clothes are *hung* on the line. The past tense of hang, *hanged,* is used only to refer to death by hanging: *He was hanged during the civil unrest of the '60s.* Use *hung* for the past tense in all other cases: *The HR department hung the fund-raising posters on each floor of the building.*

Hanukkah This holiday has three spellings. *Hanukkah* (not *Chanukah* or *Hanukah*) is the preferred spelling. Capitalize all holidays—official, unofficial, religious, secular.

harass, harassment Often misspelled.

Hawaii Do not abbreviate in text, but use *HI* (capitals without periods) with full addresses, including ZIP code. *HI* is the two-letter Postal Service abbreviation. Seven other states are not abbreviated in text: Alaska, Idaho, Iowa, Maine, Ohio, Texas, Utah. See **state abbreviations** entry.

he, him, his, thee, thou It is no longer necessary to capitalize these pronouns when referring to a deity.

headcount One word.

heading When writing a long document, it is generally useful to break it up with headings. Choose a style for headings and use it consistently throughout the document.

- Decide whether to capitalize only the first word or each of the main words in the heading: *Status of new safety requirements* or *Status of New Safety Requirements.*

- Decide how to differentiate the heading: bold, italics, capitals, larger type.

- Decide whether the headings will be flush left or centered.

- Ensure that spacing above and below the heading is consistent.

headline Write most headlines in the present tense. Briefly describe what the article is about or highlight a significant fact in the article (without distorting the article's essence). Space is usually a factor in headlines, so the fewer words the better. Writing a good headline takes extra effort, so remember the following rules:

- For capitalization in headlines, follow these guidelines: Capitalize the first and last words in a headline. Capitalize all principal words (such as nouns, pronouns, verbs) and all other words of four or more letters (such as *About, Though, Between, Against*). Lowercase articles (such as *the, a, an*), conjunctions (such as *and, or, but*) and prepositions (such as *of, with, from, for, by*). Also lowercase the *to* in infinitives (such as *to Drive, to Work*).

- When using hyphenated or compound words in headlines, capitalize the word following the hyphen, as in *E-Taxis to Operate in Boston, Cross-Border Trade Increases in 2002, Sales of Over-the-Counter Medicine Rise.*

- Be sure spelling and numbers in headlines are exactly the same as the information in the text.

- Single quotation marks are often used on quoted words if the headline is in large, bold type. This is a graphic decision. Establish a style and use it consistently.

- Use standard English (do not shorten the word *neighborhood* to *nabe).*

- Keep it short and simple.

- Use short, active verbs and make sure an omission of words (such as the articles *a, an, the)* does not confuse the reader.

- Good headlines draw the reader into the material. Clever headlines can be tricky.

- Avoid foreign phrases in headlines.

- Avoid sensational headlines.

- In headlines referring to court cases, lowercase *vs.* or *v.*

headquarters This noun can take a singular or plural verb. This stylebook favors a singular verb: *Headquarters is in Dublin.* This stylebook also favors using *headquarter* as a verb form, even though it may be considered nonstandard. *The company is headquartered in Dublin.*

healthcare This noun can be one or two words. This stylebook favors the one-word form.

healthful, healthy It is acceptable to use these words interchangeably, according to *The American Heritage Dictionary.* Both words mean conducive to good health. Still, many grammarians insist on making a distinction between the two: *healthful* means conducive to good health while *healthy* means possessing good health. *Healthy* also means indicative of sound, rational thinking or frame of mind. *The programmer demonstrated a healthy eclecticism in his choice of software.*

heap, heaps A *heap* is a pile; *heaps* is slang meaning a lot.

he is a man who This construction is wordy, according to *The Elements of Style. He is a man who* is easily replaced with the single word *he.* One word is better than five. Be concise in business writing.

heretofore, hitherto Both words mean until now. Avoid using them in business writing not concerned with legal matters.

highflying One word.

highway designations Follow this format: *U.S. Route 9, state Route 17, U.S. Route 66, Interstate 95* (in later references, use *I-95*). When a letter is attached to a number, capitalize it, but do not use a hyphen: *Route 9S.*

high yield No hyphen is needed whether used as a noun, as in *The bonds have a high yield,* or as an adjective, as in *Goldman Sachs underwrote the company's* *high yield debt offering.* A *high yield debt offering* is noninvestment grade. It is also called a *junk bond.*

hike This is used widely as a noun or verb to designate a sudden or abrupt increase in price or salary. *The government hiked public-sector salaries to compensate for the previous month's spike in inflation.* In some documents (such as an annual report), it may be too informal; use *increase* or *raise* instead.

his or her Avoid the assumption of maleness, as in *Each speaker will use slides with his presentation.* To avoid the wordy *his or her* construction (*Each speaker will use slides with his or her presentation),* it is often better to rewrite the sentence in the plural: *Speakers will use slides with their presentations.* Business writers should pay attention to gender issues.

Hispanic Persons who trace their ancestry to a Spanish-speaking country. *Hispanic* is the broadest term. The term *Latino* is less formal but may be preferred by some because it de-emphasizes the tie to Spain.

historical references Capitalize important historical events or periods, such as *the Renaissance, the Depression, the French Revolution, Prohibition.* Lowercase indefinite periods, as in *nuclear age.* Also lowercase centuries, such as *the 20th century.*

hoi polloi It is a term meaning the common people, not the elite. (Although many writers insert *the* with this expression, it is not necessary because the Greek word *hoi* means *the).*

holiday Capitalize all holidays—official, unofficial, religious, secular—including the word *Day,* as in *Martin Luther King Day.*

homemaker This one-word term is preferred to *housewife,* which defines by marital status as well as gender.

home page Write as two words, even though many technology companies write it as one word. It is the introductory page of a Website. For companies, the copyright and official name of the company usually appear on the home page.

hopefully Avoid writing *Hopefully we will have the survey results by May.* Although many writers use *hopefully* this way, some readers will protest. *Hopefully* should describe a verb, not express an attitude about the statement that follows.

hors d'oeuvre Often misspelled. The singular is *hors d'oeuvre* and the plural can be either *hors d'oeuvre* (same as the singular) or *hors d'oeuvres.* This stylebook favors *hors d'oeuvres.*

host This is a noun, as in *The host made a speech after dinner.* This stylebook favors using *host* as a verb, even though it may be considered nonstandard. *The company will host a dinner.*

hotline Lowercase and write as one word, even though some stylebooks write this as two words (*hot line).*

hours For time of day, use figures, as in *We will meet at 9 a.m. in the conference room* (not *nine a.m.).* Note the space between the number and *a.m.* Lowercase *a.m.* and *p.m.* with periods. If the time is on the hour, it is not necessary to include a colon and two zeros. Just write *9 a.m.* Use the colon to separate minutes from hours, as in *9:15 a.m.* It is better to specify *a.m.* or *p.m.* than to use the *o'clock* form. If the *o'clock* form is used, spell out the number, as in *nine o'clock,* not *9 o'clock.*

however This word works better in the middle of a sentence than at the beginning: *We cannot finalize the report until Monday. We will, however, give* *you a draft to review over the weekend.* Note the commas on either side of the word.

how-to, how-tos Use a hyphen.

HTML Use *HTML* in all references. *HTML* stands for *Hypertext Markup Language,* the codes and formatting instructions for interactive Internet documents.

http://www In a Web address, it is not necessary to include the protocol *http://* as long as *www* is part of the address, as in *See www.yourdomain.com for more information.* If *www* is not part of the address, then include *http://*. Be sure slashes are leaning in the right direction.

Also, when a Web address has a protocol other than *http://* (e.g., *ftp, https),* then include that protocol.

human resources Spell out and lowercase in the first reference; use *HR* afterward. *The new head of human resources called a meeting with the entire HR department.* Many companies capitalize the names of departments, but unless it is already established practice, lowercase department names.

Note that *human resources* and *HR* take a singular verb because the phrase refers to the department. *Human resources is responsible for the employee survey.* If that sounds awkward, rewrite the sentence, as in *The human resources department is responsible for the employee survey.*

hundredth Often misspelled.

hyperbole This is a figure of speech that uses exaggeration for effect, as in *Tara **waited an eternity** for the report.*

hyperlink No hyphen is needed for this word. It is a cross-referencing tool on a Website. Clicking on a hyperlink refers the browser to another page or site.

hypertext Text that links electronic documents with a hyperlink.

hyphen A hyphen links words and is often inserted to establish clarity. It has no space on either side of it. Many communications professionals surveyed for this book noted that they often use their stylebooks to check hyphenation on particular words. Use hyphens:

- To link two or more words that serve as an adjective: *collective-bargaining talks, cross-border transaction, 28-year-old manager, $4 billion-dollar company, 2-for-1 stock split.* **But avoid overuse.** If the meaning of a phrase is clear without a hyphen, don't use one: *best seller list, real estate agent, income tax form, word processing program, foreign exchange rates.*

- To join two or more words to form a single idea: *African-American.*

- To avoid double letters: *semi-independent, pre-existing.*

- To avoid writing words that may be unclear without a hyphen: *re-form.*

- With the prefixes *ex-, self-: ex-banker, self-explanatory.*

- To join a single letter to another word: *X-rated, y-axis, T-shirt.*

- To form a title that joins two equal nouns: *secretary-treasurer.*

- At the end of a word or number to avoid repetition: *The 65- and 66-year-old employees retired last week; The second- and third-quarter results will be released next month; The medium- and long-term goals must be linked.* This is called the *suspensive hyphen.*

- To spell out numbers when they cannot be written as numerals (for instance, at the beginning of a sentence): *Twenty-five.*

- To spell out fractions in amounts less than 1 in text. *Approximately one-third of Americans have access to the Internet through work.*

- To break words at the end of lines by syllable.

Other points to remember:

- A common error is to use hyphens in phrases with the word *very* and adverbs ending in *-ly*. Do not use hyphens with such phrases: *eagerly awaited proposal, newly elected board member, very talented writer.*

- Note that many combinations that are hyphenated before a noun are not hyphenated when they come after the noun: *a full-time job* versus *She worked full time.*

- Use an en dash in place of a hyphen in a compound adjective if one element consists of a hyphenated word: *quasi-corporate–quasi-government body, self-employed–ex-accountant.* This can make a sentence unwieldy, but occasionally it is unavoidable.

- When using hyphenated words in headings or headlines, capitalize the word following the hyphen, as in *Cross-Border Trade Increases in 2002.*

. I .

I Using the first-person *I* can change the tone in writing. Always write with your audience in mind. See Chapter 4 for more on the use of *I.*

icon Always lowercase, regardless of the meaning. *He changed the icon for Acrobat Reader. Joel Good, a conservative icon, squirmed during his speech to the National Organization for Women.*

ID Use *ID* in the first reference as long as it is clear in context. It stands for identification. *After the merger the company will issue new ID cards.*

Idaho Do not abbreviate in text, but use *ID* (capitals without periods) with full addresses, including ZIP code. *ID* is the two-letter Postal Service abbreviation. Seven other states are not abbreviated in text: Alaska, Hawaii, Iowa, Maine, Ohio, Texas, Utah. See **state abbreviations** entry.

i.e. This abbreviation stands for *id est,* which is Latin for that is. In general, use *i.e.* for parenthetical material. It is lowercased, has two periods, is not italicized and is followed by a comma. *The designer developed the new company's* *branded materials (i.e., letterhead, signage, business cards).* It is not interchangeable with *e.g.,* which means for example and stands for *exempli gratia.*

if In *if* clauses that describe hypothetical situations, use the following verb tense (called the *subjunctive): If I were you, I'd go to the meeting.* Do not write *If I was you, I'd go to the meeting.* See **subjunctive** entry.

ifs, ands or buts No apostrophes are needed in this expression.

illegal Use *illegal* only if a law has been broken. It is not applicable to the breaking of contracts.

illicit, elicit These words differ in meaning. *Illicit* means illegal or prohibited, as in *The company fired the director because of his illicit trading activities. Elicit* means to bring forth or draw out, as in *What response did the manager elicit when he reported the budget shortfall?*

immune from Write this phrase with *from* (not *immune to). The company is immune from weak market conditions in Europe and Asia.*

impact *Impact* as a noun means a strong effect: *The peso's depreciation is having a positive impact on exports.* This stylebook favors using *impact* as a verb, even though it may be considered nonstandard. *How will the price war impact margins?*

imply, infer These words have similar meanings, but a distinction exists between actor and reactor. Writers and speakers *imply* (suggest or convey an idea without stating it) while readers and listeners *infer* (they draw conclusions or figure out what is being suggested). *Mike implied layoffs were imminent. The staff inferred from Mike's comments that layoffs were imminent.*

impresario Do not italicize this Italian term.

inasmuch as This phrase is two words.

in between, in-between The first is an adverb or preposition, as in *Bob is in between jobs at the moment*. The second is an adjective or noun, as in *The new-economy companies, the old-economy companies and the in-betweens were at the conference*.

inbox One word. *Outbox* is also one word.

Inc. In the first reference to a company, write and punctuate this exactly as the company does (*Incorporated* or *Inc.*, with or without a comma before it). In the second reference it is not necessary to include this part of the formal name. The same applies to *Ltd., S.A., P.L.C., A.G., SpA, N.V., GmbH* and other corporate appellations.

Use a comma after the company name with *Inc.*, if a comma precedes *Inc.*, as in *Wal-Mart Stores, Inc., announced its earnings*. Do not use a comma if the company name does not use a comma before *Inc.*, as in *Tara works for Newell Rubbermaid Inc. at its headquarters*.

incentivize This stylebook favors using this word (created from the noun *incentive)*, even though it may be considered nonstandard.

including This implies a partial list. *The firm has capital markets experience in sectors including technology, healthcare and entertainment*. If the subject is negative, as in *No one* (the subject), *including John Forde, will be laid off next year,* it is better to use *not even,* as in *No one, not even John Forde, will be laid off next year*.

index Write the plural as *indexes: Both indexes, the S&P 500 and the Nasdaq composite, were down for the third quarter. Indexes* is preferred to *indices* for the plural.

indiscreet, indiscrete Use *indiscreet* when the meaning is lacking judgment or prudence (*indiscreetness* and *indiscretion* are the nouns). *Indiscrete* means not separated into distinct parts.

industry-wide Use a hyphen for *industry-wide, company-wide, enterprise-wide, firm-wide. Nationwide* and *worldwide* are one word.

infarction, infraction Do not confuse these terms. *Infarction* is a medical term referring to an area of tissue that dies because of an obstruction of the blood supply. *Infraction* is a term meaning violation.

infinitive An infinitive is a verb form that usually can be identified by the word *to,* as in *to eat, to purchase, to win, to split.* Nowadays most writers ignore the grammar rule that says not to **split infinitives** by putting a word in the middle, as in *to easily purchase.* The constructions that result from never splitting infinitives are often awkward. But don't put too many words between the *to* and the verb or the reader may lose track of the verb.

information services Spell out and lowercase in the first reference; use *IS* afterward. *The new head of information services called a meeting with the entire IS department.* Many companies capitalize the names of departments, but unless it is already established practice, lowercase department names. Note that *information services* and *IS* take a singular verb because the phrase refers to the department. *Information services is responsible for software development.* If that sounds awkward, rewrite the sentence, as in *The information services department is responsible for software development.*

information technology Spell out and lowercase in the first reference; use *IT* afterward. *The new head of information technology called a meeting with the entire IT department.* Many companies capitalize the names of departments, but unless it is already established practice, lowercase department names.

Note that *information technology* and *IT* take a singular verb because the phrase refers to the department. *Information technology is responsible for sys-*

tems testing. If that sounds awkward, rewrite the sentence, as in *The information technology department is responsible for systems testing.*

initial When an individual prefers two initials to a first name, use periods and no space between the initials so the computer does not break the name between initials: *P.T. Barnum, T.C. Boyle.* Avoid using the first initial in place of the first name. *Russell Bleemer* is preferable to *R. Bleemer.* It is more specific.

initialism An initialism is an abbreviation pronounced by letter, as in *IRS* (for *Internal Revenue Service* and pronounced *I-R-S)* or *CBOE* (for *Chicago Board Options Exchange* and pronounced *C-B-O-E).* Most initialisms are capitalized without periods.

An initialism is not the same as an acronym, which is a word formed from the first letter or letters of a series of words. Acronyms are pronounced as single words, as in *NASA, NATO, NOW.* If the acronym is longer than four letters, capitalize the first letter and lowercase the remaining letters, as in *Nasdaq, Nafta.* Company names are an exception to this guideline. Follow a company's style, as in *AFLAC* (not *Aflac).* Most acronyms do not require periods. When acronyms cross over and become generic terms, lowercase them, as in *radar, modem, abend (abnormal end of task).*

To write initialisms or acronyms, follow this guideline: Spell out the entire phrase in the first reference; use just the initialism/acronym afterward: *John Andrews is employed by the Brotherhood of Locomotive Engineers (BLE). He works at BLE headquarters in Cleveland.* If an initialism or acronym is widely recognizable, however, it's not necessary to spell out in first reference, as in *Nasdaq.*

in line, on line People wait *in line.* To wait *on line* is a regional preference in the New York area. Use *in line.* When referring to skating, *inline* is one word. Write *online* as one word, as in *Steve buys electronics online* or *Esther coordinates the company's online sales program.*

inoculate Often misspelled; it has a single *n.*

input, output Use *input* as a noun, meaning something (such as information) put into a system to achieve *output* (a result). This stylebook also favors two usages of *input* that may be considered nonstandard: *input* to mean a contribution of information, a comment or a viewpoint and *input* as a verb. *We need input from customers to determine whether the product modifications meet their needs. Diane input the salary information on a spreadsheet.*

in regard to There is no *s* at the end of *regard* in this phrase. A common error is to write *in regards to.*

institution Capitalize the full name and always follow the institution's style in the first reference; use the abbreviation or shortened name afterward, as in *She is an economist at the National Labor Relations Board. She has worked at the NLRB for five years.* Use *it/its* when referring to an *institution* (not *they/their*). *The World Bank held **its** meeting in Santiago* (not **their** *meeting*). *It invited all Latin American countries to attend* (not **They** *invited*).

insure, ensure *Insure* refers to insurance. *The company insured the computer equipment for $2 million. Ensure* means to guarantee. *The airline canceled the flight to ensure passenger safety.*

interesting Use this word sparingly. Let the reader judge whether something is interesting. This also applies to terms like *funny, fascinating, stimulating, awe-inspiring, unique.*

interface Even though it may be considered nonstandard, this stylebook favors using *interface* as a verb, in the sense of to meet and exchange ideas. *The manager needs to interface more with her staff.*

interjection An exclamation that expresses strong feeling: *Bravo! Kudos! Scram!*

Internal Revenue Service *Internal Revenue Service* and *IRS* may be used interchangeably.

Internet Capitalize and use in the first reference. Use *the Net* interchangeably afterward.

A Web address is a URL (for uniform resource locator). Include it when referencing a Website that readers might want to consult. Follow capitalization, no matter how idiosyncratic it may be, because some addresses are case-sensitive. Write the sentence so that normal punctuation (such as a comma) does not cause confusion. It is not necessary to include the protocol *http://* as long as *www* is part of the address, as in *See www.yourdomain.com for more information.* If *www* is not part of the address, then include *http://*. Be sure slashes are leaning in the right direction.

Also, when a Web address has a protocol other than *http://* (e.g., *ftp, https),* then include that protocol.

Internet service provider Spell out in the first reference (note that only *Internet* is capitalized); use *ISP* afterward.

intranet Lowercase. This is part of an organization's internal network, which is usually linked to the Internet.

intrapreneur This is a person within a company who is responsible for turning an original idea into a finished product.

intriguing Nowadays this word is used to mean fascinating or alluring. Its original meaning suggested subterfuge, an underhanded scheme.

investor relations Spell out and lowercase in the first reference; use *IR* afterward. *The new head of investor relations called a meeting with the entire IR department.* Lowercase the names of departments within companies, unless it is already established practice to capitalize.

Note that *investor relations* takes a singular verb because the phrase refers to the department. *Investor relations is responsible for financial information.* If that sounds awkward, rewrite the sentence, as in *The investor relations department is responsible for financial information.*

IOU Write *IOU* in all references. It comes from the pronunciation of *I owe you.*

Iowa Do not abbreviate in text, but use *IA* (capitals without periods) with full addresses, including ZIP code. *IA* is the two-letter Postal Service abbreviation. Seven other states are not abbreviated in text: Alaska, Hawaii, Idaho, Maine, Ohio, Texas, Utah. See **state abbreviations** entry.

IP Spell out *intellectual property* in the first reference; use *IP* afterward.

IPO Spell out *initial public offering* in the first reference; use *IPO* afterward.

IQ Use *IQ* in all references. It stands for *intelligence quotient.*

it Use *it* to refer to a company, an organization, a school, a department within a company or a country. *The company had an outstanding year. It* (not **They**) *increased sales by 30%.*

Other ways to use *it:*

- To refer to something previously mentioned, as in *I saw* In the Mood for Love *last weekend; it was fabulous.*

- For someone whose identity is unknown, as in *Someone left this package on my desk, but I don't know who it was.*

- To refer to a general condition or state of affairs, as in *He couldn't take it anymore, so he resigned.*

- To emphasize a word that is not the subject of the sentence, as in *It is incredible that he finished the project so quickly.*

- For an animal, as in *It bit my leg.*

- For a ship, as in *The ship sailed Friday; it is fully booked.* It is outdated to use *she.*

italics Use italics to differentiate text but with less emphasis than bold. Also use italics for the titles of periodicals, books, movies and foreign words that may be unfamiliar to readers. Put the punctuation following italicized words in italics, as in Does Michael read the *New York Times?* Use italics for words as words, as in I looked up the word *verisimilitude* in the dictionary.

It is Sentences beginning with *It is, There is, There are* can become monotonous. Rewrite and combine sentences to show a closer connection: *Relationships are everything is a deeply rooted business maxim* as opposed to *There is a maxim in business that relationships are everything. It is deeply rooted.*

it's, its Confusing these forms is one of the most common mistakes in writing. *It's* is short for *it is* or *it has. It's your turn* or *It's been a productive week. Its* indicates possession in the singular. *The board made its decision at the July meeting.*

-ize This stylebook favors using *-ize* to create verbs from nouns because it's useful in business, even though this practice may be considered nonstandard. Examples include *finalize, prioritize, customize, moisturize, revolutionize, optimize, incentivize.*

· J ·

"The immediacy of e-mail has led to a lot of sloppy writing."

—Dan Vecchioni, principal communications specialist, employee communications

Detroit Edison

Japanese names In Japanese, names are written with the family name first, followed by the given name: *Matsumoto* (family name) *Kazuyuki* (given name). Although many English-language publications follow that style and would write *Matsumoto Kazuyuki,* this creates confusion about first and last names. To avoid such confusion when writing for business, put Japanese names in the same order as names written in English: given name first, followed by the family name: *Kazuyuki Matsumoto* or *Mr. Matsumoto.*

jargon This is the language of the inner circle, often exclusionary in nature. In some instances certain terms may be appropriate and necessary in business writing, but for a wider readership, include explanations. Do not assume all readers know the terms. See Chapter 2 for more details.

Java Capitalize when it is a reference to the computer language or the island in Indonesia. Lowercase the informal term, *java,* when it refers to a cup of coffee.

Jeep, jeep Uppercase the four-wheel-drive vehicle used by civilians because it is a trademark, but lowercase the military vehicle.

Jehovah's Witness Use an apostrophe and capitalize *Witness*. It refers to a member of a denomination founded in the United States.

jibe It means to conform to standard. Do not confuse with *gibe,* which means to jeer or mock.

job titles Lowercase job titles when they come after a name: *Rhonda Price, managing director.* Uppercase when the title precedes the name: *Managing Director Rhonda Price.* Lowercase when no name is used, as in *The managing director will speak at the meeting.* Note the difference between a job description (*technologist*) and a job title (*information systems manager*).

Johns Hopkins University Often misspelled. (It is not *John Hopkins University.*)

joint venture, joint-venture Do not hyphenate when used as a noun, as in *The companies formed a joint venture to develop the technology.* Write with a hyphen when used as an adjective, as in *The companies signed a joint-venture agreement.* Spell out in the first reference; for subsequent references *JV* is an alternative.

JPEG Use *JPEG* in all references. It stands for *Joint Photographic Experts Group* and is a file format for Web-based images (particularly photographs).

judge Use this title in all references. Capitalize it if it precedes a person's name. *He will meet with Judge Myles Markowitz today.* According to *The Associated Press Stylebook,* all federal courts use this title, except the Supreme Court (which uses *justice);* most civilian, criminal and family courts also use this title. But the New York State Supreme Court and its Appellate Division use *justice* instead of *judge.* Double-check to be sure which title is appropriate, *judge* or *justice.*

judgment Use the American English spelling *(judgment)*, not the British spelling *(judgement)*.

judicial, judicious *Judicial* means pertaining to courts or law. *Judicious* means wise.

jump-start Write this phrase with a hyphen. *Nelida wants to jump-start the product launch by offering rebates.*

junior, senior Use the abbreviation *Jr.* or *Sr.* with names of people. Use a comma before *Jr.* or *Sr.* For instance: *Louis V. Gerstner, Jr.* In a listing by last name, the *Jr.* or *Sr.* comes last: *Gerstner, Louis V., Jr.*

Spell out and lowercase *junior* or *senior* to designate a member of the class.

junk mail Lowercase this term, which refers to unsolicited mail.

jury-rig Hyphenate this verb, which means to assemble for a temporary purpose.

justice The Supreme Court uses the title *justice* instead of *judge.* Also, the New York State Supreme Court and its Appellate Division use *justice* instead of *judge.* Capitalize *justice* only if it precedes a person's name. *He will meet with Justice Sandra Day O'Connor.* Check to make sure the title is appropriate, *judge* or *justice.*

juvenile delinquent This term refers to someone under the age of 18 who is guilty of a criminal offense. Do not capitalize.

· K ·

karat Measures the fineness of gold. Do not confuse this term with *carat,* which is a unit of weight for gemstones. *Her future husband gave her a 14-karat gold ring with a 2-carat diamond.* A *caret* (^) is a mark used by editors and proofreaders.

ketchup This spelling is preferred to these spellings: *catsup* or *catchup.*

Keynesian Relating to the economic theories of John Maynard Keynes, especially those theories advocating government monetary and fiscal programs designed to increase employment and stimulate business activity.

Keystone Kops Often misspelled.

keystroke One word.

keystroke guideline The fewer keys it takes to form a word, the better. In most instances, this stylebook favors the keystroke guideline—as long as clarity is not jeopardized. In making this decision, determine who the readers are and the degree of formality you want to convey. This stylebook follows this suggestion from *The Chicago Manual of Style:* "Anything that reduces the fussiness of typography makes for easier reading."

khan Lowercase this term, which is a title for a ruler, an official or an important person in India and some central Asian countries.

kids Slang for *children.* The use of the word *kids* may offend some readers.

kilo(-) Words formed with *kilo* are not hyphenated, such as *kilometer* and *kilowatt.*

kilobyte Use *K* for *kilobyte* for all references. There is no space between the number and the *K,* as in *128K.* A *kilobyte* equals 1,024 bytes.

kindergarten, kindergartner This word is often misspelled (as *kindergarden* and *kindergardner).*

kind of, sort of These are colloquial expressions for *rather. She was kind of disappointed with her raise* is too informal for writing. *She was rather disappointed with her raise* is better, but both are qualifying terms that are often unnecessary. It is preferable to be more direct and write: *She was disappointed with her raise.*

These phrases can also mean *type of,* as in *What kind of car are you purchasing?* Do not insert the article *a* in this construction, as in *What kind of a car are you purchasing?* Check for agreement in these constructions: *That kind, those kinds.*

kinetic energy Lowercase this term, which refers to the energy possessed by a body because of its motion.

king Lowercase *king* when it is not part of a name, as in the *king of England,* but uppercase if it precedes the name: *King Charles.*

kiosk This is used in a business reference as a place that gives customers or employees access to computers. *The store has kiosks that enable customers to order out-of-stock items online.* A kiosk is also a newsstand.

Kleenex Uppercase this term, which is a trademark.

knot Do not write *knots per hour.* It is implied because a *knot* equals 1 nautical mile per hour.

know-how Write with a hyphen.

knowledgeable Often misspelled.

known as No quotation marks are necessary in this construction: *Jeffrey Young, known as the King of Spin, introduced the beleaguered president.*

Korean names In Korean, names are written with the family name first, followed by the given name(s): *Hong* (family name) *Ji Hoon* (given names). Although many English-language publications follow that style and would write *Hong Ji Hoon,* this creates confusion about first and last names. To avoid such confusion when writing for business, put Korean names in the same order as names written in English: given name(s) first, followed by the family name: *Ji Hoon Hong* or *Mr. Hong.*

kosher Lowercase this term, which refers to the dietary laws of Judaism. Informally this term can mean legitimate or proper.

kudos This means praise or credit. No verb is needed, as in *Kudos to Sarah for surpassing this month's sales quota.* If a verb is used, it is singular. *Kudos goes to Sarah for surpassing this month's sales quota.*

kW Use a lowercase *k* and an uppercase *W* for the abbreviation for *kilowatt.*

Kwanzaa Some African-Americans celebrate this cultural festival, which begins Dec. 26 and ends Jan. 1. This celebration is based on African harvest customs.

· L ·

lady No longer a synonym for *woman,* this word has a patronizing tone. Reserve the use of *lady* for nobility.

laissez-faire Note the hyphen. Italics are not necessary because most readers are familiar with this French phrase. This policy refers to an economic doctrine that opposes governmental regulation of or interference in business and commerce beyond the minimum necessary for a free enterprise system.

LAN Use *LAN* in all references. It stands for *local area network,* a network that connects computers over a limited distance.

languages Capitalize the names of languages and dialects: *English, Latin, Spanish, Catalan, Cajun.*

laptop One word.

largess This spelling is preferred to *largesse.* It is a generous bestowal of gifts.

last in first out Spell out in the first reference; use *LIFO* afterward. Write *last in first out* with hyphens when used as an adjective, as in *The company changed to last-in-first-out accounting in 2000.* This is a method of inventory accounting.

later The *on* isn't necessary with *later.* Write *I will see you later,* not *I will see you later on.*

Latino(s) Persons who trace their ancestry to a Spanish-speaking country. *Latino* is less formal than *Hispanic* (which is a broader term), but *Latino* may be preferred by some because it de-emphasizes the tie to Spain. Note that Brazil is not a Spanish-speaking country.

latitude, longitude Do not use the degree symbol for latitude and longitude. Instead use these forms: *45 degrees north latitude; 22 degrees west longitude.* Latitude is the distance north or south of the equator, designated by parallels, as in *17th parallel.* The distance east or west of Greenwich, England, is longitude, designated by meridians, as in *Greenwich meridian.*

latter, former *Latter* means the second of two. *He interviewed the manager and the account executive and determined the latter had more experience. Latter* also refers to nearer to the end. *He devoted the latter half of the meeting to a discussion of the budget. Former* means the first of two. *Former* also means ex. *The former mayor of Detroit was a Democrat.*

lawyer It is a generic term that covers all members of the bar. It is often used interchangeably with *attorney,* who is someone authorized to act for another. But note that an attorney does not have to be a lawyer.

lay, lie Distinguishing the correct tense of these verbs can be tricky. Confusion occurs because the present-tense *lay* (to place) is also the past tense of *lie* (to recline). Remember that *lay* (to place) takes a direct object, as in *Don't lay the blame on your staff. Lie* (to recline) doesn't take a direct object. *Martha lies* *on the floor for her back.* Here are the principal parts of these two verb forms: to place (*lay* [present], *laid* [past], *laying* [present participle], *laid* [past participle]); to recline (*lie* [present], *lay* [past], *lying* [present participle], *lain* [past participle]).

lay off, layoff This is two words when used as a verb, as in *The company will lay off 500 employees to cut costs.* Write as one word when used as a noun, as in *The layoff is intended to cut costs.* These terms apply to the removal of employees to reduce a work force or cut costs. Do not use them for terminations because of job performance.

lecture If a lecture has a formal title, write the title with capital initials and use quotation marks.

left-handed Use a hyphen.

legacy Use this to refer to previous systems or currencies. *The E.U. countries continued circulating their legacy currencies for two years after the euro was introduced. The company is converting its legacy systems to e-business systems.*

legislative body Capitalize *Congress, Senate, House of Representatives, Assembly, Legislature, Parliament, Duma,* etc. in references to a specific body.

lend This is a verb. *The bank lends to companies with a superior credit rating.* Use *loan* for the noun. *The bank is processing the loan.*

letters When a single letter appears in text, use italics: Place an *x* next to your preference. If the letter stands for a capitalized word, capitalize the letter; if it stands for a lowercase word, lowercase the letter.

leveraged buyout Spell out in the first reference (note that *buyout* is one word); use *LBO* afterward.

liable This is not just a probability but an undesirable one. *The company is liable to be sued if the tainted food is not removed from the stores.*

liaison Often misspelled. The verb is *liaise.*

libel It means injurious to a company or individual's reputation. Do not confuse with *slander,* which is a spoken statement that belittles another person.

lieutenant Often misspelled.

likable Often misspelled.

like Use *like* for comparisons. *She runs like a gazelle. Like* in this construction introduces just a noun. Use *as* instead of *like* to introduce phrases with a subject and verb. Write *The union went on strike as we expected.*

limousine Often misspelled.

liquefy Often misspelled.

L.L.B. Use *L.L.B.* in all references. It stands for *bachelor of laws.*

L.L.D. Use *L.L.D.* in all references. It stands for *doctor of laws.*

loan This is a noun. *The bank is processing the loan.* Use *lend* for the verb. *The bank lends to companies with a superior credit rating.*

loath, loathe *Loath* means unwilling or reluctant, as in *Megan Byrne was loath to predict how employees would react to the announcement. Loathe* means to feel intense dislike or disgust, as in *She loathes the Monday-morning meetings.*

local area network Use *LAN* in all references. This refers to a network that connects computers over a limited distance.

local of a union Use a figure and capitalize when giving the name of a union subdivision: *Local 25 of the UAW.* Lowercase *local* when it stands alone or in plural uses, as in *locals 23, 38, 60.* Observe the local's preference (in punctuation, capitalization, etc.).

login, logoff, logon Each is one word, no hyphen.

logo Use *logo* in all references. It is short for *logogram* and *logotype.* Most companies have guidelines to protect how their logos are used, both externally and internally (e.g., for business cards, ID cards, slide presentations). Pay attention to logo usage.

long distance, long-distance When used as a noun, no hyphen is needed. *It is a long distance from Moscow to Novosibirsk.* Write a hyphen in all references to the telephone service, as in *Mary Dee called her mother long-distance* or *The company cut its long-distance telephone costs 20% last year.*

lowercase(d) It is a verb, noun and adjective and refers to letters that are not capitalized. It is one word, no hyphen. The same goes for *uppercase.* Note the difference in how it is used: *Lowercase the word* chairman. *The word* chairman *is lowercased* (with a *d*).

Lunar New Year The Asian festival.

-ly Do not use a hyphen between adverbs ending in *-ly* and adjectives they modify, as in *a highly complex formula, a badly damaged box, a fully informed participant.*

·M·

M.A., M.S. See **master of arts** entry.

Mac/Mc When alphabetizing words beginning with *Mac/Mc,* do so as though all letters were lowercased: *MacDougal, Mackey, McDonald.* Do not separate *Mac/Mc* in alphabetical entries.

Macintosh It is a type of computer manufactured by Apple Computer, usually referred to as a *Mac.* Do not write *MacIntosh.*

mad, angry These words are not interchangeable. Use *mad* when meaning insane, *angry* when the meaning is irritation.

mafia The preferred term is *organized crime.*

magazine, newspaper names When referring to magazines or newspapers within documents, capitalize and italicize: *Wall Street Journal, Money, Miami Herald.* Do not italicize or capitalize *the* in the title of a magazine or newspaper. (Because *the* in many newspaper and magazine names may or may not be part of the official name, set it in regular type to prevent inaccuracies.)

Likewise lowercase *magazine* without italics, as in *Business Week* magazine. Use quotation marks for the titles of articles within periodicals, as in "Ten Ways to Improve Your Speaking Skills."

mailman *Postal worker* is the preferred term since it avoids reference to gender.

mailroom One word.

Maine Do not abbreviate in text, but use *ME* (capitals without periods) with full addresses, including ZIP code. *ME* is the two-letter Postal Service abbreviation. Seven other states are not abbreviated in text: Alaska, Hawaii, Idaho, Iowa, Ohio, Texas, Utah. See **state abbreviations** entry.

majority, plurality Often confused. A *majority* means more than half of the total number. A *plurality* refers to the number of votes cast for the winning choice if this number is not more than half of the total votes cast (not necessarily the *majority* of votes). Depending on the construction, *majority* can take either a singular or a plural verb. *The majority of union members **have** voted to strike* or *The majority **has** voted to strike.*

male, female Use *male* and *female* as adjectives: *He was the only male yoga instructor.* Use *man* or *woman* as a noun: *He was the only man in the yoga class.* Do not refer to gender unless it is pertinent.

maneuver Often misspelled.

man-hour Avoid terms that refer to gender; just write *hour.* This applies to *manpower* as well; instead use *personnel, labor, work force.* Note that *work force* is two words.

many, much Use *many* with nouns that can be counted, as in *How many days do you need to set up the office?* Use *much* with quantity in bulk or things that can't be counted. *How much time do you need to set up the office?*

marcom This is informal. It is an abbreviated form for *marketing communications,* often used to refer to departments within companies. It takes a singular verb, as in *Marcom writes all brochures, fact sheets and customer letters.*

Martin Luther King Day Capitalize *Day.* This is a U.S. federal holiday held on the third Monday in January. Capitalize all holidays—official, unofficial, religious, secular.

Mass Capitalize when referring to the ceremony. Use *celebrated* rather than *said. The Mass will be celebrated at 10 a.m.*

masterful, masterly *Masterful* means domineering or overpowering. *Masterly* means skillful.

master of arts, master of science Lowercase both of these terms. In most instances they can be abbreviated in all references; use the initials *M.A.* or *M.S.* It is also correct, but less specific, to write *a master's degree* (which applies to both the *M.A.* and the *M.S.).*

maverick Lowercase this word, which sometimes refers to a highly independent individual who resists the mainstream.

May Day, mayday The first term refers to May 1, which celebrates the coming of spring or is a labor holiday in many countries. The second term, which is one word, is an emergency signal, which comes from the French phrase *m'aidez,* meaning help me.

M.B.A. Use *M.B.A.* in all references in most cases. It stands for *master of business administration.*

MC The preferred form is *emcee*. This is short for *master of ceremonies.*

m-commerce Use *m-commerce* in all references, unless the audience is unlikely to be familiar with this phrase. It stands for *mobile commerce* and refers to commerce through mobile communications. It is sometimes called *m-business.*

measurement tables Always check the conversion between metrics (The International System of Units) and U.S. Customary Units. Most dictionaries have these charts.

media It takes a plural verb (the singular is *medium). The media **are** expected to comment extensively on the chairman's sudden resignation.* But note that *media* is increasingly used with a singular verb (like the word *data). The media **is** expected to comment extensively on the chairman's sudden resignation.* For formal writing, use the plural verb.

media relations Lowercase the names of departments within companies, unless it is already established practice to capitalize.

Note that *media relations* takes a singular verb because the phrase refers to the department. *Media relations is responsible for the press release.* If that sounds awkward, rewrite the sentence, as in *The media relations department is responsible for the press release.*

Medicaid, Medicare Capitalize both. Medicaid is a federal-state program designed to pay for healthcare for the needy. The state determines who is eligible and the kind of services available while the federal government partially reimburses the state. Medicare is the federal healthcare insurance program for people age 65 and over, as well as for the disabled. Both Medicaid and Medicare cover some of the costs associated with healthcare.

megabyte Use *MB* in all references in technical writing. In other writing, spell it out in the first reference; use *MB* afterward.

megahertz Use *MHz* in all references in technical writing. In other writing, spell it out in the first reference; use *MHz* afterward. Note the capitalization.

memento Often misspelled. (Not *momento.*)

memo, memorandum, memorandums The shortened form (*memo*) is preferred to the longer forms in all references.

menswear This is the preferred form. It is often written as *men's wear.*

mergers and acquisitions Spell out in the first reference (including the word *and*); use *M&A* (no spaces) afterward. When used as an adjective, the spelled-out phrase takes hyphens and drops the *s*'s, but the abbreviation does not. *The firm has extensive merger-and-acquisition experience in the biotech industry* or *The firm has extensive M&A experience in the biotech industry.*

meridians *Meridians* designate longitude, the distance east or west of Greenwich, England, as in *Greenwich meridian.* See **latitude, longitude** entry for additional information.

metaphor A metaphor is a comparison between dissimilar terms that gives the phrase a whole new meaning, as in *spaghetti code* (unstructured computer program code that is impossible to follow). Do not mix metaphors. A mixed metaphor occurs when the comparison between the dissimilar terms is too outlandish for association, as in *a playground of red tape.*

metric measurements Although metric measurements (The International System of Units) are increasingly recognized in the United States, it is still necessary to list the U.S. equivalent in parentheses. For specifics, consult a metric conversion chart or the measurement table in most dictionaries. For international documents, it may be useful to follow this suggestion from *Wired Style:* "Use the measurement system of the place you're writing about." But still provide an equivalent for U.S. readers.

micromanage No hyphen is needed for this term, which refers to a style of managing that is too hands-on and detail-oriented.

mid- Many *mid-* words use a hyphen: *By mid-year we will know the results of the market survey.* Check the dictionary if unsure.

middle age, middle-aged Do not capitalize. Use a hyphen and a *d* in *aged* when used as an adjective, as in *The middle-aged man began a second career.* This term usually refers to people between 40 and 65 years of age.

middle initials They are often a part of a name, so in the first reference include them when they are offered or relevant, as in *George W. Bush.* If two people in one organization have the same name, use the middle initial to distinguish between them.

midnight Write *midnight,* not *12 midnight.* It is the end of a day. The new day begins at 12:01 a.m. Also write *noon,* not *12 noon.*

mile A mile equals 5,280 feet, 1,760 yards or 1,609 meters.

miles per hour Use *mph* in all references.

Millennial Generation Note the capitalization in this term, which describes students entering the work force as of 2000.

millennium Remember that *millennium* has two *l*'s and two *n*'s. The preferred plural of *millennium* is *millenniums,* not *millennia.*

million, billion Use the word *billion* or *million* instead of writing out the zeros. A *billion* is equal to a thousand million. (FYI: a *billion* in British usage is equal to a million million.)

Use figures with the words *million* and *billion,* as in *The surplus was $2 billion* (note it is not *$2 billions*). Use decimals instead of fractions: *2.5 million* rather than *2½ million.* Do not use a hyphen to join the figures and the word *million* or *billion,* even in the following example: *The board approved the $1 million investment.* Use hyphens **after** the word *million* or *billion* when the amount forms a phrase that serves as an adjective, as in *The meeting is a $2 million-a-year event.*

For slide shows, charts, spreadsheets, etc., abbreviate *million* to *M* or *mn* (without periods). Abbreviate *billion* as *B* or *bn* (without periods). *Total Value of Deal: $10B* (no space between the number and *B*) or *Total Value of Deal: $10bn* (no space between the number and *bn*).

mindset One word. *His mindset remains positive despite the complaints from customers.*

Minnesota Mining and Manufacturing Company In formal writing, spell out in the first reference; use *3M Company* or *3M* afterward. In informal writing, use *3M Company* or *3M* in all references.

minuscule Often misspelled. (Not *miniscule.*)

minus sign Use the minus sign with negative numbers for charts, slide shows, etc., writing it with a dash if possible; otherwise use a hyphen. The alternative is to put negative numbers in parentheses. Whichever style you choose, use it consistently.

Use a word, not a minus sign, to indicate temperatures below zero: *minus 10°* or *40° below zero.* In text, spell out the word *minus,* as in *We will receive the shipment, minus the spare parts, next week.*

minutiae Often misspelled. It means small details and is the plural of *minutia.*

mips Spell out *millions of instructions per second* in the first reference, except in technical writing. Use *mips* afterward. Note it is lowercased.

miscellaneous Often misspelled.

modem Use *modem* (all lowercased) in all references. It stands for *modulator-dem*odulater and refers to the device that converts computer data over telephone lines.

modifier A modifier is any word or phrase that describes a noun, pronoun or verb. Modifiers function as either adjectives or adverbs. Modifiers make the meaning more exact, as in *tall* man, *part-time* employee, *2-for-1* stock split, *billion-dollar* deal. Keep modifiers close to the words they describe.

momentarily This adverb means either for a moment or moment by moment. A frequent error is to use it to mean at any moment. Write *The support person will be online in a moment,* not *The support person will be online momentarily.*

Monday Capitalize days of the week.

Monday morning quarterback No hyphen is needed for this term. It describes a person who second-guesses.

money Do not use the plural of *money* (*moneys* or *monies*). It sounds awkward to most readers. Use symbols for dollars and cents. See **foreign currency** entry.

moneymaker It is one word, as are these three other words: *moneylender, moneygrubber, moneyman.*

month Abbreviate *Jan., Feb., Mar., Apr., Aug., Sept., Oct., Nov., Dec.* in text as long as they are followed by numerals: *Dec. 27, Jan. 29, Sept. 15.* Do not abbreviate *May, June* or *July,* even if followed by a numeral: *June 16.* Spell out the month if it appears alone or with just the year: *December, October 1984.* Tabular material follows a different style.

monthlong One word.

more important, more importantly Use these phrases interchangeably, according to the most recent edition of *The American Heritage Dictionary*, as in *More important, all managers must attend the conference* and *More importantly, all managers must attend the conference*. Note that some grammarians may object on the grounds that *more importantly* is an adverbial (as is *hopefully)*, which means it must modify a verb.

more perfect Avoid this phrase. It is either *perfect* or not.

more than Use *more than* when referring to amounts (not *over),* as in *The consultant makes more than $200 an hour*. Exact figures, however, are preferable. If exact figures are unavailable, *approximately* and *about* are alternatives, as in *The consultant makes approximately $200 an hour*.

morph This verb is a buzzword meaning to change or evolve. It is derived from *metamorphosis*. *The image on the Website morphs from a dollar sign into a euro sign*.

mother Lowercase *mother* unless it serves as a proper noun: *The CEO's mother is a major stockholder. Tell Mother her broker is on the telephone.* The same goes for *mom*.

mouse, mouses The plural for the clickable appendage of the computer can be either *mouses* or *mice*. *Mouses* is preferred because it distinguishes between the computer attachment and the rodents.

movie, television titles Titles of movies and television shows are italicized. Capitalize the first letter of the main words (but lowercase articles [*the, a, an]*, conjunctions [*and, or, for, nor]* and prepositions, unless they are more than four letters or they are the first or last words of the title or subtitle. Also lowercase the *to* in verb forms, as in *to Speak). The Wizard of Oz, The Garden of* *the Finzi-Continis, Who Wants to Be a Millionaire.* Put individual episodes of television shows in quotation marks, not italics, as in "Daveless in New York" on *NYPD Blue.*

Mr., Mrs., Ms. In text, do not include these titles in the first reference to an individual. Use the full name, as in *Andrea Sholler* (not **Ms.** *Andrea Sholler) will join the company effective March 5.* Afterward the title can be used, as in **Ms.** *Sholler has extensive experience in business development.* Other options for subsequent references are to use the first or last name only, as in *Andrea has extensive experience* or *Sholler has extensive experience.* . . . Whichever style you choose, use it consistently. Many newspapers use the full name first, then just the last name in later references. For women, use *Ms.* unless *Mrs.* is a known preference.

In addresses, use *Mr.* or *Ms.* when sending out a direct mailing; it simplifies matters to refer to all women as *Ms.*

The plural of *Mr.* is *Messrs.* The plural of *Mrs.* is *Mmes.* The plural of *Ms.* is *Mss.*

much, many Use *much* with quantity in bulk or things that can't be counted. *How much time do you need to set up the office?* Use *many* with nouns that can be counted, as in *How many days do you need to set up the office?*

multi(-) Do not hyphenate words beginning with *multi* unless followed by an *i* or unless the word could be confusing. *The company signed a multiyear, multicurrency agreement in November* but *The World Bank announced the initiative would be a multi-agency effort.*

multislacking Do not hyphenate this word, which means to play around on the computer instead of working.

Murphy's law Note the apostrophe. This law states that if something can go wrong it will.

music Use quotation marks for the titles of songs, popular as well as classical ("Layla," "Ave Maria"). Also use quotation marks for national anthems ("The Star-Spangled Banner"). Italicize long classical music compositions (operas, oratorios, tone poems), as in *Don Giovanni.* Many musical compositions do not have descriptive titles but are identified by the name of a musical form. When used as the title of a work, the name of the form and the key are usually capitalized but not italicized or put in quotation marks, as in Sonata in E-Flat.

Muslim This is the preferred term to describe adherents to Islam. Do not differentiate between *black Muslims* and *Muslims.*

· N ·

NAACP Use *NAACP* in all references. It stands for the *National Association for the Advancement of Colored People.*

Nafta See **North American Free Trade Agreement** entry.

names Follow these guidelines. Pay particular attention to the correct spelling of personal names. People don't like to see their names misspelled or their titles cited incorrectly, so double-check both.

- In the first reference, use full names, as well as initials if given or relevant: *Jöelle Delbourgo, Carlos Estrella, Maureen Moore, Betsy K. Harrington, Martin S. Simmons.* Include the person's title if it is relevant. Capitalize the title only if it precedes the name, as in *Managing Director Lisa Smith;* lowercase if it follows the name, as in *Lisa Smith, managing director.*

- In text, do not include *Mr., Mrs., Ms.* in the first reference. Write *John Banville* (not *Mr. John Banville*). Use *Mr., Mrs., Ms.* for addresses. For subsequent references, decide whether to use first names, last names or names with titles. For example: *John Banville is the guest speaker.* **John** *is an acclaimed author* or **Banville** *is an acclaimed author* or **Mr. Banville** *is* *an acclaimed author.* Whichever style you choose, use it consistently for every name throughout the document.

- Do not use abbreviations for names (as in *Thom.*) unless that is the person's preference.

- As long as the identity is clear, refer to people as they prefer to be known, as in *Bill Gates.*

- Use *Jr., Sr.* or *III* if part of the name, as in *John F. Welch, Jr.* Note that names with Roman numerals, as in *Thomas Walsh III,* do not take a comma. In an alphabetical listing by last names, put the *Jr., Sr.* or *III* last, as in *Welch, John F., Jr.*

nano Most *nano* words do not need a hyphen, as in *nanosecond. Nano* is a prefix denoting one-billionth of a unit.

NASA Use *NASA* in all references. It stands for the *National Aeronautics and Space Administration.*

Nasdaq Use *Nasdaq* in all references. Note that only the first letter is capitalized. (If an acronym is longer than four letters, uppercase the first letter and lowercase the remaining letters.) *Nasdaq* stands for *National Association of Securities Dealers Automated Quotation System.* It is the electronic stock market operated by the National Association of Securities Dealers (NASD), the parent company of Nasdaq and the American Stock Exchange. It is the second-largest stock market in the United States, after the New York Stock Exchange.

Nasdaq composite index Capitalize only the word *Nasdaq* when referring to this index. Write out *Nasdaq composite index* in the first reference; use *Nasdaq composite* afterward. Do not refer to the index simply as *Nasdaq* because this would be a reference to the entire market.

nation, national Lowercase these terms unless they are part of a formal name. *The nation is relieved the economy is growing again. The National Security Council meets this week.*

national anthem Put a specific national anthem in quotation marks.

National Association of Securities Dealers Spell out in the first reference; use *NASD* afterward. NASD is the parent company of Nasdaq and the American Stock Exchange.

National Institutes of Health Spell out in the first reference (note the *s* at the end of *Institutes);* use *NIH* afterward. This is an agency within the Department of Health and Human Services and is the primary biomedical research arm of the federal government.

nationality Capitalize the proper names of nationalities, as in *Chinese, Japanese, Irish, American Indian* (not *Native American), Italian, Polish, Colombian, African-American, Swedish,* but lowercase racial descriptions, as in *black* or *white.*

National Labor Relations Board Spell out in the first reference; use *NLRB* afterward.

National Organization for Women Spell out in the first reference; use *NOW* afterward. Note it is *for Women,* not *of Women.*

nationwide *Nationwide* and *worldwide* are one word. Use a hyphen for *company-wide, enterprise-wide, firm-wide, industry-wide.*

NATO Use *NATO* in all references. It stands for *North Atlantic Treaty Organization.*

Navy   Capitalize when referring to the U.S. forces (as in *Navy policy, the Navy, the U.S. Navy);* lowercase when referring to the naval forces of other countries, as in *the Dutch navy.*

NC-17   Use a hyphen. This is the movie rating designating that individuals under age 17 are not admitted (formerly referred to as an *X rating).*

Negro(es)   Use this term only if it is part of a proper noun or in historical contexts. *African-American* is the preferred term.

neither/nor   This means not either of two. It is not interchangeable with *none* or *not one. Neither the CFO nor the CIO is authorized to speak to the media.* After a *neither/nor* construction, use a singular verb if both subjects are singular; use a plural verb if both subjects are plural; if one of the subjects is singular and one is plural, use the number of the one nearer the verb, as in *Neither the director nor her managers know how to use the new software.*

Net, the   Spell out *Internet* in the first reference; use *the Net* interchangeably afterward.

net income   Lowercase *net income,* the amount left after taxes are paid.

netiquette   Lowercase; this refers to accepted practices for using the Internet, including e-mail. The word *netiquette* is derived from *network etiquette.*

new economy, old economy   The first is a reference to the Internet economy. The second is a reference to the pre-Internet economy. Lowercase both *new economy* and *old economy.* Write with a hyphen only when they serve as adjectives, as in *Many new-economy companies are postponing their IPOs until next year. Pablo's portfolio consists primarily of old-economy stocks.*

newspaper names   Do not capitalize *the* in a newspaper or magazine's name, as in the *Wall Street Journal* (see **magazine, newspaper names** entry).

newsstand One word.

New Year's Day It can also be referred to as the *New Year.* (Lowercase *new year* if it refers to the 12-month period.) Other examples: *Chinese New Year, Jewish New Year, Lunar New Year.* Since the New Year is the first day of the calendar year and a holiday, write *Happy New Year* (not *Happy new year* or *Happy New Year's).*

New Year's Eve Capitalize all three words.

New York Stock Exchange Spell out in the first reference; use *NYSE, the stock exchange, the exchange* or the *Big Board* for other references. The New York Stock Exchange is the largest stock market in the United States.

nicknames If nicknames are preferred, honor them: *Jimmy Carter, Babe Ruth.* It is not essential to put the nickname in quotation marks if it is a substitute for the name, as in *the Great Emancipator, the Wizard of Menlo Park.*

nighttime One word.

no, yes It is not necessary to use quotation marks, except in direct discourse: *He answered yes to the question. "No," he grumbled as he hung up the telephone.*

No. Use this abbreviation for the word *number* only with an accompanying figure, as in *Her office is No. 15 on the second floor.* Capitalize *No.*

No. 1 Use *No. 1* (rather than spell out *number one)* in all references, as in *The company ranked No. 1 for safety* or *Nanette's No. 1 fear about using a credit card online is identity theft.* The same holds for other numbers, as in *The No. 2 Internet service provider announced plans to merge with the No. 3 cable company.*

noes and yeses This form is preferred to *nos.*

non(-) Most words starting with *non* need no hyphen, as in *nonbinding, noncompliance.* But if the word might be confusing without a hyphen, use a hyphen, as in *non-negotiable.* Also use a hyphen when *non* precedes a word with a capital letter: *non-American, non-Canadian.*

nonprofit One word. It is preferable to *not-for-profit.*

noon Write *noon*, not *12 noon.* Also write *midnight*, not *12 midnight.*

North American Free Trade Agreement Spell out in the first reference; use *Nafta* afterward. Note that only the first letter in *Nafta* is capitalized. If an acronym is longer than four letters, uppercase the first letter and lowercase the remaining letters. Company names are an exception to this guideline. Follow a company's style, as in *AFLAC* (not *Aflac*).

not-for-profit Use *nonprofit* instead.

noun A noun is a word that names a person, place, thing, idea or quality. Using nouns as verbs is common practice (e.g., *access, incentivize, stylize, bullet, fast-track)* in business writing. Even though many of these constructions are considered nonstandard, this stylebook favors them because of their obvious usefulness.

number Use a singular verb when *number* stands alone, as in *The number is not available yet.* Use a plural verb after *a number of,* as in *A number of employees are scheduled to attend the workshop.*

number, amount Use *number* for things that can be counted one by one, as in *She put a number of coins on the counter* or *The number of days spent on the reports varies each quarter.* Use *amount* for things that cannot be counted one by one, as in *The amount of time spent on the reports varies each quarter.*

number cruncher Lowercase this term.

numbers Spell out numbers under 10 in text; use figures for numbers 10 and above. There are exceptions to this general rule:

- Use figures for ages of people and animals; building numbers; headlines, slide shows, charts and other tabular material; some financial contexts (as in *The stock edged up 2 points);* figures that include decimals (*2.8 inches of rain);* results from voting; percentages (*1%, 10%);* proportions (*2 tsp.);* data-driven references (*8 bits);* references to money (*$2 million, 5 pence);* time of day (*1 a.m.);* days of the month; degrees of temperature; latitude and longitude; dimensions; numbered expressions (*Page 1);* sports points or scores.

- Use figures in a series, even if one of the numbers is below nine: *The director has 3 assistants, 10 managers and 12 account executives reporting to her.*

- Use the word *billion* or *million* instead of writing out the zeros. Do not use a hyphen to join the figures and the word *million* or *billion,* even in the following example: *The board approved the $1 million investment.* If the amount is used as an adjective, use hyphens only **after** the amount, as in *The meeting is a $2 million-a-year event.*

- Round long numbers. In general, round off figures in the millions to one decimal place (*4.5 million),* those in the billions to two places (*6.58 billion)* and those in the trillions to three (*4.768 trillion).* Be mindful that rounding numbers can be misleading.

- When fractions in amounts less than one appear in text, spell out and hyphenate: *Approximately one-third of Americans have access to the Internet through work.* If fractions consist of whole numbers and fractions, use figures. *Wayne poured 2 ⅞ gallons into the mold.* For ages or pairs of dimensions, use numerals plus fractions, as in *Children must be 2½ years old to be admitted to the preschool in town* or *The supervisor used the 2¾"-by-5¼" plank to secure the shelf.* In tabular material, use figures, expressing fractions preferably with decimal points (*5.5 instead of 5½).*

- For numbers in names, use Roman numerals (without a comma): *John M. Dawson III.* In an alphabetical listing by last name, the number comes last: *Dawson, John M. III.*

- Spell out all numbers that begin a sentence: *Eighty-four employees attended the conference.* Use hyphens between words that form one number: *twenty-three, forty-one.* It is sometimes better to rewrite a sentence to avoid starting with a number, as in *Approximately 84 employees attended the conference.*

- Spell out casual expressions: *Thanks a million.*

- For ordinal numbers, spell out *first* through *ninth.* Use figures starting with *10th.* If an ordinal number is part of a name, use figures: *1st Fleet.*

- Use words or numerals according to an organization's practice: *3M, Twentieth Century Fund.*

- When numbers are used to designate sections, chapters, pages, etc., capitalize the word that precedes the number, as in *Chapter 4, Page 6, Version 7, Section 8.*

- **Remember:** Always take the time to ensure that all the numbers cited are correct and, if appropriate, add up. Also be sure any numbers appearing in graphs, charts, headings or captions match the numbers in the text.

·O·

"Organize your thoughts around the objective of each communiqué, what it's trying to achieve, the messages that need to be conveyed and any adverse consequences you anticipate. Be sure to edit your own work, then have someone with fresh eyes view it."

—Lynne S. Butterworth, senior manager, corporate communications
Williams Communications Group

observance, observation These words are not interchangeable. *Observance* is the act of complying with prescribed rites while *observation* is something that is noted. *In observance of the holiday, the banks will be closed. His observation that the company needs to develop an Internet-centric model met with agreement.*

occasion Often misspelled.

Occupational Safety and Health Administration Spell out in the first reference; use *OSHA* afterward.

occupational titles Lowercase job titles when they come after a name: *Christina Greer, managing director.* Uppercase when the formal company title precedes the name: *Managing Director Christina Greer.* Lowercase all titles/job descriptions when no name is used, as in *The receptionist resigned Monday* or *The chairman asked for a status report on the new legislation.*

occur, occurred, occurring (v.), occurrence (n.) Often misspelled.

ocean Lowercase *ocean* if it stands alone, but uppercase it if it is part of the name of one of the five oceans: *Pacific Ocean, Atlantic Ocean, Indian Ocean, Antarctic Ocean, Arctic Ocean.* When more than one ocean is mentioned, lowercase *ocean,* as in *the Atlantic and Indian oceans.*

o'clock It is better to specify *a.m.* or *p.m.* than to use the *o'clock* form, as in *We will meet at 9 a.m. in the conference room* rather than *We will meet at 9 o'clock in the conference room.* Note the space between the number and *a.m.* If the time is on the hour, it is not necessary to include a colon and two zeros. Just write *9 a.m.,* not *9:00 a.m.* Use the colon to separate minutes from hours, as in *9:15 a.m.* If the *o'clock* form is used, spell out the number, as in *nine o'clock,* not *9 o'clock.*

off Do not write *off of.* The *of* is unnecessary. *She fell off the stage,* not *She fell off of the stage.*

offsite One word. *The company's senior management team had an offsite meeting in January.*

Ohio Do not abbreviate in text, but use *OH* (capitals without periods) with full addresses, including ZIP code. *OH* is the two-letter Postal Service abbreviation. Seven other states are not abbreviated in text: Alaska, Hawaii, Idaho, Iowa, Maine, Texas, Utah. See **state abbreviations** entry.

OK This is informal but OK (capitals without periods). The past is *OK'd.* To ensure consistency in a document, change any *O.K., okay* or *ok* forms to *OK.*

old-boy network, old-girl network Use a hyphen, but do not capitalize these terms, which refer to an informal system of mutual assistance. *The old-girl network at Colgate helped Elise get a job at Unicom Corp.*

omission Often misspelled. There are several ways to indicate *omission* in text. See **ellipsis** entry.

on It is not necessary to use *on* before a date or day of the week. *She heard about the promotion Tuesday.* If, however, confusion would occur, include *on: Harold met Mary on Friday.*

on account of Use *because* instead.

one When using *one* in the sense of a person (as a pronoun), do not substitute *his* or *her* later in the sentence. Write *One does not need one's calculator to figure out the sum* (not *One does not need his calculator to figure out the sum*). In American English, this pronoun is considered overly formal and is rarely used in business writing.

one(-) In text hyphenate *one-* in fractions: *one-third, one-half.* The same applies for other fractions: *two-thirds, five-eighths.* Use figures for slides, tabular material, etc.

one another, each other Use *one another* when referring to more than two people. *Martha, Tara and Alice will help one another with the project.* Use *each other* when referring to two people. *They looked at each other in disbelief.* To form the possessive of *one another*, write *one another's. They read one another's reports and synthesized the findings into a single document.*

onetime, one-time *Onetime* means ex- or former, as in *The onetime management consultant now works at the Fed. One-time* with a hyphen means once, as in *The company marketed the sale price as a one-time offer.*

ongoing One word. Alternatives are *continuing* and *developing.*

on line, in line To wait *on line* is a regional preference in the New York area. People wait *in line* in other parts of the country. Use *in line* instead of *on line*. In reference to a type of skating, use *inline* (one word).

online Write *online* as one word, whether it's used as a noun or an adjective, as in *Luisa went online to find the address* or *The company offers various online services.*

online shorthand Use these informal abbreviations that are common in e-mail for friendly communication but not for formal correspondence. *IMHO (in my humble opinion), IOW (in other words)* and *IRL (in real life)* are examples. See Chapter 5 for other abbreviations.

OPEC Use *OPEC* in all references. It stands for *Organization of Petroleum Exporting Countries.*

op-ed Note the hyphen. An op-ed expresses the personal viewpoints of individual writers in a publication and is usually located opposite the editorial page. An editorial is an opinion piece that reflects the views of the publisher. For op-eds, verify the spelling of the writer's name.

operations Note that *operations* takes a singular verb when used to refer to a department. *Operations is responsible for securities processing.* If it sounds awkward, rewrite the sentence, as in *The operations department is responsible for securities processing.* Lowercase the names of departments within companies unless it is already established practice to capitalize.

ophthalmologist, optometrist, optician The first is a doctor who treats eye disease. The second measures the eye to prescribe glasses. The third makes the glasses.

ordinal number A number indicating position in a series or order is an *ordinal number*. The ordinal numbers are *first (1st), second (2nd), third (3rd)* and so on. In text, spell out *first* through *ninth;* use the numeral form afterward (*10th, 20th*). The exception is for addresses or tabular material, when *1st* through *9th* should be used. Also use figures if an ordinal number is part of a name: *1st Fleet.*

organization, institution In text, always follow the organization's style in the first reference. Refer to an organization by its shortened form afterward. If the word *company* or *companies* appears alone in a subsequent reference, always spell it out and lowercase. *The Bank of New York Company, Inc., will release the annual earnings report in a few weeks. The company did not specify the reason for the delay.* For internal parts of an organization, lowercase, as in *personnel, corporate affairs, accounting, operations, human resources,* unless it is already established practice to capitalize. These departments take singular verbs. Use *it/its* when referring to an *organization* or *institution* (not *they/their*). *The World Bank held its meeting in Santiago* (not **their** *meeting*). *It invited all Latin American countries to attend* (not **They** *invited*).

Oriental Use *Asian* instead.

orthodontics Use a singular verb.

orthodox Capitalize only when it is part of the name of a religion, as in *Eastern Orthodox Church.* Do not capitalize when the meaning is traditional, as in *Her orthodox approach to staff meetings is inappropriate for a company comprised mostly of telecommuters.*

ounce Spell out in text, but it is acceptable to abbreviate to *oz.* for tabular material. A fluid ounce equals two tablespoons or six teaspoons. An ounce in weight is equal to 28.35 grams.

outbox One word. *Inbox* is also one word.

outline style The bulleted list has overtaken outline style in business writing, but for long enumeration outline style may be a better choice. Follow this example for outline style (format from *The Chicago Manual of Style)*:

    I. Executive summary

    II. Ideas for implementing a program

        A. Role of facilities and human resources departments

          1. Risk manager's assessment

          2. Facilities manager's cost assessment

        B. Outsourcing

          1. Bid accepted from XYZ Company

          2. Time frame for implementation

            a) XYZ Company will complete first stage in January 2003

              (1) Facilities department time frame

              (2) Construction proposal

                (*a*) Areas affected by construction

                (*b*) Noise level and inconvenience

over Do not use *over* when referring to amounts. Instead use *more than,* as in *The consultant makes more than $200 an hour.* Exact figures, however, are preferable. If exact figures are unavailable, *approximately* and *about* are alternatives, as in *The consultant makes approximately $200 an hour.*

overall One word. Most over(-) words do not use a hyphen, but check the dictionary if you are uncertain.

over the counter, over-the-counter Spell out in the first reference; use *OTC* afterward. Do not use a hyphen when used as a noun, as in *She bought the medication over the counter.* Write with hyphens when used as an adjective, as in *The numbers exclude over-the-counter trades.*

overuse One word.

oxymoron It is a combination of contradictory terms, as in *deafening silence, jumbo shrimp.*

· P ·

Pablum, pablum, pabulum Capitalize if it is the food for infants, which is a trademark. Lowercase *pablum* if the meaning is bland and uninspired. *The press release was such pablum that the business media ignored it.* The term *pabulum* comes from the Latin word for food and means insipid intellectual nourishment, as in *The miniseries turned the book by Dickens into pabulum.*

page number Capitalize the word *Page,* as in *Page 1 story* and *Page B15.* In tabular material, abbreviate, as in *P. 5* or *pp. 4, 9, 10.* Lowercase the abbreviation for *pages,* which is *pp.* If it begins a sentence, use *Pp.*

pan- Use a hyphen in words formed with *pan* and proper nouns, as in *The company's pan-Asian strategy fails to take into account differences among the individual markets.*

paperwork One word.

papier-mâché Often misspelled. Note the accents. It is not necessary to italicize this French phrase.

paradox A seemingly contradictory statement that may in fact be true. *The paradox is that inertia may be more exhausting than vigorous activity.*

paragraph A paragraph typically deals with one idea or topic. Paragraphs are designed to develop an idea, so the size of a paragraph varies. Most range between three and five sentences. The one-sentence paragraph can be effective in a document, but avoid overuse. Long paragraphs can put off some readers, so refrain from writing paragraphs that consistently exceed six or seven sentences. Paragraphs begin on a new line, indicated either by an indent (use the tab, not five spaces) or by a blank line of space.

paragraph number Capitalize the word *Paragraph,* as in *Paragraph 3.*

parallel Often misspelled. When used in reference to location, parallels designate latitude, the distance north or south of the equator, as in *17th parallel.* Use figures, as in *Operation Timber will take place at the 4th parallel north.* Meridians designate longitude, the distance east or west of Greenwich, England, as in *Greenwich meridian.* See **latitude, longitude** entry.

parameters This word is often used when *perimeter* (meaning the outer boundary) is the intended meaning. The origin of the word *parameter* is from science, meaning a factor that determines what is possible or what results. Using this scientific term to mean scope or boundaries is widespread in business writing, even though many grammarians object. This stylebook accepts that usage: *The board expanded the project's parameters to include the entire organization.*

parentheses Use parentheses *( )* to enclose an explanation or clarify material. Do not use parentheses and brackets *[ ]* interchangeably. See **brackets** entry. To punctuate parentheses:

- If an entire sentence is in parentheses, put a period (or question mark or exclamation point) inside the parentheses. *Executives at the company believe their pensions are secure. (Industry insiders confirm this.)* With a question mark: *Executives at the company believe their pensions are secure. (Do industry insiders confirm this?)*

- If the phrase in parentheses is entirely within the sentence, the punctuation goes outside the parentheses. *She did not confirm her leave of absence with the manager (which explains why they were looking for her Monday).* The punctuation goes outside even if the phrase could stand as a complete sentence. *She did not confirm her leave of absence with the manager (they were looking for her Monday).* Note that the first word in the parentheses is not capitalized because the parenthetical material is part of the sentence.

- Do not precede an opening parenthesis with a comma, semicolon or colon.

- Use parentheses sparingly.

parenthetical documentation This method for citing sources is informal but generally preferred in business writing. Follow this style, which cites a quote from a newspaper article: "The earnings outlook right now is even slower" ("Two Views of a Marked-Down Market," *New York Times,* Nov. 26, 2000). In academic and scientific writing, usually footnotes and endnotes are preferred to parenthetical documentation to cite sources, but on the rare occasion when a source needs to be cited in science style within the text, follow this example: He called "XML the lingua franca of the Web" (Sagar 2001, *Computing Puzzles,* 10).

part from, part with Use *part from* for persons and *part with* for things. *She will part from her colleagues with regret. He is reluctant to part with his old laptop.*

partial quotes See **quotation marks** entry.

part time, part-time This takes no hyphen when used as an adverb, as in *He works for the company part time.* Write a hyphen when it is used as an adjective, as in *She has a part-time job with an advertising agency.*

passenger lists Arrange alphabetically according to the last name and include full addresses if available. Use a paragraph break for each name.

passive voice Avoid using verbs in the passive voice and write in the active voice whenever possible. In the passive voice, the action is done to the subject, as in *The account executive was corrected by the sales manager.* In the active voice, the subject acts. *The sales manager corrected the account executive.* The emphasis changes. The active voice is stronger and more direct. It is preferred in most business writing.

While the active voice is preferred, there are instances where the passive voice is necessary. Richard Lauchman, author of *Plain Style: Techniques for Simple, Concise, Emphatic Business Writing,* says, "The passive is often necessary and writers who believe it is 'bad' or 'weak' will often emphasize the wrong idea." See Chapter 4 for more information.

pastor Lowercase because it is not a formal title. A pastor in the Catholic church leads a parish. A pastor in the Lutheran or Baptist church is a minister who leads a congregation. In the Catholic, Lutheran and some other Protestant religions, the first reference should read *pastor Dennis Cohan of St. Catharine Roman Catholic Church* or *Rev. Dennis Cohan, pastor of St. Catharine Roman Catholic Church.*

patrolman Most police departments use the term *police officer,* which avoids reference to gender. Capitalize either term if it precedes the name, as in *Patrolman James Whitcomb* or *Police Officer Joan Petersson.*

PC Use *PC* for *personal computer* in all references. The plural is *PCs. PC* is also used informally to mean politically correct.

pd., p.d. The first is an abbreviation for *paid;* the second is an abbreviation for *per diem,* which stands for *per day.* Do not use the *p.d.* abbreviation for a general audience as it is not recognizable to some readers.

PDF Use *PDF* in all references. It stands for *portable document format.* A PDF preserves the look of an original document (both images and typeface), so that no matter which computer or printer is used, the document will look the same.

P/E See **price-earnings ratio** entry.

peacock This name refers only to the male. A female is called a *peahen.* Male and female are *peafowl.*

per annum Write *p.a.* (lowercased with periods) instead of *per annum* in reports, slide shows and other internal documents. In formal documents *yearly, a year* and *annually* are preferable to both *p.a.* and *per annum.*

percent Use the symbol *(%)* instead of the word *percent.* The exception is when a sentence begins with a number, in which case both the number and the word *percent* must be spelled out. *Forty percent of the budget goes to salaries.* (Note that many stylebooks spell out *percent,* as in *5 percent,* but most business publications do not.)

  Percent takes a singular verb when standing alone: *The director said 10% was insufficient.* When a word follows *% of,* it takes a singular or plural verb depending on the word that follows: *Approximately 20% of her time is spent on customer service. Sixty percent of employees drive to work.*

  Use decimals instead of fractions, as in *7.5%.* For amounts less than *1%,* put a zero before the decimal, as in *0.3%.* Repeat *%* with each individual number, as in *He has tabulated 30% to 60% of the study.*

  A common error is to confuse *percent* with *percentage point.* If the company grew market share from 35% to 40%, write *We grew market share to 40%, up five percentage points from last year,* not *We grew market share to 40%, up 5% from last year.*

period This is the final stop in a sentence. Periods are also used for many abbreviations. In Internet and e-mail addresses, this is called a *dot.*

period, era Do not capitalize *period* when referring to a specific time frame, as in the *Romantic period.*

periodicals See **magazine, newspaper names** entry.

perk Use *perk* (not *perq)* in all references. It is a shortened form of *perquisite,* which is a fringe benefit.

personal names See **names** entry.

personnel Note the spelling. When used to refer to employees in general, it takes a plural verb, as in *All personnel are invited to the holiday party.* When referring to a department within a company, lowercase and use a singular verb, as in *This year personnel is coordinating the holiday party.* If that sounds awkward, rewrite the sentence, as in *This year the personnel department is coordinating the holiday party.*

Peter Principle Note the capitalization. This theory is from a book by Laurence J. Peter that claims employees are promoted until they reach their level of incompetence.

PG, PG-13 Movie ratings that recommend parental guidance. The *-13* indicates that children under age 13 must be accompanied by an adult.

Ph.D., Ph.D.s Note the punctuation. Put this title for someone who holds a doctorate after the name. Mention the area of specialty when appropriate, as in *Arturo Salazar, Ph.D. in economics, will discuss public-private partnerships.*

The abbreviation *Dr.* can also be used for people with Ph.D.s, as in *Dr. Arturo Salazar,* but it is redundant to write *Dr. Arturo Salazar, Ph.D.*

phone Use this interchangeably with *telephone.*

pica It is a unit of measurement in printing that equals just less than one-sixth of an inch.

PIN Use *PIN* in all references. It stands for *personal identification number,* so don't write *PIN number,* which is redundant.

pint A unit of volume or capacity equal to one-eighth of a gallon or 16 ounces. It is part of the U.S. Customary System.

pixel Use *pixel* in all references. It is the shortened form for *picture element* and stands for the dots that make up an image or character on a computer or TV screen. Resolution improves as the number increases.

play both ends against the middle No hyphens are needed. This phrase means to maneuver opposing forces to personal advantage.

plays Italicize the titles of plays (do not put in quotation marks). Capitalize the principal words, as in *Death of a Salesman.*

plural Double-check the endings of plurals in the dictionary if uncertain. If using foreign words, don't assume the plural is formed by adding an *s.* For example, the plural of the Italian *lira* is *lire;* the Korean word *chaebol* is both singular and plural.

plus Use a singular verb with the construction *108 plus 233 is 341.*

plus fours This term is interchangeable with *+4s,* which are the four-digit add-on ZIP codes. Note the hyphen, as in *90452-2511.*

podium, pulpit, rostrum, lectern Pay attention to the prepositions (*on, in, behind)* for these terms. A speaker stands *on a podium* or *rostrum, in a pulpit* or *behind a lectern.*

poem Individual poems that are part of a collection take quotation marks, as in Walt Whitman's "Song of Myself." The title of a collection of poetry, however, is italicized, as in *Paradise Lost.*

policeman, police officer Use *police officer,* which avoids reference to gender. Capitalize when it precedes a name, as in *Police Officer Robin Walsh.*

police stations Lowercase *station,* as in *56th Street station.*

policyholder One word.

policymaker It is one word, as in *If the economy starts to overheat, Fed policymakers will move to dampen inflation.*

political parties Capitalize, as in *Democratic Party, Republican Party, Labor Party, Party for Social Democracy, Green Party, Socialist Party.*

political party labels For a representative from the U.S. Congress or a state legislature, write *Congressman Bill Jones, Democrat from New Jersey; Sen. John Smith, Republican from California; Assemblyman David Hathaway, Republican from Maine.* An alternative is *Congressman Bill Jones, D-N.J.; Sen. John Smith, R-Calif.; Assemblyman David Hathaway, R-Maine.* Use standard state abbreviations with this form. See **state abbreviations** entry.

Note that when preceding a name, *senator* can be abbreviated to *Sen.* (with a capital *S)* and *representative* to *Rep.* (with a capital *R).* There are no short forms for *assemblyman/assemblywoman* and *congressman/congresswoman.* They are not capitalized, unless preceding a name.

portal Lowercase this word, which is used for a Website designed to be the place of entry for people using the Web. A portal usually has a search engine and a list of sites and may offer other services such as e-mail. Yahoo! Inc. is one example of a portal. The word *portal* predates the Internet and more broadly means a major entrance or door. James Joyce wrote, "Mistakes are the portals of discovery."

Portuguese names Some people from Portuguese-speaking countries use both their mother's and father's family names. Note that the father's surname comes last. For example, in the case of *Amanda Teixeira Netto,* the mother's name is *Teixeira* and the father's name is *Netto.* For shortened references to the person's last name, write *Ms. Netto* or *Netto.* It is also correct to list both family names in shortened references, if that is how the person is known, as in *Ms. Teixeira Netto* or *Teixeira Netto.*

When alphabetizing Portuguese names in which both family names are used, use the father's surname, as in *Netto, Amanda Teixeira.*

Many married women retain their father's name before the husband's name. If *Amanda Teixeira Netto* married *João Macedo,* she could be known as *Amanda Netto Macedo.* In second references, write *Ms.* or *Mrs. Macedo* or *Macedo.*

To alphabetize in this instance, write *Macedo, Amanda Netto.*

Note the difference from Spanish, where the mother's name comes last. See **Spanish names** entry.

possessives See **apostrophe** entry.

Postal Service Use *Postal Service* interchangeably with the *United States Postal Service.*

Post-it Capitalize the *P,* use a hyphen and lowercase the *i* when referring to the trademarked paper product. The plural is *Post-its.*

post office Lowercase *post office* because it is not a formal name. A postmaster is the person in charge of a post office. Lowercase unless it is part of a formal title.

pounds and pence Spell out when the amount is indefinite. *The company invested millions of pounds in an infrastructure upgrade.* Use the symbol (£) with figures. *The company invested £10 million in an infrastructure upgrade.* Note there is no space between £ and the number. (Also note that many e-mail systems do not have the £ symbol, so spell out *pound* or write *GBP* in e-mails.) Spell out *pence* and *penny* (which is singular for *pence)* when they appear alone in sums: *1 penny (not 1 pence), 4 pence.* See **foreign currency** entry.

pre(-) Most words beginning with *pre-* do not need a hyphen, as in *precursor, prepaid.* But use a hyphen when *pre-* is followed by the letter *e,* as in *pre-eminent, pre-existing.* Also use a hyphen if the letter following *pre-* is capitalized, as in *pre-Darwinian, pre-Nafta.*

predominant, predominantly These are the preferred spellings (not *predominate* and *predominately).*

prefixes Usually words with these prefixes are one word: *pre-, post-, over-, under-, intra-, extra-, infra-, ultra-, sub-, super-, pro-, anti-, re-, un-, non-, semi-, pseudo-, supra-, meta-, multi-* and *co-,* as in *superabundant, cofounder, infrared, semiautomatic, multithreaded, intravenous, reintroduce, nonstandard.*

prepositions A preposition is used to relate a noun or pronoun to some other word in the sentence, as in *at, by, in, from, above, against, toward, with.* It is acceptable to end a sentence with a preposition, as in *The consultant said the hardware incompatibility problem is nothing to be concerned about.* If the sentence sounds awkward, revise it to avoid ending with a preposition, as in *The consultant said we had no reason to be concerned about the hardware incompatibility problem.* At one time, grammarians insisted that a sentence should not end in a preposition, but this is no longer the case.

presently It means in a little while or soon, but because it can also mean currently or now, *currently* is clearer when the meaning is now.

presidency Lowercase in all instances.

president For organizations, uppercase the word *President* only if it precedes a name, as in *President Armand D'Agostino will meet with the board this afternoon.* If no name is used, lowercase *president,* as in *D'Agostino has been the company's president since 1999.*

Presidents' Day Note the placement of the apostrophe. This holiday commemorates the birthdays of George Washington and Abraham Lincoln.

preventative, preventive These terms are interchangeable.

price-earnings ratio Spell out *price-earnings ratio* in the first reference; use *P/E ratio* or just *P/E* afterward. Note this takes a slash (/) and both letters are capitalized.

prime rate Do not capitalize. It is the lowest rate of interest on a bank loan offered to preferred borrowers.

principal, principle These terms are often confused. *Principal* means main party, owner, chief or leader. *French law firms represent the principals in the merger. Principal* also means the amount, excluding interest or premium, due on a loan or to a security holder at maturity. *The government has started paying down principal on its foreign debt. Principal* is also used as an adjective, as in *His principal contact at the firm is in marketing.*

   Principle means a truth or belief, as in *The department's guiding principle is customer satisfaction.*

print out, printout Use two words for the verb, as in *Julio will print out the document for Margaret.* Write as one word when used as a noun. *Julio will give Margaret a printout of the document.*

privately held This does not take a hyphen, regardless of how it is used. *The company is privately held* or *It is a privately held company.* The same is true for other words ending in *ly,* as in *highly complex formula, remarkably astute analyst.*

private sector, private-sector No hyphen is needed when used as a noun, as in *The former ambassador now works in the private sector.* Write with a hyphen when used as an adjective, as in *The former ambassador now works in a private-sector foundation.* The same holds for *public sector.*

privilege Often misspelled.

proactive No hyphen is needed.

producer price index Spell out in the first reference; use *PPI* afterward. This measures prices paid to producers for their goods.

professor Always lowercase before a name and never abbreviate as *prof.*

pronoun A pronoun is a word used in place of a noun or noun phrases, as in *I, you, he, yours* (all personal pronouns), *who* (a relative or interrogative pronoun), *these* (a demonstrative pronoun), *each* (an indefinite pronoun), *himself* (a reflexive pronoun).

proportions Use figures instead of spelling out the numbers. *The recipe called for 6 cups of flour and 2 cups of sugar.* Do not abbreviate proportions in text, although it is acceptable to use abbreviations in tabular material, as long as their meanings are clear, such as in recipes: *2 tsp. salt.*

proposition Lowercase unless it refers to a specific ballot question. When a figure appears with *proposition,* capitalize and abbreviate, as in *Voters have many unanswered questions about Prop. 13.*

prostate, prostrate Do not confuse these terms. The first refers to the prostate gland; the second refers to the act of reclining.

protester Often misspelled (not *protestor).*

Public Broadcasting Service Spell out in the first reference; use *PBS* afterward. This is a nonprofit association, not a network of public television stations.

public schools Lowercase unless used with a figure, as in *Public School 9.*

public sector, public-sector This takes no hyphen when used as a noun, as in *She has worked in the public sector since 1995.* Write with a hyphen when used as an adjective, as in *She has worked in public-sector organizations since 1995.* The same holds for *private sector.*

punctuation Its primary purpose is to help readers understand the written word. Style may vary from one organization to the next, but the key issues are clarity and consistency. Avoid using punctuation for effect, as in *She quit without giving notice!!!*

"Writing clearly is thinking clearly."

—Ken Terrell, executive director, employee communication
Bell Atlantic Corporation (now Verizon)

Q1, Q2, Q3, Q4 These abbreviations can be used for *first quarter (Q1)*, *second quarter (Q2)*, etc. in slide shows, charts, tabular material and other internal documents, depending on the audience and degree of formality. Include the year if necessary. *In Q1 2003 the company plans to launch its new product line.* In formal documents, such as annual reports, do not use the abbreviation. *In the first quarter of 2003, the company plans to launch its new product line.*

Q&A Use *Q&A* in all references. It stands for *question and answer.* The plural is *Q&A's.* If writing a *Q&A,* choose a style that is readable and clear. Often the question is in bold or italics while the answer is in normal (roman) type.

Quakers Use this for Religious Society of Friends in all references.

quandary Often misspelled.

quart Spell out in text, but abbreviate as *qt.* in tabular material. A *quart* equals 32 ounces or 2 pints. To convert to liters, use a conversion chart.

quasi, quasi- This is a separate word when used with a noun, as in *a quasi success.* Hyphenate when used as an adjective, as in *quasi-official policy.* It means to resemble something.

queen Lowercase unless it appears before a name as an official title, as in *Queen Elizabeth.*

query This refers to a request for information from a database. In publishing, authors send query letters and editors write queries on manuscripts. It means to inquire or question.

question mark Use a question mark (*?)* at the end of a direct question, as in *What time is it?* Do not use a question mark after an indirect question, as in *I wonder what time it is.* See **quotation marks** and **parentheses** entries.

questionnaire Often misspelled.

quick This is an adjective, as in *Steve is a quick study.* A common error is to use it as an adverb, as in *Come quick.* Write *Come quickly* instead.

quick-and-dirty This expression means rough estimate or to get the task done quickly, without worrying about details. *The client asked for a quick-and-dirty report to expedite the budget request.*

quid pro quo This has two plural forms, *quid pro quos* or *quids pro quo.* This stylebook favors *quid pro quos.* Choose one form and be consistent. Italics are not necessary, unless the expression may be unfamiliar to readers. It is Latin for an equal exchange or substitution.

quincentenary It is the 500th anniversary. *Quincentennial* is an alternative. Offer an equivalent in parentheses if readers may not know these terms.

quindecennial It means occurring every 15 years or a 15th anniversary. This is an unfamiliar word to many readers. If used, offer an equivalent in parentheses.

quitclaim One word. It is the transfer of a title, right or claim to another.

quotation marks Follow these guidelines:

- Use double marks (") for direct quotations of speech or writing. *CFO Thomas Rider said, "We plan to close the German office in 2003 or sooner, depending on market conditions." The memo said, "It has been a year of change at our company."*

- Use single marks (') for a quotation within a quotation. *"The CFO explained that 'market conditions' would determine the timing for closing the German office," said the managing director.*

- Use quotation marks the first time to introduce a new word in text, as in *The analyst told the investor about the "whisper numbers." The whisper numbers boosted the investor's interest.*

- When single and double quotation marks fall together, separate them with a space, as in *"The CFO explained that the timing for closing the German office would depend on 'market conditions,'" said the director.* If quotation marks occur within single quotation marks, use double quotation marks, as in *Kathleen said, "John told me, 'The "whisper number" had a negative impact on the stock.'"*

- With indirect quotations, do not use quotation marks, as in *Thomas Rider discussed the timing for closing the German office.*

- For multiple paragraphs of quoted material, begin each paragraph of the quoted material with quotation marks, but use ending quotation marks only at the end of the quoted material. Put the attribution for the multiple-paragraph quotation at the beginning or in the first paragraph of the quotation, not at the end. Another option is to set off long quotations from the text as block quotations, in which case they are not enclosed in quotation marks but indented (usually 10 spaces). In a block quotation, change any single quotation marks to double marks.

- For unusual wording or unfamiliar expressions, use quotation marks, as in *The head of media relations called the reporter a "hack" after reading the article.*

- Use quotation marks for the titles of speeches, chapters, lectures, paintings, songs (popular and classical), national anthems, articles in periodicals, short stories, poems that are part of a larger collection, individual episodes in television shows.

- If a term is used differently from its original meaning, put it in quotation marks, as in *"Gang of Four"* when referring to Erich Gamma, Richard Helm, Ralph Johnson and John Vlissides, authors of the book, *Design Patterns* (as opposed to the *Gang of Four* associated with Mao's Cultural Revolution).

Punctuation with quotation marks:

- A **period** always goes inside quotation marks that end a sentence. *Lynn said, "The electricians are incompetent." The first chapter of the book is entitled "Dealing with Local Municipalities."*

- A **comma** goes inside quotation marks when the quotation does not end the sentence. *"I need to call my agent," said Kevin. If you want to be known as a "player," join the M&A group. The best chapters of the book are entitled "Romancing the Inspectors," "Getting Tough with Contractors" and "The Zoning Board Shuffle."*

- A **comma** precedes a direct quotation when the attribution comes first, as in *Kevin said, "I need to call my agent." The memo said, "It has been a year of change at our company."*

- Do not use a **comma** at the start of a partial quotation. *Yuri Fridman said we needed "to start from scratch."*

- A **question mark** goes inside quotation marks if it is part of the direct quotation, as in *"Where is the money?" asked Tyson.* No comma is used here.

- A **question mark** goes outside the quotation marks if the whole sentence containing the quotation is a question, as in *What did he really mean when he said, "Where is the money"?*

- An **exclamation point** goes inside the quotation marks if the quoted words are an exclamation, as in *Simpson told the reporters, "Buzz off!"* No period is necessary in this case.

- An **exclamation point** goes outside the quotation marks if the whole sentence is exclamatory, as in *Simpson actually admitted the experience was "humbling"!*

- A **colon** and a **semicolon** always go outside the quotation marks, as in *Nora said, "I have a migraine"; she added, "I need a vacation."*

quotations Accuracy is the primary consideration when quoting an individual. Never take a statement out of context. If the person quoted is cast in a negative light, the quotation should be exact—verbatim. Otherwise, clean up grammar and spelling.

quote, quotation *Quote* is the verb, though writers often use it incorrectly as a noun. The noun is *quotation.* Write *He gave me the quotation over the phone,* not *He gave me the quote over the phone.*

· R ·

R This is a movie rating meaning restricted.

rabbi Lowercase *rabbi* unless it is a formal title that precedes a name, as in *Rabbi Levy led the panel discussion.* The only other formal title in the Jewish congregation is *cantor,* the individual who leads the congregation in song. Also lowercase *cantor,* except when preceding a name.

race Unless relevant to the material, avoid identifying individuals by race. Lowercase all racial descriptions, as in *black, white.*

racket The light bat used in tennis and badminton; however, *racquet* is the bat used in racquetball.

R&D Spell out *research and development* in the first reference; use *R&D* afterward (with the ampersand [*&*] and no spaces).

radio station Use the letters without periods, as in *WNYC.* If the station may not be familiar to readers, write *radio station WNYC.*

railroad If it is part of a name, capitalize it; otherwise, lowercase *railroad*. Always double-check railroad company names for the official spelling.

rainmaker One word. This refers to someone who generates business for an organization, bringing in clients and money.

RAM Use *RAM* in all references. It stands for *random access memory*, the memory of a computer.

ratio Use figures and hyphens, as in a *3-to-1 ratio*.

really Avoid this word when possible. It rarely adds meaning. The same holds for *very*.

real time, real-time Write as two words when used as a noun, as in *The Website allows customers and service representatives to communicate in real time.* Write with a hyphen when used as an adjective, as in *The company's goal is to provide real-time account information to all customers.*

Realtor Use *real estate agent*, the generic term, unless the individual is a member of the National Association of Realtors; then write *Realtor*, which is a service mark.

rebut, refute These are not interchangeable. *Rebut* means to take issue; *refute* means to disprove.

recession Lowercase. This is an economic downturn that may be temporary or may continue into a depression (also lowercased).

recipes Always use figures. It is acceptable to abbreviate measurements in listings to save space, such as recipes: *⅛ teaspoon of sugar (⅛ tsp. sugar), 2 tablespoons of butter (2 T. butter).*

record In the sense of setting a record, do not use *new*. Write *The sales department set a record this month,* not *The sales department set a **new** record this month.* The *new* in this sentence is redundant.

recur, recurred, recurring Often misspelled.

red herring Facts, statements, accusations, actions that are used to draw attention away from the main point and throw the reader or opponent off balance.

redline The verb is one word, as in *The bank cannot redline this neighborhood* or *The technologist redlined my specifications.*

redundancy Avoid unnecessary repetition in all writing. The following are examples of redundancies: *ATM machine, $500 million dollars, new record, PIN number, dead carcass, absolutely necessary, rarely ever, consensus of opinion, close proximity, surround on all sides, Dr. Heidi Waldorf, M.D.*

reengineer No hyphen is needed as this word is clear without it.

refer back When using the construction *refer back,* make sure the *back* is necessary for clarification. Some grammar books claim the *back* is redundant because the prefix *re-* means *back,* however, the latest edition of *The American Heritage Dictionary* claims this construction can clarify in some instances, as in *Refer back to the first page for the telephone number and refer ahead to the last page for the Website.*

regardless There is no such word as *irregardless.* It is a double negative. Write *regardless* instead.

regional names Uppercase the names of recognized regions, as in *New England, the Pacific Northwest, Latin America, Southeast Asia, the Baltics, Western Europe.*

registered trademark When a product is a registered trademark, it means it is recorded and verified by an authorized association. Registration puts on public record the exact details of the claim. Capitalize all registered trademark names, as in *Coca-Cola, Gold Medal flour.* The symbol for it is ®, but the symbol is not required in general text, although some companies require it in advertising and marketing materials.

reign, rein *Reign* is a period of rule or dominance, as in *He had a short reign as CEO. Rein,* which is literally the strip of leather attached to the bit in a horse's mouth, is used for expressions such as *give free rein to, pull in the reins* and *rein in. Aleksei gave his staff free rein to develop the new software.*

release time Follow this boldface style if a press release is embargoed until a specific time: *For release 9 a.m. EST.*

religious references Many religious references are capitalized; however, do not capitalize pronouns (e.g., *he, thou, thee)* when referring to a deity.

repellent This is the preferred spelling.

rescission Often misspelled (not *recision).* It means the act of making void (from *rescind).*

research and development Spell out in the first reference; use *R&D* afterward (with the ampersand [*&*] and no spaces).

restrictive clauses See **comma** entry.

résumé Note the two accents.

return on investment Spell out in the first reference; use *ROI* afterward.

Rev. Capitalize and abbreviate as a title that precedes a name, as in *Rev. John Bailey.* Lowercase *reverend* when it is not followed by a name. *The reverend will hold a meeting at 4 p.m.*

RFP Spell out *request for proposals* in the first reference; use *RFP* afterward. The plural is *RFPs*.

Rh factor Also written *RH factor.* The term comes from Rhesus monkeys; the Rh factor was first detected in the blood of this animal.

rhythm Often misspelled.

right-handed Use a hyphen.

rise Use *raise* instead of *rise* for an increase in pay.

ROI Spell out *return on investment* in the first reference; use *ROI* afterward.

Rolodex This is often misspelled (not *Roladex).* Capitalize because it is a brand name, even though this term is used generically.

ROM Use *ROM* in all references. It stands for *read-only memory.*

Roman numerals The numeral system uses seven letters: *I, V, X, L, C, D, M.* The equivalents are: *I* = 1, *V* = 5, *X* = 10, *L* = 50, *C* = 100, *D* = 500, *M* = 1,000. Add when a letter follows one of equal or greater value, as in *XV* = 15. Subtract when a smaller number precedes a larger one, as in *IV* = 4. Do not put a comma before the Roman numeral when it appears in a name.

roman type Do not capitalize *roman* when referring to upright typefaces.

room names Capitalize the names of special rooms or numbered rooms: *Rainbow Room, Oval Office, Room 23.*

rostrum, podium, pulpit, lectern Pay attention to the prepositions (*on, in, behind*) for these terms. A speaker stands *on a rostrum* or *podium, in a pulpit* or *behind a lectern.*

Route Capitalize *Route* when it appears in the names of roads, as in *Route 66.* In tabular material, use the abbreviation *Rte.* with the number, as in *Rte. 9S.*

rpm Use *rpm* in all references. It stands for *revolutions per minute.*

RSVP Use *RSVP* in all references. It stands for the French *répondez s'il vous plaît,* meaning please reply.

Russian(s) Use this term only for the people of Russia. Always double-check the spelling of Russian names. Use familiar forms, as in Tchaikovsky (not Chaikovsky), when possible.

Refer to people from the other former Soviet republics according to country, as in *Ukrainian, Belarussian, Georgian, Moldovan, Armenian.* The term *Soviet* applies to all nationalities that made up the former Soviet Union.

· S ·

saccharin (n.), saccharine (adj.) Often misspelled. The first is a sugar substitute; the second means overly sweet.

sacred writings Capitalize the names of sacred writings, as in *Upanishads, Old Testament, Gospels, Holy Bible, Koran.*

safe deposit box This phrase is not hyphenated. Avoid using this form: *safety box.*

salesperson Avoid a reference to gender by using *sales clerk, salesperson* (one word) or *sales representative.* If you need to express gender, use *saleswoman* instead of *salesgirl.*

salutation If the gender of the addressee in correspondence is unknown, drop the *Mr.* or *Ms.* and use the full name in the salutation, as in *Dear Pat Wilson:.*

sanction It can mean either approve or penalty. Be clear in context. *The doctor sanctioned prescribing the medicine* or *The United Nations issued a report on the Iraqi trade sanctions.*

Saturday Capitalize days of the week.

savings and loan association Spell out in the first reference; use *S&L* (with the ampersand [*&*] and without spaces) afterward. The plural is *S&Ls*. This is not interchangeable with *bank* or *thrift*.

scalable Note the spelling (no *e*). This term refers to an idea or technology that can be borrowed and turned into something else by others.

school Lowercase unless it is part of a proper noun, as in *St. Luke's Grammar School, Public School 3, Richard E. Byrd School*. For colleges and universities, capitalize only when they are part of the name, as in *McGill University* or *Vanderbilt University*.

scientific terms There are many style matters regarding scientific terms. It is best to double-check specific stylebooks (for instance, *American Medical Association Manual of Style*). If a stylebook is unavailable, always check the dictionary.

scissors It takes a plural verb and pronoun, as in *The scissors **are in their** place, beside the Scotch tape.*

screen saver Write as two words.

sculpture Capitalize the titles of sculptures and put into italics, as in Rodin's *The Thinker*.

seasons Lowercase all seasons: *winter, spring, summer, fall* or *autumn*.

second, secondly When enumerating, use *second*, not *secondly*, as in *First plug it in, second turn it on.*

second-guess Write with a hyphen. It means to criticize or correct someone after an outcome is known. The person who does this is a *second-guesser.*

second hand, secondhand Write as two words in the sense of the hands on a clock. When used as an adverb, also write as two words, as in *She heard about the layoffs second hand.* Write as one word when used as an adjective. *She bought a secondhand car* or *The secondhand smoke bothered Mary Adele.*

Securities and Exchange Commission Spell out in the first reference; use *SEC* or *commission* (lowercased) afterward.

self(-) Many words with this prefix are hyphenated, as in *self-governing, self-addressed, self-service.* Check the dictionary if uncertain.

semi(-) Most words with this prefix are not hyphenated, as in *semicircle, semiconductor.* But use a hyphen to avoid writing two consecutive *i*'s, as in *semi-informal.*

semiannual, semiyearly Both mean twice a year. These words are not familiar to all readers, so use *twice a year* when possible.

semicolon A semicolon (*;*) adds more emphasis than the comma but is weaker than the colon (*:*). Follow these guidelines:

- Use a semicolon to join closely related statements: *Human resources deals with personnel issues; auditing deals with risk issues.*

- Use semicolons to mark off phrases or items in a series that would ordinarily be separated by commas except that the phrases or items already contain commas: *Sue Ciezcko, director of human resources, asks employees to read the Employee Manual; the Insurance Booklet, including the preface; the Employee Stylebook, even though it is more than 300 pages; and the Code of Ethics.*

- The semicolon goes outside quotation marks or parentheses: *Naomi read "Bartleby the Scrivener"; she then quit her job at the post office.*

Senate Capitalize references to the *Senate*.

senator Lowercase unless it precedes a name. Before a name, capitalize and abbreviate, as in *Sen. John Glenn.*

senior, junior Use the abbreviation *Sr.* or *Jr.* with personal names. Use a comma before *Sr.* or *Jr.* For instance: *Anthony Forde, Sr.* In a listing by last name, the *Sr.* or *Jr.* comes last: *Forde, Anthony, Sr.*
   Spell out and lowercase *senior* or *junior* to designate a member of the class.

separate Often misspelled.

sergeant Often misspelled. Lowercase unless it precedes a name. Before a name, capitalize and abbreviate as *Sgt.*

serviceable Often misspelled.

service mark This refers to a name, brand, symbol or slogan that distinguishes a services company or its products and is protected by law. Capitalize service marks in text. In some instances, companies follow service marks with the abbreviation ^{SM}, written as a superscript, as in *TradeSuite^{SM}*. Use of registration symbols, such as ^{SM} or ^{TM}, depends on practice already established by individual companies.

services Write this with a singular verb when referring to an industry, as in *Services is a counter-cyclical business.*

service sector Lowercase this term, which refers to the part of the economy that employs approximately 80% of the work force in the United States.

shall, will In American English, *shall* is used infrequently and tends to sound overly formal or mannered. In British English the distinction between *shall* and *will* is still observed.

shareholder, share owner The first is one word; the second is two.

she Do not refer to ships or countries as *she*. Use *it* instead.

s/he Some publications use *s/he* as a gender alternative to *he or she*. It takes a singular verb, as in *The person who wrote the letter did not include a name, although s/he* **expects** *a reply.* This stylebook does not recommend this construction.

shortfall One word. It is the amount by which something falls short of expectation, need or demand. *Analysts project a shortfall in demand for PCs.*

signs When the words in short signs and notes appear in textual matter, capitalize the first letter in each word, but don't italicize or use quotes. *There is a No Smoking sign in the lobby.*

sitdown This is one word when it is used as a noun, as in *HR scheduled a sitdown with the new secretary to explain office protocol.*

Six Sigma Capitalize this term, which refers to a corporate approach to quality management that is fact-based and data-driven and aims to bring defects to near zero.

slash This is also known as a virgule. It is a diagonal mark (/) used primarily to separate alternatives as in *and/or* or *his/her;* or to replace the word *per* as in *miles/hour.* The double-slash (//) is used for Web addresses after the protocol, as in *http://.*

slowdown Write as one word when used as a noun. *Investors expect an economic slowdown in the third quarter.*

slug This is a printing term. A slug names the various stages in the editing of a document.

slugfest This informal term is not hyphenated. It means a heated argument, where blows—real or imagined—are exchanged.

small-business man, small-business woman Use a hyphen. Note that in this usage, *businessman* and *businesswoman*, which are usually one word, become two-word forms.

snail mail Coined to mean the alternative to e-mail, this term is used for mail sent through the post office.

so-called Write with a hyphen. *Ireland, the so-called Celtic Tiger, experienced strong economic growth during the 1990s.*

Social Security Capitalize this reference to the government insurance program, as in *Please include your Social Security number.*

soft money Lowercase this term meaning the unlimited contributions made to political parties. Also lowercase *funny money, dumb money.*

software Capitalize the principal words in program names, as in *Microsoft Word.* There is no need to use quotation marks or italic type.

some time, sometime, sometimes *Some time* means a portion of time, as in *Rosalie will have some time to meet with you Tuesday. Sometime* means at an indefinite time in the future, as in *Rosalie will meet with you sometime next week. Sometimes* means occasionally. *Rosalie sometimes schedules meetings for 8 a.m.*

spacing Use the tab key instead of fives spaces for a paragraph indent. Use a single space between sentences (not a double space).

spam Lowercase this term, which is another word for electronic junk mail.

Spanish names Many people from Spanish-speaking countries use both their mother's and father's surnames, with the mother's surname last. For example, in the case of *Vicente Fox Quesada, Fox* is the father's name and the mother's name is *Quesada.* Shortened references use the father's last name: *President Fox, Mr. Fox* or *Fox,* but never *President Quesada, Mr. Quesada* or *Quesada.* It is also correct to list both family names in shortened references, as in *President Fox Quesada, Mr. Fox Quesada* or *Fox Quesada.*

When alphabetizing Spanish names in which both family names are used, always put the father's surname first, as in *Fox Quesada, Vicente* (not *Fox, Vicente Quesada).*

Many married women retain their father's family name and use *de* before the husband's name, as in *Violetta Barrios de Chamorro.* In second references, write *Ms.* or *Mrs. Chamorro.*

Note the difference from Portuguese, where the father's name comes second. See **Portuguese names** entry.

spec(s) Spell out *specification(s)* in the first reference; use *spec(s)* afterward. *The vendor e-mailed the specs for the new PCs. Specs* on a manuscript deal with typeface, headline style, etc. This stylebook favors using *spec* as a verb, even though it may be considered nonstandard. *Sue will spec the manuscript before Friday.*

speeches Put the titles of speeches in quotation marks and capitalize the main words. *The keynote speech is entitled, "The Challenges of Leadership in Times of Change."*

spell check, spell checker, spelling checker Use *spell check* for the verb, as in *Spell check the document before you print it.* This stylebook prefers *spell* *checker* to *spelling checker* when used as a noun, as in *I ran the document through the spell checker.*

When you spell check a document or e-mail, follow this guideline: Always use it; never trust it. This is because the spell checker only detects misspelled words. It will not detect the wrong form, as in *you* instead of *your.*

spinoff Write as one word when used as a noun, as in *The spinoff of the health-care division is scheduled for the third quarter.*

split infinitive See **infinitive** entry.

spokesman, spokesperson, spokeswoman Use *spokesperson* if you don't know or don't want to refer to the gender of the speaker.

sports sponsorship Capitalize the name of the event, as in *Buick Open.*

spouse Use *spouse* instead of *wife* or *husband,* as in *The candidate invited executives and their spouses to the banquet.*

spreadsheet One word.

spring Lowercase seasons.

St. Use this abbreviation for *Saint,* as in *St. Anthony, St. Paul, Minn.*

Standard & Poor's Spell out in the first reference. Note the hyphen, the use of *&* (spaces on either side) and the placement of the apostrophe. Use *S&P* afterward.

When citing the index, write *Standard & Poor's 500-stock index* in the first reference; use *S&P 500-stock index* or *S&P 500* afterward.

startup Write as one word, whether used as a noun or an adjective. *Marc works in a startup* or *Marc works in a startup company.*

state There are 50 states in the United States, but four are *commonwealths* (Kentucky, Virginia, Massachusetts and Pennsylvania). Lowercase all *state of* and *commonwealth of* constructions, as in *state of California.* Lowercase *state* when it precedes a level of jurisdiction, as in *state Rep. Thomas Feldman.* Apply the same style to phrases such as *town of Warwick, city of Milwaukee.*

state abbreviations The Postal Service prefers the two-letter postal abbreviations when ZIP codes are included. Both letters are capitalized, no periods are used after the letters and no commas are used between the state and the ZIP code. But use these abbreviations only with full addresses.

In text, do not use the Postal Service abbreviations. Instead use the standard state abbreviations in conjunction with a city or town. Spell out the state name if no city or town is included. (Note that some cities do not require state names. See **cities** entry.) Many of the standard abbreviations are the same as those used by the Postal Service, but note the different use of capitalization and periods. In text a comma goes between the city and state and after the state abbreviation (unless it falls at the end of the sentence). *Margaret Sinsky is moving to San Diego, Calif., next spring* or *Next spring Margaret Sinsky is moving to San Diego, Calif.*

Note that eight states are never abbreviated in text: Alaska, Hawaii, Idaho, Iowa, Maine, Ohio, Texas, Utah.

Alabama: Ala. AL	Delaware: Del. DE
Alaska: Alaska AK	Florida: Fla. FL
Arizona: Ariz. AZ	Georgia: Ga. GA
Arkansas: Ark. AR	Hawaii: Hawaii HI
California: Calif. CA	Idaho: Idaho ID
Colorado: Colo. CO	Illinois: Ill. IL
Connecticut: Conn. CT	Indiana: Ind. IN

Iowa: Iowa IA

Kansas: Kans. KS

Kentucky: Ky. KY

Louisiana: La. LA

Maine: Maine ME

Maryland: Md. MD

Massachusetts: Mass. MA

Michigan: Mich. MI

Minnesota: Minn. MN

Mississippi: Miss. MS

Missouri: Mo. MO

Montana: Mont. MT

Nebraska: Nebr. NE

Nevada: Nev. NV

New Hampshire: N.H. NH

New Jersey: N.J. NJ

New Mexico: N. Mex. NM

New York: N.Y. NY

North Carolina: N.C. NC

North Dakota: N. Dak. ND

Ohio: Ohio OH

Oklahoma: Okla. OK

Oregon: Oreg. OR

Pennsylvania: Pa. PA

Rhode Island: R.I. RI

South Carolina: S.C. SC

South Dakota: S. Dak. SD

Tennessee: Tenn. TN

Texas: Texas TX

Utah: Utah UT

Vermont: Vt. VT

Virginia: Va. VA

Washington: Wash. WA

West Virginia: W.Va. WV

Wisconsin: Wis. WI

Wyoming: Wyo. WY

stationary, stationery Often confused. *Stationary* means standing still, while *stationery* means writing materials.

stellar Note the spelling (not *steller*). *The board rewarded the CEO for the company's stellar performance.*

stratum, strata The singular is *stratum;* the plural is *strata. The proportion of the population in the lowest stratum of society is growing.*

streaming media This refers to audio, video, newsfeeds and other media content that flows (or streams) live over the Web (as opposed to a downloaded file that is played from a desktop).

street Spell out and capitalize in this construction: *Sue Levine lives on Grove Street.* If more than one street is mentioned, lowercase, as in *The building is on Knoll and State streets.* Use *St.* with figures, in tabular material and with complete addresses. See **addresses** entry for more information.

Street, the Capitalize *Street* when it refers to the financial community in the Wall Street area of New York: *The Street expects the Fed to lower interest rates.*

Student Loan Marketing Association Spell out in the first reference; use *Sallie Mae* afterward. Note the spelling of *Mae.*

subjunctive Use this form of the verb for wishful thinking, as in *If I were a millionaire, I would buy the company* (not *If I was a millionaire).*

subpoena Often misspelled. When used as a verb, the past tense is *subpoenaed,* as in *The company's legal team subpoenaed court records.*

summer Lowercase seasons.

Sunday Capitalize days of the week.

supersede Often misspelled. It means *to take the place of.*

supposed to Remember the *d* at the end of *suppose* in this construction: *He was supposed to leave the information with his secretary.*

Supreme Court Capitalize in all references. This is the highest court in the United States, consisting of nine justices and having jurisdiction over all other courts in the nation. Also capitalize references to the state supreme courts, as in *Connecticut Supreme Court.*

suspensive hyphen Rather than repeat the words in a series of similar phrases that form adjectives, use the suspensive hyphen, as in *The facilities manager*

ordered one-, two- and three-inch nails for the project. The company released first-
and second-quarter earnings results.

sync Use *sync* not *synch,* as in *She is out of sync with the rest of the department.*
It is short for *synchronization.*

synchronicity Often misspelled. Synchrony is a form of synchronicity.

synergy This means combined or cooperative action and is also used in the
sense of complementary areas, as in *The CEO appointed a committee to iden-*
tify synergies in the merged companies. Note the plural is *synergies.*

systemic This term is used by computer programmers to denote something
that affects an entire system or multiple systems. For formal writing, avoid *sys-*
temic (it is a medical term) and use *systematic* instead.

$\cdot T \cdot$

24/7 Use figures and a slash. It is sometimes written *24/7/365.*

20/20 Write this with figures and a slash. *With 20/20 hindsight Sheila admitted that the other position would have been a better career move.*

10-K Use *10-K* in all references (note the hyphen and capital *K*). This refers to the SEC's Form 10-K, which is a financial statement that publicly held companies must file each year. (The 10-Q is filed each quarter.)

For kilometers, write *10K* (without the hyphen), as in *Crystal finished the 10K race in record time.*

3D Use *3D* in all references, as in *The oceanographers used 3D imaging to map the ocean floor.* It stands for *three-dimensional.*

360-degree review Include the word *degree,* using a hyphen, in the first reference. In subsequent references, this can be used interchangeably with *360 review* or *360,* as in *Barbara received the results of her 360 last week.* This refers to performance reviews that include feedback from a person's supervisor, peers, direct reports and, in some cases, customers. It is also correct to use the degree symbol, as in *360° review,* though this usually takes longer to write on a computer.

tablespoon, tablespoonful(s) Spell out in text, but abbreviations are acceptable in tabular material. *Tablespoon* has three abbreviations: *T., tbs., tbsp.* Choose one and be consistent. A tablespoon is equal to 3 teaspoons or ½ a fluid ounce.

tabular material Space is always a consideration in tabular material, so figures and abbreviations are preferred, regardless of spell-out and first-reference rules in text.

take-home pay Note the hyphen. This is the amount of salary after taxes.

takeover It is one word when used in the sense of acquisition. *The proposed takeover will require Justice Department approval.*

taskmaster One word. This is someone who assigns burdensome tasks.

tax-exempt Write with a hyphen.

tchotchke(s) Often misspelled. It means knickknacks (one word).

teaspoon, teaspoonful(s) Spell out in text, but abbreviations are acceptable in tabular material. *Teaspoon* has two abbreviations: *t.* and *tsp.* Choose one and be consistent. It equals ⅓ of a tablespoon.

tech, technology When used as an adjective, *tech* is interchangeable with *technology,* as in *It was a tough week for tech stocks* or *It was a tough week for technology* stocks. But when *technology* is used as a noun, it is not interchangeable with *tech. The company spent more than $1 billion to upgrade its technology* (not *to upgrade its tech).*

techies This informal term is often misspelled (not *tekkies*).

technical vocabulary It may be tempting to use technical vocabulary when writing about work. Remember it's usually best to keep matters simple. Always explain terms that may be unfamiliar to readers. If a paragraph is weighed down with words like *blue lasers, solar cells* and *liquid electronic display*, don't assume readers will understand. Offer simple explanations.

technology, media and telecom sector Spell out in the first reference; use *TMT sector* or *TMT* afterward.

teenage, teenager Do not use a hyphen.

telecom This is the shortened version of *telecommunications*. Spell out *telecommunications* in the first reference; use *telecom* afterward. *Telecoms* and *telcos* are shortened forms for *telecommunications companies*. Spell out the entire phrase in the first reference; use *telecoms* or *telcos* afterward.

telephone Use this interchangeably with *phone*.

telephone calls, telephone messages *Return* calls; *answer* messages.

telephone numbers Follow these guidelines:

- For the United States and Canada, start with *1*, put the area code in parentheses and use a hyphen after the exchange, as in *1 (415) 493-4762*.

- When a business uses a word instead of numbers, put a hyphen after the exchange and provide the numbers in parentheses, as in *1 (614) 556-ERGO (3746)*.

- If extensions are necessary, write *1 (206) 591-0860, Ext. 5564*. Decide whether to capitalize *Ext.* or lowercase it (*ext.*). Choose one form and be consistent.

- If the telephone numbers are internal to an organization and all readers have the same area code and exchange, just write the extension, as in *Call Toni Akerejah, Ext. 2781.*

- If a number is toll-free, write *1 (888) 664-3427 toll-free.* It is not necessary to specify *toll-free* with 800 numbers because readers are already familiar with this exchange.

- If a number is pay-per-call, write the cost after the number, as in *1 (900) 687-5412, 90 cents per minute.*

- If writing international numbers for a U.S. audience, give the U.S. international access code *(011)*, followed by the country and city codes, as in *011 44 171 775 3400.* Use spaces instead of punctuation (such as hyphens) for international numbers. International numbers vary as far as punctuation goes and also in terms of how numbers are grouped. In addition, not all countries use seven numbers.

- If writing international numbers for an international audience, do not include *011*, since this is the international access code for calls made from the United States.

- Follow the same guidelines for fax numbers.

television titles Capitalize the principal words and italicize the title, as in *Who Wants to Be a Millionaire.* For individual episodes with names, use quotation marks: "Daveless in New York" episode of *NYPD Blue.*

temperature To indicate temperature, use figures and the degree symbol for all numbers except zero: *It was 98° in Dallas yesterday* or *Do you think the temperature will rise above zero today?* Use a word, not a minus sign, for temperatures below zero, as in *The pipes froze because it was minus 10°.*

Fahrenheit is the temperature scale used in the United States. If it is necessary to specify the temperature scale, write *32 °F* (with a capital *F,* without a space before or after the degree symbol and without a period after the *F°).*

Celsius is the temperature scale used in the metric system. If using this scale, specify *32° C* (with a capital *C,* without a space before or after the degree symbol and without a period after the *C°.* To convert Celsius or centigrade temperature to Fahrenheit, multiply by 9, divide by 5 and add 32. Note that both *Fahrenheit* and *Celsius* are capitalized.

Also note that everyone has a temperature, usually 98.6°, so do not write *Mark has a temperature.* Instead write *Mark has a high temperature* or *Mark has a fever.*

tense Try to minimize the unnecessary shifting of verb tenses. If the sentence begins in the past tense, the other verbs in the sentence should relate logically to that tense, as in *She **said** she **was** happy to see me.* When it is necessary to switch back and forth among past, present and future to express time, be sure the verb tenses are logical throughout. Shifting tenses indiscriminately gives the appearance of uncertainty. In addition try to stick to the simple present or past tense when writing because it is more concise. For example, *The company plans to roll out the new product in March* is more concise than *The company is planning to roll out the new product in March.*

Texas Do not abbreviate in text, but use *TX* (capitals without periods) with full addresses, including ZIP code. *TX* is the two-letter Postal Service abbreviation. Seven other states are not abbreviated in text: Alaska, Hawaii, Idaho, Iowa, Maine, Ohio, Utah. See **state abbreviations** entry.

than, then Use *than* to introduce a second element in a comparison, as in *Karen is a better tennis player than John.* Use *than* when referring to amounts, as in *He earns more than $100,000 a year.*

Use *then* as an adverb in the sense of *at that time,* as in *I was still at the office then.* It is also used in if/then constructions. It is used as a noun, as in *By then the systems had crashed* or *The meeting is at 10 a.m.; until then let's rehearse the presentation.* Avoid using *then* as an adjective, as in *At the summit, then–Prime Minister Margaret Thatcher addressed her European counterparts,* which sounds awkward. Better to revise the sentence, as in *At the summit, Margaret Thatcher, then prime minister, addressed her European counterparts.*

Thank you in advance Just write *thank you* (without a hyphen).

that, which To decide whether to use *that* or *which,* determine whether the information is **essential** (*that*) to the meaning of the sentence or merely helpful or **nonessential** (*which*).

Follow these examples: *I am looking for the file that has everyone's address in it. I am looking for the blue file, which was on the desk yesterday.* Use a comma before *which.* See **comma** entry for additional information.

that, who Use *that* when referring to things: *The software company that Melissa Gerardi cofounded has 10 employees.* Use *who* when referring to persons: *Melissa Gerardi, who is the keynote speaker, cofounded a software company.* For animals use *that,* as in *The owner of the dog that bit me apologized profusely.*

A common error is to refer to organizations as *who: For companies that haven't changed their policies, the court ruling was a wake-up call* (not *For companies who haven't changed*).

that is Follow with a comma if used in text. The Latin abbreviation for *that is* is *i.e.,* which stands for *id est.* In general, use this abbreviation for parenthetical material. It is lowercased, has two periods, is not italicized and is followed by a comma. *The design company developed the new company's branded materials (i.e., letterhead, signage, business cards).* It is not interchangeable with *e.g.,* which means for example and stands for *exempli gratia.*

their, there, they're Occasionally these forms are confused. *Their* is a possessive pronoun: *their house, their briefcases, their domain. There* is an adverb indicating direction, as in *Don't go there. They're* is a contraction, meaning *they are,* as in *They're planning a trip to Africa.*

there is, there are Sentences beginning with *There is, There are* (and *It is*) can become monotonous. Rewrite and combine sentences to show a closer connection: *Relationships are everything is a deeply rooted business maxim* as opposed to *There is a maxim in business that relationships are everything. It is deeply rooted.*

When using *there is, there are,* be sure the verb agrees with the noun. *There are five programmers in the department* not *There is five programmers in the department.* This mistake is especially common with the contraction *there's.* Do not write *There's five programmers in the department;* write *There are five programmers.*

theretofore This has a legal connotation. Use *until then* instead.

thinking outside the box The *of* isn't necessary (*thinking outside of the box*).

third generation Spell out in the first reference; use *3G* afterward. This is used in reference to advanced wireless communications networks, as in *third-generation technology* or *third-generation services.*

three Rs They are *reading, 'riting and 'rithmetic.*

Thursday Capitalize days of the week.

till It is interchangeable with *until.* Do not use the literary form *'til.*

time Use figures, as in *We will meet at 9 a.m. in the conference room* (not *nine a.m.*). It is better to specify *a.m.* or *p.m.* than to use the *o'clock* form. Note the space between the number and *a.m.* If the time is on the hour, it is not necessary to include a colon and two zeros. Just write *9 a.m.* Use the colon to separate minutes from hours, as in *9:15 a.m.* If the *o'clock* form is used, spell out the number, as in *nine o'clock,* not *9 o'clock.*

timecard, timeline, timetable Each is one word.

time frame Two words.

time zone Spell out and capitalize time zones in the first reference, as in *Pacific Standard Time, Central Standard Time, Eastern Standard Time*. However, if a time accompanies the time zone, use abbreviations in the first reference, as in *11 a.m. CST*. Note that a comma is not needed after *a.m.* or *p.m.*

titles Lowercase *titles* unless they precede a name, as in *Chief Executive Officer Jill Considine* or *Jill Considine, chief executive officer*. Unofficial titles (job descriptions) are lowercased, even when they precede a name, as in *psychologist Mary Warwick, trustee Allen Burke*.

to, too Occasionally these words are confused. Use *too* to mean excessive, as in *too long, too much, too willing*. It also means in addition, as in *John Reilly will speak, too*. Note that a comma is necessary when *too* ends a sentence.

today Be specific. It is better to use the date in business writing, especially for correspondence between different time zones. Avoid using *today, this morning, tonight, yesterday, tomorrow*.

to-do Note the hyphen. *Nancy assured the staff that salary reviews were at the top of her to-do list.* Another meaning of this phrase is commotion: *Bill Gates's appearance created a big to-do at the conference.*

toll-free Write with a hyphen.

tonight Not *tonite*.

topics Capitalize the names of topics, as in *Topics discussed at the conference included Belt-Tightening in Q3 and Diversity in the Workplace.*

tortuous, torturous These terms are often confused. *Tortuous* means winding or twisting while *torturous* means anguishing.

totaled, totaling The preferred spelling in American English uses one *l.*

Total Quality Management Spell out in the first reference; use *TQM* afterward. This refers to programs used by corporations to improve quality.

touchtone Interchangeable with *push-button* for telephone dialing. Lowercase it; *touchtone* is now a generic term.

toward This is preferred to *towards.*

To Whom It May Concern Capitalize all words in this formal greeting, which is followed by a colon (*:*).

trademark It is a name, symbol or slogan used by a manufacturing business and protected by law. In most textual material it is not necessary to use the registration symbols (®, ™), but this decision will vary at companies. The ® symbol and ™ (capitalized without periods) are usually written as superscripts (in small type above the line), a function word processors can perform. Advertising and marketing departments should contact the International Trademark Association for additional information.

trans(-) Compounds formed with *trans-* are one word, as in *transoceanic, transshipment.* It is no longer necessary to capitalize proper names that follow *trans-,* as in *transatlantic, transpacific* (not *trans-Atlantic, trans-Pacific*).

travel, traveled, traveling, traveler The preferred spelling in American English uses one *l.*

traveler's check(s) Note the placement of the apostrophe.

trickle-down theory Note the hyphen. This economic theory holds that financial benefits accorded to big business enterprises will in turn trickle down to smaller businesses and consumers.

T-shirt Capitalize the *T,* even in the middle of a sentence, and use a hyphen.

Tuesday Capitalize days of the week.

TV This is interchangeable with *television,* but use *TV* in all references to *cable TV.*

· U ·

"At least do a brief outline if you are writing a document of any length."

—Ann Collier, vice president, financial and public relations
Circuit City Stores, Inc.

U.K. Use *U.K.* as an adjective, as in *The U.K. office is headquarters for all of Europe.* Spell out *United Kingdom* when referring to the region, as in *The United Kingdom is headquarters for all of Europe.*

United Kingdom is not interchangeable with *Great Britain* or with *England.* The United Kingdom comprises Great Britain (England, Scotland and Wales) and Northern Ireland.

uncharted waters Not *unchartered waters.* It means new territory.

Uncle Sam Capitalize personifications. *Mother Nature* and *John Barleycorn* are other examples of personifications.

under way Write as two words, as in *The renovation will be under way before yearend.*

unemployment rate Write this as a percentage figure: *The unemployment rate for August was 4%.* This statistic is compiled monthly by the Bureau of Labor Statistics.

uninterested This word has a different meaning from *disinterested. Uninterested* means not interested. *Disinterested* means neutral or impartial. *The companies signed an arbitration agreement to ensure that disinterested parties handle all disputes.*

union names In the first reference, give the full name of the union. Use a shortened form afterward. Shorten *United Brotherhood of Carpenters and Joiners of America* to *carpenters' union* or *the Brotherhood of Carpenters.*

United Kingdom Spell out *United Kingdom* when referring to the region, as in *The United Kingdom is headquarters for all of Europe.* Use *U.K.* when it is an adjective, as in *The U.K. office is headquarters for all of Europe.*

United Kingdom is not interchangeable with *Great Britain* or with *England.* The United Kingdom comprises Great Britain (England, Scotland and Wales) and Northern Ireland.

United Nations Spell out when used as a noun, as in *Thord Palmlund works at the United Nations.* When used as an adjective, write *U.N.,* as in *Thord Palmlund works at U.N. headquarters.*

United States Spell out *United States* when referring to the country, as in *The United States is increasing its production of fossil fuels.* Note the singular verb: *The United States is* (not *The United States are).* Also note the singular possessive: *The United States is increasing its production of fossil fuels* (not *their production).*

Write *U.S.* when used as an adjective, as in *U.S. production of fossil fuels is increasing.* When a distinction is necessary with the symbol for dollar, write *US$2.1 billion* (no periods in *US;* no space between *US* and *$).*

universities Verify the names and spelling of universities and colleges by checking Websites. Use the full name in the first reference, as in *Rutgers University.* Use the shortened version *(Rutgers)* afterward.

unprecedented It means for the first time.

uppercase(d) It means capitalized and is a verb, noun and adjective. It is one word, no hyphen. The same goes for *lowercase*. Note the difference in how it is used. *Uppercase days of the week* or *Days of the week are uppercased* (with a *d*). To uppercase a word means to capitalize the first letter; it does not mean to use all capitals.

upside One word. *Downside* is also one word.

uptime One word. *The systems have two years of continuous uptime. Downtime* is also one word.

URL Use *URL* in all references if readers are likely to be familiar with this term. It stands for *uniform resource locator*. Pronounce *URL* letter by letter. Use *Web address* if readers will not be familiar with *URL*. Otherwise *Web address* and *URL* are interchangeable.

It is helpful to readers to include URLs when referencing a Website. Follow capitalization, no matter how idiosyncratic it may be, because some addresses are case-sensitive. Write the sentence so that normal punctuation (such as a comma) does not cause confusion. It is not necessary to include the protocol *http://* as long as *www* is part of the address, as in *See www.yourdomain.com for more information.* If *www* is not part of the address, then include *http://.* Be sure slashes are leaning in the right direction.

Also, when a URL has a protocol other than *http://* (e.g., *ftp, https),* then include that protocol.

U.S. Write *U.S.* as an adjective, as in *U.S. production of fossil fuels is increasing.* When a distinction is necessary with the symbol for dollar, write *US$2.1 billion* (no periods in *US;* no space between *US* and *$*). Spell out *United States* when referring to the country, as in *The United States is increasing its production of fossil fuels.* Note the singular verb: *The United States is* (not *The United*

*States **are**).* Also note the singular possessive: *The United States is increasing **its** production of fossil fuels* (not ***their** production).*

user-friendly Write with a hyphen.

Utah Do not abbreviate in text, but use *UT* (capitals without periods) with full addresses, including ZIP code. *UT* is the two-letter Postal Service abbreviation. Seven other states are not abbreviated in text: Alaska, Hawaii, Idaho, Iowa, Maine, Ohio, Texas. See **state abbreviations** entry.

utilize In most cases it is more concise to use *use*.

U-turn Use a hyphen and uppercase *U.*

. V .

"Eliminate jargon and 'corp-speak' as much as possible."

—Barbara J. Gustafson, manager, corporate communications

UnitedHealth Group Corporation

v., vs. See **versus** entry.

value-added Use a hyphen.

vaporware This is a negative term for new versions of software that appear every year like clockwork.

VCR Use *VCR* in all references. It stands for *videocassette recorder.* The plural is *VCRs.*

venture capitalist Spell out in the first reference. Use *VC* afterward only if the meaning is obvious in context; otherwise you may confuse readers. *VC* may mean venture capitalist to one reader and Vietcong to another.

verb It is a word or group of words denoting action, occurrence or state of being. The verb, along with any words that modify its meaning, forms the predicate of a sentence: *am, worked, will retire, have worked, will have completed.*

verbal, oral *Verbal* refers to both spoken and written words. *Oral* refers to spoken communication only. Using *verbal* for just spoken communication is correct, but *oral* is more precise. *He needs to work on his verbal skills.*

versus Spell out *versus* in text when not referring to court cases, as in *At the company softball game, it was the Titans versus the Bullets.* Use either *v.* or *vs.* for *versus* in court cases. (Whichever abbreviation you choose, use it consistently.) The *v.* or *vs.* is set in a different font from the names, as in *Hirsch* v. *3Com* or Anderson *vs.* McKiernan. If used in a headline, lowercase the abbreviation: Roe *v.* Wade Battle Begins.

very Use this word sparingly. It adds little meaning to a sentence.

Veterans Day No apostrophe is needed for this holiday (unlike *Presidents' Day*). Veterans Day is a U.S. federal holiday held November 11 to commemorate the end of World War I.

vice president Do not hyphenate. The title is lowercased when it comes after a name, as in *Sean Murray, vice president, will retire in June.* Capitalize when it precedes the name. *Vice President Sean Murray will retire in June.*

Vietnam War Capitalize the names of all wars. Write *Vietnam* as one word (not *Viet Nam*). Also use *Vietcong,* not *Viet Cong.*

VIP Use *VIP* for *very important person* in all references. The plural is *VIPs.*

vis-à-vis Note the accent and hyphens. No italics are necessary. This means in comparison with or in relation to.

vitamin Write *vitamin* in lowercase, but capitalize the letter for the vitamin, as in *vitamin A, vitamin B$_{12}$.*

VJ Use *VJ* in all references to a video jockey, who is the host of a television program featuring music videos. *VJ* derives from *DJ,* which means disc jockey.

voice mail This is two words, as in *The photographer left a voice mail and followed up with a letter of introduction.* Use the abbreviated forms *v-mail* or *vmx* only in informal correspondence. Most people refer to individual voice mail messages as just *voice mail(s),* even though *voice mail* is the system.

votes Use figures when they are paired, as in *The committee voted 10 to 6 in favor of launching the Internet service* (even though *six* is normally spelled out). When the number of votes stands alone, spell out numbers under 10, as in *A total of six committee members voted against launching the Internet service.*

· W ·

wake-up call Note the hyphen.

Wall Street This is a name for the financial district in lower Manhattan. It also can be referred to as *the Street,* with a capital *S.*

WAN Use *WAN* in all references. It stands for *wide area network,* an office network that usually connects several offices or buildings.

war It is lowercased, unless it is part of the name of a specific conflict: *Gulf War, Iraq-Iran War, Six Day War, World War II.*

warrantee, warranty A *warrantee* is a person who gets a *warranty,* which is a guarantee.

Washington's Birthday Note the apostrophe in this U.S. federal holiday, which is the third Monday in February. It is also called Presidents' Day, which includes Lincoln.

weak-kneed Often misspelled.

Web Use *the Web* (capital *W)* interchangeably with *World Wide Web.*

Web address This refers to an address on the World Wide Web. Another way to write *Web address* is *URL,* which stands for *uniform resource locator.* When writing for widespread comprehension, *Web address* may be preferable to *URL,* a term some readers may not know.

Include Web addresses when referencing a Website that readers might want to consult. Follow capitalization, no matter how idiosyncratic it may be, because some addresses are case-sensitive. Write the sentence so that normal punctuation (such as a comma) does not cause confusion. It is not necessary to include the protocol *http://* as long as *www* is part of the address, as in *See www.yourdomain.com for more information.* If *www* is not part of the address, then include *http://.* Be sure slashes are leaning in the right direction.

Also, when a Web address has a protocol other than *http://* (e.g., *ftp, https),* then include that protocol.

Web browser software Netscape Navigator, HotJava and Microsoft Internet Explorer are brand names; capitalize accordingly (but do not italicize).

Webmaster One word. The role of Webmaster varies by organization, but generally it's the person who builds and manages a Website.

Website Write as one word. Other variations (website, Web site) are correct, but the key is consistency. It is common to see *Website* written several ways within a document. Whichever form you choose, use it consistently throughout documents and any related materials. Use a global search to check.

Webzine Write as one word and uppercase. Italicize the names of Webzines (like newspapers and other periodicals), as in *Failure.* Also called *e-zines* or *zines,* these are online magazines.

Wednesday Capitalize days of the week.

weekend One word.

weeklong One word.

weight Use figures and spell out the unit of weight, as in *The baby weighed 7 pounds, 11 ounces.*

well-being Write with a hyphen.

West Capitalize when referring to a region of the United States, as in *The West is experiencing a dry spell.* In the United States, the term *West* encompasses 13 states broken into two divisions: **Mountain** (Arizona, Colorado, Idaho, Montana, Nevada, New Mexico, Utah, Wyoming) and **Pacific** (Alaska, California, Hawaii, Oregon, Washington).

If *west* is a direction and not a region, lowercase it, as in *I plan to drive west on Route 208.*

West Point Spell out *U.S. Military Academy* in the first reference; use *West Point* afterward.

whereabouts Most dictionaries allow either a singular or a plural verb. *His whereabouts is unknown* or *His whereabouts are unknown.* Choose one and be consistent.

white paper Lowercase this term, which refers to a position paper. *The Securities Industry Association issued a white paper on decimalization.*

who, whom Many dictionaries say to use *whom* only when it is preceded by a preposition (e.g., *to, with, for, from*) because otherwise it sounds overly formal even when used correctly.

If that suggestion for *who* and *whom* is unsatisfactory, follow this guideline: use *who* when pronouns serve as subjects, as in *Who finds this distinction unclear?* Use *whom* when pronouns serve as objects, as in *Whom did you ask?*

Sometimes it is difficult to figure out whether the word is functioning as a subject or an object. In this case, follow the advice of William Safire, the language pundit from the *New York Times:* "When 'whom' is correct, recast the sentence."

wholesale price index Spell out in the first reference; use *WPI* afterward. This measures the prices that businesses pay for a basket of goods.

who's, whose The first is a contraction for *who is,* as in *Who's the point person for the press release? Whose* is the possessive for both people and things, as in *Clara Marshall, whose background is in journalism, edited the white paper* or *The Canadian company, whose head office is in Toronto, announced it would acquire a Finnish company.*

why It is not necessary to put *why* in quotation marks or to use a question mark in constructions such as *Joe asked why it was necessary to meet twice a week.*

wide area network Use *WAN* in all references. This refers to an office network that usually connects several offices or buildings.

widgetmakers Do not capitalize this term, which refers to companies that produce the unnamed internal workings of new gadgets.

wildcard Use the one-word form when referring to the computer symbol.

windfall One word. It is a sudden or unexpected gain.

Windows Capitalize when referring to the operating system.

winter Lowercase seasons.

win-win Write with a hyphen, as in *The internship program is a win-win for the company and for the students* or *It is a win-win program.*

with regard to Do not write *with regards to.*

words as words Italicize a word used in text as a word: I looked up the word *verisimilitude* in the dictionary.

word selection Try to use short instead of long words. Use "words that are short and strong; words that sedate are words of three, four and five syllables, mostly of Latin origin, many of them ending in 'ion' and embodying a vague concept," according to William Zinsser, author of *On Writing Well.*

work Many compound *work* words are one word: *workstation, workday, workweek, workbook, workhorse, workload, workman, workout.* An exception is *work force,* which is two words.

workers' compensation Note the apostrophe. This insurance system was formerly known as *workmen's compensation.*

work force Use two words.

works of literature When characters in plays or fiction are quoted, use the present tense, as in *Hamlet says, "To be or not to be."*

world-renowned Use a hyphen and don't forget to add the *ed.*

World Trade Organization Spell out in the first reference; write *WTO* afterward.

worldwide It is one word, except when referring to the World Wide Web. *Nationwide* is also one word. Use a hyphen for *company-wide, enterprise-wide, firm-wide, industry-wide.*

World Wide Web Separate each word with a space. *World Wide Web* is interchangeable with *the Web* (capital *W*). The World Wide Web "is a graphics intensive environment running on top of the Internet," according to *Wired Style*. It was conceived in 1989 but did not take off until 1993. It comprises all the Websites on the Internet that are linked globally.

worth Write an apostrophe in expressions using *worth,* as in *He did a day's worth of work in four hours* or *She got her money's worth when she bought the new computer.*

would-be Use a hyphen, as in *The IT department invited all would-be Web designers to submit ideas for the new Website.*

wrongdoing This is one word, as in *The employee insisted he had engaged in no wrongdoing, despite the videotaped evidence.*

·X·

"I can teach you to type. I can't teach you to write."
—Russ Robinson, director, global business markets public relations
Sprint National Consumer Organization

x-axis Use a hyphen. This refers to the horizontal line on a graph.

Xmas Do not use this form; write *Christmas* instead.

XML This stands for *Extensible Markup Language*. Use *XML* in all references.

X-rated It can mean obscene, but the movie listing has been replaced by the NC-17 movie rating.

X-ray Note the hyphen. The letter *X* can be capitalized or lowercased, as in *x-ray*. Whichever form is chosen, use it consistently.

XY recorder An output device for a computer. Do not uppercase the *r* in *recorder*.

· Y ·

Y2K This means year 2000 and gained widespread usage at the turn of the century. It was often used in *Y2K bug,* which referred to problems related to how computer programs read years.

Yahoo! Inc. The name of this company includes an exclamation point (*!*), so include it in the first reference. Use *Yahoo* afterward.

yard It is equal to 3 feet, or 36 inches. Spell out *yard* in text, but abbreviate as *yd.* in tabular material.

y-axis Use a hyphen. This refers to the vertical line on a graph.

yearend, yearlong Each is one word.

years Follow these guidelines:

- Use figures for specific years, as in *1999, 2005.*

- When reducing a year to two digits, use an apostrophe if the year stands alone, as in *The project will be completed in early '03.* In charts and graphs and other tabular material, *03* is another option.

- When referring to a span of years, write *2001–05,* dropping the century in the second year. The exception is when referring to a time span across two centuries: *1999–2004.* Note there are no spaces on either side of the dash or hyphen.

- When referring to a decade, use *1990s* or *'90s* (whichever is chosen, use it consistently).

- Do not use a comma between the month and year when they stand alone: *January 2003.*

- When the year follows a specific date, use a comma before and after the year, as in *Daniel was born November 7, 2000, in Seattle.*

- If writing the entire date with numerals, use two digits each for the month, the day and the year: *03/10/03.* Note that in American English the month comes first, followed by the day, so that 03/10 refers to March 10. In many countries, 03/10 refers to October 3. If you are writing for an international audience and confusion could occur, spell out the month instead.

- Do not begin sentences with numbers, as in *2003 was a record year for the company.* Rather than spell out 2003, revise the sentence: *The company had a record year in 2003.*

- In text, write out *year.* Use *yr.* for *year* in tabular material, slide shows, etc.

year to date In most cases it is best to spell this out in the first reference and use the abbreviation *YTD* afterward. *Year to date the company's sales in Taiwan are above forecast.* This phrase takes hyphens when used as an adjective, as in *Year-to-date sales in Taiwan are above forecast, but YTD sales in mainland China are below forecast.* Hyphens are not needed with YTD.

yellow pages Lowercase.

yeses and noes This is the preferred form (not *noes*).

yes man Do not capitalize or hyphenate.

yesterday Be specific. It is better to use the date than the day in business writing, especially for international correspondence. Avoid using *yesterday, today, this morning, tonight, tomorrow.*

yet When you mean up to now, write *He **hasn't started** yet* (the present perfect tense) rather than *He **didn't start** yet* (the past tense).

yield Express this as a percentage. It is a rate of return on an investment.

yogurt Do not spell it *yoghurt.*

your, you're The word *your* indicates possession, as in *Your new computer will be installed Tuesday. You're* is a contraction for *you are,* as in *You're going to receive a new computer Tuesday.*

yo-yo Use a hyphen. It can mean abrupt changes or reversals.

yr. Use *yr.* for *year* in tabular material, slide shows, etc. In text, write out *year.*

Yule Capitalize when referring to the Christmas season.

yuppie Use in informal writing only. It means *young urban professional* and is considered a hackneyed expression.

· Z ·

Zagat Note the spelling. When referring to any of the Zagat surveys, use an apostrophe, as in *Zagat's gave the Thai restaurant an excellent rating.*

zeitgeist In business writing, avoid this term, which is German for spirit of the age and may not be familiar to many readers. It is often seen in literary writing. If used, italicize.

zeppelin Lowercase this word, which is now a generic term, even though the gas-filled flying apparatus is named after Count Ferdinand von Zeppelin.

zero(s) Note the spelling of the plural. Spell out *zero* in text and in references to temperature. Use the figure in tabular material, slide shows, etc.

zero hour The scheduled time for the start of an operation or action.

zero-sum game Note the hyphen.

zigzag One word. Often misspelled.

zine One word. Italicize the names of zines, as in *Failure*. Also called *e-zines* or *Webzines,* these are online magazines.

ZIP code Capitalize *ZIP;* lowercase *code.* Do not use a comma between the state abbreviation and the ZIP code. When giving the nine-digit version, use a hyphen, as in 90022-5284. The extra four digits in a ZIP code are called *plus fours* or *+4s.* The phrase *ZIP code* is a service mark.

zodiac Lowercase.

SOURCES WE LIKE

WHILE THE BIBLIOGRAPHY AT THE END of the *The Business Style Handbook* is comprehensive, it doesn't give you a full assessment of the books we favor for style and guidance. Without a doubt some sources are better than others. The following books and Websites are particularly helpful, clear and informative. Try to use the most current editions.

STYLEBOOKS

The Chicago Manual of Style: This is the mother of all stylebooks, one of the most comprehensive books of its kind. It is expensive but also an invaluable resource. Its major drawback is that answers are sometimes difficult to find. *The Associated Press Stylebook:* One of the most accessible stylebooks on the market, this book is used by 90% of the Fortune 500 participants. It is comprehensive, simple and inexpensive. A drawback is that the business and Internet entries are in different sections from the bulk of the alphabetical entries. *The New York Times Manual of Style and Usage:* This book does not have the same direct approach as AP, but style decisions are thoughtful and penetrating. The book's editors are explicit about the degree of formality needed for their discriminating and "grammar-conscious readership." It does not have a business focus. *Wired Style, Principles of English Usage in the Digital Age:* It may be too irreverent to provide direction to the mainstream, but it is helpful in resolving questions about technology. Besides providing a lot of background information about the digital age, it focuses on online language. It also encourages writers to "appreciate unruliness." It is, as a result, short on usage and style guidelines. *The Elements of Style:* This is a useful, brief and accessible book that offers invaluable advice on writing simple, clear prose. It's a classic. Business writers will need more specific answers, but it's good introductory material to jump-start the writing process.

DICTIONARIES

The American Heritage Dictionary of the English Language: We prefer this dictionary to *Merriam-Webster's,* even though the majority of Fortune 500 participants use various editions of *Merriam-Webster's.* (Make sure it is a *Merriam-Webster's* [originating from Springfield, Mass.]. The *Webster's* name is used by other publishers.) *The American Heritage Dictionary* is lively, and it also has more than 500 usage entries that give background as well as direction. Keep dictionaries as current as the company budget will allow. As a supplement to the main dictionary, use *Microsoft Computer Dictionary* for technology terms.

GRAMMAR BOOK

The Scott, Foresman Handbook for Writers: This is a useful textbook on grammar, punctuation and writing. Anyone who wants to improve writing skills would be wise to supplement a stylebook with a good grammar book that is simple yet comprehensive.

WRITING BOOKS

The Oxford Essential Guide to Writing: This book gets high marks for its clarity and approach. The focus is for the general writer, but people who write on the job could make significant strides in understanding language by reading this book in its entirety. *Plain Style: Techniques for Simple, Concise, Emphatic Business Writing:* This is not a stylebook but is highly recommended for those who want to cut away the verbosity of their prose. Its focus is business writing, so it specifically tackles the issues that arise in this environment. The author has a lot to say about clarity, emphasis, brevity and simplicity. *The Art of Clear Thinking:* All the books we came across by Rudolf Flesch during our research were valuable, even though they were written more than a quarter-century ago. He was an early advocate of plain English in the workplace and everywhere else, and his work is as pertinent today as it was back in the '50s, '60s and '70s—perhaps even more so. *On Writing Well:* All of William Zinsser's books are worth reading for those who want to deepen their knowledge of the writing process. His work is accessible, current, clear and simple. *Words Fail Me:* This is a lively, brief book about some major stumbling blocks in the English language by Patricia O'Conner, a former editor of the *Wall Street Journal.* You won't have to read any of her paragraphs twice. They are concise, friendly and full of good sense.

WEB SOURCES

For abbreviations, emoticons and other e-mail conventions:
    www.squareonetech.com
    www.anrecs.msu.edu/technology (See E-mail Etiquette Guide.)
    www.everythingemail.net
    www.windweaver.com/emoticon.htm
For foreign currency information:
    http://pacific.commerce.ubc.ca (See Exchange Rate Service link.)
    www.thefinancials.com/vortex/CurrencyFormatsTable.html

www.jhall.demon.co.uk/currency/index.html

www.bsi-global.com/Technical+Info.../Publications/_Publications/
tig90.xalter

www.xe.net/gen/iso4217.htm

For technology references:

www.whatis.com

www.techweb.com/encyclopedia

For information on companies:

www.hoovers.com

For information on citing online sources:

http://owl.english.purdue.edu

www.bedfordstmartins.com (Search for Online!)

For an online dictionary:

www.m-w.com

BIBLIOGRAPHY

BOOKS

American Heritage Dictionary. 3rd ed. Boston/New York: Houghton Mifflin Company, 1997.

American Heritage Dictionary. 4th ed. Boston/New York: Houghton Mifflin Company, 2000.

American Management Association. *The AMA Style Guide for Business Writing.* New York: amacom, American Management Association, 1996.

Booker, Dianna. *Would You Put That in Writing?* New York: Facts on File, 1983.

Chicago Manual of Style. 14th ed. Chicago: University of Chicago Press, 1993.

Flesch, Rudolf. *The Art of Clear Thinking.* New York: Harper & Row, 1951.

Flesch, Rudolf. *Say What You Mean.* New York: Harper & Row, 1972.

Geer, Sean. *Pocket Internet.* 2nd ed. London: Profile Books Ltd, The Economist Newspaper 2000.

Goldstein, Norm, ed. *The Associated Press Stylebook and Briefing on Media Law.* Cambridge, Mass.: Perseus Publishing, 2000.

Goldstein, Norm, ed. *The Associated Press Stylebook and Libel Manual.* Reading, Mass.: Perseus Books, 1998.

Hairston, Maxine, and John J. Ruszkiewicz, eds. *The Scott, Foresman Handbook for Writers.* Glenview, Ill.: Scott, Foresman and Company, 1988.

Hale, Constance, ed. *Wired Style, Principles of English Usage in the Digital Age.* San Francisco: HardWired, 1996.

Haslem, John A., ed. *Webster's New World Pocket Style Guide.* New York: Macmillan General Reference, a Simon & Schuster Macmillan Co., 1997.

The IFR Financial Glossary. 3rd ed. London: IFR Publishing Ltd, 1992.

Kane, Thomas S. *The Oxford Essential Guide to Writing.* New York: Berkley Books, 2000.

Lauchman, Richard. *Plain Style: Techniques for Simple, Concise, Emphatic Business Writing.* New York: amacom, American Management Association, 1993.

Merriam-Webster's Collegiate Dictionary. 10th ed. Springfield, Mass.: Merriam-Webster, 2000.

Microsoft Computer Dictionary. 4th ed. Redmond, Wa.: Microsoft Press, 1999.

O'Conner, Patricia. *Words Fail Me.* New York: Harcourt Brace & Company, 1999.

Piotrowski, Maryann V. *Effective Business Writing.* New York: HarperPerennial, 1996.

Rifkin, Jeremy. *The Age of Access.* New York: The Putnam Publishing Group, 2001.

Siegal, Allan M., and William G. Connolly, eds. *The New York Times Manual of Style and Usage.* New York: Times Books, 1999.

Standard & Poor's Register of Corporations, Directors and Executives. 3 vols. Charlottesville, Va.: Standard & Poor's, 2000.

Strunk, William, Jr., and E. B. White. *The Elements of Style.* 3rd ed. Needham Heights, Mass.: Allyn & Bacon, 1979.

Winokur, Jon, ed. and comp. *Advice to Writers.* New York: Pantheon Books, 1999.

Zinsser, William. *On Writing Well.* 6th ed., rev. and updated. New York: HarperPerennial, 1998.

ARTICLES

Fortune 500 List. *Fortune,* 14 June 1999.

"Grammar Rules." *Wall Street Journal,* 4 Aug. 2000.

Kelly, Erin. "A Shift in Style." *Fortune,* 13 Nov. 2000.

Kirn, Walter. "Happy Families Are Not All Alike." *New York Times Book Review,* 11 June 2000.

Leonhardt, David. "In Language You Can Understand." *New York Times,* 8 Dec. 1999, sec. C: 1+.

Ragan Report, The Weekly Survey of Ideas and Methods for Communications Executives, 15 May 2000.

Shrage, Michael. "Need Innovation? Start by Locking Up the Tech Toys." *Fortune,* 8 Dec. 2001.

Shrage, Michael. "Take the Lazy Way Out? That's Far Too Much Trouble." *Fortune,* 5 Feb. 2001.

Useem, Jerry. "Conquering Vertical Limits." *Fortune,* 9 Feb. 2001.

INDEX

ABOUT THE AUTHORS

HELEN CUNNINGHAM HAS MORE THAN 20 years' experience as a business writer and editor. She is a director of corporate communications at The Depository Trust & Clearing Corporation. Previously she worked at The Economist Group, as editor of the weekly publication *Business Latin America.* At Philip Morris International, Cunningham worked as a business communications specialist in the international planning department, and at the law firm of Shearman & Sterling she was in the media/communications and marketing department. She also worked in Moscow on a joint venture.

Brenda Greene has more than 20 years' experience as a writer and editor. An editor at SYS-CON Media, she is married and the mother of three children. Her other publishing experience includes working as an editor at *Working Woman, North Jersey Herald & News,* and Whitney Communications. On the corporate side, Greene has worked as marketing manager for a business-to-business venture. She was also the writer and editor for a project to create a health and fitness guide for children with asthma, jointly sponsored by Theracom Communications and Pfizer Pharmaceuticals. She worked on various projects at Dugan Farley Communications (a medical advertising specialist), Agora Publications and the University of Maryland.